Women as Transformational Leaders

Women as Transformational Leaders

FROM GRASSROOTS TO GLOBAL INTERESTS

VOLUME I: CULTURAL AND ORGANIZATIONAL STEREOTYPES, PREJUDICE, AND DISCRIMINATION

Michele A. Paludi and Breena E. Coates, Editors

Women and Careers in Management
Michele A. Paludi, Series Editor

 PRAEGER

AN IMPRINT OF ABC-CLIO, LLC
Santa Barbara, California • Denver, Colorado • Oxford, England

15 38042

MAY 0 8 2012

Library of Congress Cataloging-in-Publication Data

Women as transformational leaders : from grassroots to global interests / Michele A. Paludi and Breena E. Coates, editors.

v. ; cm. — (Women and careers in management)

Includes bibliographical references and index.

ISBN 978–0–313–38652–7 (hardcopy : alk. paper) — ISBN 978–0–313–38653–4 (ebook) 1. Women executives. 2. Leadership—Psychological aspects. 3. Sex role in the work environment. 4. Sex discrimination in employment. I. Paludi, Michele Antoinette. II. Coates, Breena E.

HD6054.3.W635   2011

658.4'092082—dc23   2011022815

ISBN: 978–0–313–38652–7
EISBN: 978–0–313–38653–4

15 14 13 12 11   1 2 3 4 5

This book is also available on the World Wide Web as an eBook.
Visit www.abc-clio.com for details.

Praeger
An Imprint of ABC-CLIO, LLC

ABC-CLIO, LLC
130 Cremona Drive, P.O. Box 1911
Santa Barbara, California 93116-1911

This book is printed on acid-free paper (∞)

Manufactured in the United States of America

Whether there are innately female leadership styles … is not really the right question. It is more important to ask why there has been so little attention paid to women leaders over the years as well as why the styles of leading more often exhibited by women are particularly useful at this critical moment in history.

—Charlotte Bunch

We dedicate this book set to women leaders past, present, and future.
—Michele A. Paludi and Breena E. Coates

Contents

CHAPTER 14

Leading a "Dis-Organization": Being a Queen Mother of a Red Hat
Society, 245

Series Foreword

Ma muaka kite a muri
Ma muri ka ora a mua
(Those who lead give sight to those who follow,
Those who follow give life to those who lead.)
—Pauline Tangiora

Welcome to Praeger's "Women and Careers in Management" series. This series examines the status of women in management and leadership and offers discussions of issues that women managers and leaders face, including:

- Differences in leadership styles
- Traditional gender roles reinforcing women's subordinate status in the workplace
- Obstacles to advancement and pay
- Benefit and resource inequity
- Discrimination and harassment
- Work–life imbalance

This series acknowledges that gender is one of the fundamental factors influencing the ethics, values, and policies of workplaces and that the discrimination against women managers and leaders explains the pervasiveness of institutionalized inequality. This series also discusses interconnections among equality issues of sex, race, class, age, sexual orientation, religion, and disability. Thus, this series brings together a multidisciplinary and multicultural discussion of women, management, and leadership.

"Women and Careers in Management" encourages us all to think criti-
cally about women managers and leaders, to place value on cultural experiences, and to integrate empirical research and theoretical formulations
with experiences of our family, friends, colleagues, and ourselves. It is
my hope that the books in "Women and Careers in Management" will
serve as a "life raft" (Klonis, Endo, Crosby, and Worrell, 1997), especially
for the millennial and subsequent generations.

I am honored to have *Women as Transformational Leaders: From
Grassroots to Global Interests* published in the "Women and Careers in
Management" series. These volumes share Pauline Tangiora's sentiment:

> Those who lead give sight to those who follow,
> Those who follow give life to those who lead.

—Michele A. Paludi
Series Editor

Reference

Klonis, S., Endo, J., Crosby, F., & Worrell, J. (1997). Feminism as life raft.
Psychology of Women Quarterly, 21, 333–345.

Acknowledgments

Michele A. Paludi

I extend my appreciation to my friend and colleague, Breena Coates, for collaborating with me on this multivolume set. I have been honored to work with Breena and appreciate her graciousness and sage advice.

I also thank my sisters, Rosalie Paludi and Lucille Paludi, for their continued support and encouragement.

The following family and friends also deserve my appreciation for their discussions throughout the writing and editing of this book set: Carmen A. Paludi, Jr., Tony LoFrumento, Steven Earle, Florence L. Denmark, Catherine Raycroft, and David Raycroft.

Students who collaborated with me on the chapter dealing with women entrepreneurs also deserve recognition: Lindsay Baker, Janet Boyce, Jennie D'Aiuto, Jodi Stein, and Heather Stein. You have honored me by referring to me as your professor.

I also thank the planning committee, reviewers, and presenters at Union Graduate College's conference, "Women, Management and Leadership: Organizational Practices and Individual Strategies for Women," at which I was fortunate to be a co-chair. I learned a great deal from each of you.

Breena E. Coates

First and foremost, it was a great pleasure collaborating with Michele Paludi, whose work I have admired for many years. I would also like to extend my appreciation to my husband, Sharad K. Singh, for his support and help. I thank Professors Louise Comfort and Jay Shafritz, who have mentored and encouraged me ever since I was a student of theirs at the

University of Pittsburgh. I also appreciate the many insights and growth opportunities afforded me by interactions with my students at San Diego State University, the United States Army War College, and California State University, San Bernardino.

Foreword: Thinking about Women and Leadership

There are a myriad of lenses through which to view women's leadership issues. To be sure, in this century compared to last century, there is vastly less overt discrimination against women who have assumed or are seeking to assume leadership positions. But, and this is an important but, discrimination and related challenges particular to women leaders have not evaporated. Stated most simply, in recent decades, women face more subtle forms of discrimination.

What is at once difficult and troubling is identifying strategies to address the more subtle forms of discrimination. It is equally challenging to provide assistance to women leaders (or aspiring leaders) that prepares them for the challenges they face. Part of the reason for the difficulty is that when one form of bad behavior against women leaders is identified, it may be eradicated or curtailed, but it is then replaced with another form of bad behavior that was not necessarily even on the proverbial radar screen.

It is also true that women leaders themselves may not be fully aware of what distinguishes their leadership styles and approaches from that of their male counterparts. It is for this reason that I think it is important for women leaders to be vigilant—to be aware of the areas in which their leadership may be affected by their gender, affecting both how they perceive and handle situations and how others perceive and respond to them in a leadership position.

As is often the case, some areas impacted by gender may not initially be obvious. If these areas can be identified, women leaders' awareness can be heightened. This, in and of itself, can have a salutary effect. That is also why books and conferences and conversations about women and leadership are so important—for women and for men.

To reinforce this point, I want to identify one example of a less-than-obvious area in which women's attitudes and perceptions can profoundly impact leadership and how thinking more about the identified area can affect change. The topic is money; it is ubiquitous, but we are often blissfully unaware of the profound impact that money and our attitude and behaviors with respect to money has on our lives.

Start with this observation: Leadership requires dealing with money in a host of ways—budgets, salary negotiations for oneself and others, borrowing, lending, refinancing, donations, programmatic development... the list goes on. As a college president, virtually every issue I address has a monetary implication: from adding a new faculty member, to seeking a grant or a donation, to determining whether to add an athletic team or dismiss a student for academic failure.

The research data support the conclusion that women think about, handle, and address money issues differently than their male counterparts (recognizing, of course, the risk of homogenizing all women when talking about gender). Money means something different for women and men, and these differences have leadership implications that cannot be ignored.

Consider that some women have a fear of numbers and math (call it arithmophobia), and score lower on quantitative literacy tests than their male counterparts. This can lead to women delegating financial issues to others. The leadership implications of not being comfortable with budget requests, budget analyses, and budget projections and relying on others within an organization to deal with the "money" part of business decision making are obvious.

Consider that the research shows that women find investing difficult, stressful, and time-consuming and are more risk-averse than their male counterparts. Indeed, research shows that when women handle money, they feel like they are gambling as opposed to making wise decisions. If these perceptions, attitudes, and emotions with respect to money carry into the workplace, they can affect business choices, decisions, and behavior.

There is research showing that women negotiate differently than their male counterparts. As Babcock and Laschever point out in their *Women Don't Ask: Negotiation and the Gender Divide*, men are socialized in a "scrappier paradigm" and learn in their childhood to take charge and recognize opportunity. Pine and Gnessen, authors of the book *Sheconomics*, conducted a survey in 2010 that showed that 8 of 10 women didn't like asking for money, 9 out of 10 women found that asking was embarrassing, and both men and women would rather ask men than woman for money.

Results like these have real impact. They affect women asking for raises for themselves, handling salary negotiations with employees, and seeking public office, where asking for money is part and parcel of success. They affect women's fund-raising capacities and their comfort level with pursuing a myriad of opportunities for the organizations they lead.

While there are no easy answers to improving how women view and handle money, my point here in this Foreword is that if we want to encourage more and more women to be successful leaders, we need to help them learn more about those areas where gender-based attitudes, behaviors, and belief systems impact how they function as leaders.

I appreciate that recognition and vigilance alone will not change women's leadership success, but it is a good first step. Importantly, books like this on leadership can make that recognition and vigilance possible.

—Karen Gross

Introduction

It's an uphill struggle, to be judged both a good woman and a good leader.

—Rosabeth Moss Kanter

During the course of developing and preparing this two-volume book set, the topic of women's leadership and leadership styles gained national and international media attention, for example:

- In May 2010, President Obama selected Solicitor General Elena Kagan as his nominee to the United States Supreme Court. During his nomination speech, President Obama cited what he called Kagan's "openness to a broad array of viewpoints" and her "fair-mindedness."

- In August 2009, Evelynn M. Hammonds, Dean of Harvard College, addressed the Women's Leadership Conference and said this:
  "I've been thinking a lot about leadership during this time of great political change and financial uncertainty in the world . . . Because in times of crisis, the need for leaders with courage, discipline, and vision is palpable. We all look to our leaders to help us through difficult times—indeed, we often demand a solution from them for the most difficult of our problems."

- In May 2009, President Obama selected Judge Sonia Sotomayor to become the first Latina U.S. Supreme Court Justice. In his nominating speech, President Obama described Judge Sotomayor as someone who " . . . inspires young people to achieve their dreams."

- In January 2009, Secretary of State Hilary Clinton's first meeting with her staff included an acknowledgment of their contributions. She stated: "This is a team . . . you are members of that team . . . we will be the better because we have heard from you."

All of these comments echo research findings from the social sciences that suggest women leaders embrace the following values in their work: inclusion, honesty, nurturance, participation, collaboration, communication, and gender and race equity. For example, research conducted by two consulting firms, Caliper and Aurora (2005), reported that women leaders:

- Are more persuasive than their male counterparts.
- Learn from adversity and carry on with an "I'll show you" attitude.
- Demonstrate an inclusive, team-building leadership style of problem solving and decision making.
- Are likely to ignore rules and take risks.

In addition, Wachs Book (2001) described the careers of 14 top women executives and found results similar to the Caliper and Aurora study: women are willing to reinvent rules and sell their visions, they are determined to reframe challenges into opportunities, and they remain focused on "high touch" in a business world that is high tech.

Rodgers-Healey (2003) surveyed 193 women leaders and asked the following questions:

- Do you believe that a woman can be as good a leader as a man?
- Do you feel that women in a work and personal setting help each other become leaders?
- What is your vision as a leader?
- What forms of support do you need to make this possible?

The majority of women in this research defined leadership in terms of listening, empowering others, being collaborative, facilitating change, mentoring others, and being effective communicators. In addition, most of the women indicated that encouragement, equality, and the presence of role models are necessary in order to achieve their visions of being good leaders.

Chin (2008, p. 714) also noted that the objectives of feminist women leaders include empowering others in the following ways:

- Creating the vision.
- Social advocacy and change.
- Stewardship of an organization's resources.
- Changing organizational cultures to create gender-equitable environments.
- Promoting feminist policies and agendas.

Eagly, Johannesen-Schmidt, and van Engen (2003) further noted that for women, an effective leadership style is *transformational*, a style that incorporates empowerment, ethics, inclusiveness, nurturance, and encouraging innovation and social justice. Thus, transformational leadership describes leaders who "motivate subordinates to transcend their own self-interests for the good of the group or organization" (Powell, Butterfield, and Bartol, 2008, p.159). Burns (1978) described transformational leadership as occurring ". . . when one or more persons engage with others in such a way that leaders and followers raise one another to higher levels of motivation and morality . . . transforming leadership ultimately becomes moral in that it raises the level of human conduct and ethical aspirations of both the leader and led, and thus, has a transforming effect on both."

In contrast, *transactional* leaders form exchange relationships through using rewards and punishment as incentives for employee performance. Transactional leadership is associated with aggression (Powell, Butterfield, and Bartol, 2008). According to Duff-McCall and Schweinle (2008), a transactional leadership ". . . suits the masculine social interaction and leadership style, because men internalize the male gender role, which supports an agentic desire for competition, aggression, and assertion" (p. 90). Thus, transactional leadership rewards competition, aggression, and an authoritarian managerial style (Eagly and Johannesen-Schmidt, 2001). Eagly et al. (2003) found that women score higher than men on only one aspect of transactional leadership that is related to positive outcomes: rewarding their employees for good performance. Thus women who are transformational leaders exhibit caring and nurturing attitudes toward employees through praise and other forms of rewards.

The research on a transformational leadership style would predict that women, who are more likely to use this style, should not face any barriers to becoming leaders. However, this is not the case: women experience significant barriers, including dealing with gatekeepers, pay inequity, lack of work–life integration, and discrimination, which keep them from reaching their full potential as leaders. Eagly and Karau (2002) noted that there is an incongruity between agentic leadership and femininity. Thus, women are perceived as ineffective as leaders no matter what leadership style they use. When women engage in behaviors stereotypically linked to men (e.g., leadership), they are not perceived similarly to men and are often evaluated more negatively than when conforming to stereotypes of women. (Doyle and Paludi, 1998): According to Heilman, Wallen, Fuchs, and Tamkins (2004):

> The mere recognition that a woman has achieved success on a traditionally male task produces inferences that she has engaged in counternormative behavior and therefore causes similarly negative consequences. (p. 3)

Thus, women will be perceived negatively since they are engaging in "unfeminine" behavior, referred to as the "double bind." (Denmark, Baron, Klara, Sigal, Gibbs, and Wnuk, 2008; Oakley, 2000)

Jandeska and Kraimer (2005) found that most organizations are structured by a traditional and stereotypical masculine culture that values and rewards men who exhibit these stereotypical traits more so than women. Women struggle to find their place within these organizations. According to Jandeska and Kraimer (2005):

> This "code of conduct" in masculine cultures, while recognizable to males, can be completely alien to females and thus would be considered less hospitable towards women's careers. For example, an "old-boy network" excludes women from centers of influence and valuable sources of information, often trivializing or ignoring their contributions. (p. 465)

Jandeska and Kraimer (2005) further found that collective organizational cultures exist that reward more stereotypic feminine behaviors.
These collectivistic cultures focus on cooperation and empowerment.
They are conducive to women being more satisfied with their careers
and more engaged to the organization's success. As Jandeska and Kraimer
(2005) noted:

> Even women in senior roles in large corporations find themselves "on
> the outside looking in" when it comes to information sharing and
> access to the inner circle, where decisions are made.... Women char-
> acterize such a culture as exclusionary and claim that upper manage-
> ment often lacks awareness of the barriers it creates to women's
> assimilation and advancement. (p. 465)

Yoder (2001) also noted that a transformational leadership style would
be perceived as effective in "a congenial setting," one in which empowering and nurturing subordinates is valued. Denmark, Baron, Klara, Sigal,
Gibbs, and Wnuk (2008) further suggested that organizations must be supportive of transformational leadership "... by legitimizing and encouraging women leaders and by ensuring that the male/female ratio of
employees is not skewed in favor of male employees" (p. 38). This
research is echoed by women's accounts. For example, Barbara Adachi
(2010) stated:

> They say it's lonely at the top...I say it's lonely to be the only
> woman at the table. It was not long ago when I arrived at my first man-
> agement committee meeting at Deloitte and my feelings of excitement
> were quickly reduced to feelings of isolation upon seeing the room
> filled merely with men. Not only was I outnumbered, I felt over-
> looked—as if I were invisible.... Putting aside my personal feelings
> as a woman, there's a much bigger issue at stake: the underrepresenta-
> tion of women is having a profoundly negative effect on company bot-
> tom lines. (pp. 1, 2)

Margaret Chesney (2007) once quipped with regard to women and
leadership: "The ceiling is breaking—but watch out for falling glass."
Nevertheless, the breaking up of the glass ceiling is still slow, and this

has led Eagly and Carli (2007) to create a more updated metaphor—the *labyrinth*. This metaphor captures the multiple complex challenges, false starts, and barriers that women encounter as they navigate the lanes to leadership victories in the twenty-first century.

It is our hope that these two volumes will serve as a (wo)mentor for women who aspire to become leaders. We echo the sentiment of Denmark, Baron, Klara, Sigal, Gibbs, and Wnuk (2008) who recommend the following to empower women to become leaders:

> ... women should band together and actively participate in groups that unite women. Whether this be a union or a group of women within a department, it has been through this action of uniting and supporting that women have made progress in the past and which provides a key to progress in the future. (p. 54)

On January 4, 2007, Nancy Pelosi became the first women to hold the Speakership of the House of Representatives. She accepted the Speaker's gavel, affirming her vision for "partnership" over "partisanship." She then addressed the historical importance of being the first female to hold the position of Speaker:

> It is a moment for which we have waited more than 200 years ... but women weren't just waiting; women were working. Never losing faith, we worked to redeem the promise of America, that all men and women are created equal. For our daughters and granddaughters, today, we have broken the marble ceiling ... the sky is the limit, anything is possible for them.

This two-volume set on women as transformational leaders features scholarly research about work environments that welcomed them and those that prevented them from being transformational. Contributors discuss the continued struggle of women leaders to break the glass ceiling, social stigma attached to women leaders, sexism and homophobia in hiring and evaluating lesbian leaders in organizations, women leaders in nonprofit organizations, and the interface of sex and race in evaluating and promoting women of color. We take a multicultural approach to women and leadership, including discussing leadership of Czech and Latina women. We also offer readers resources on women's leadership institutes, organizations concerned with women and leadership, and global feminist leadership programs.

In addition, we feature personal accounts from women in business, academia, and in community organizations about their experiences as leaders and with women leaders. This idiographic approach (Paludi and Fankell-Hauser, 1986) to understanding women's leadership styles and experiences illustrates how women differ in the strength of their striving for achieving leadership and in the roles that elicit this striving. These personal accounts also highlight organizational factors and personal factors that facilitated or hindered their career development. Our goal is that these personal accounts stimulate additional research agendas on women and leadership that make women leaders central, not marginal and visible, and not invisible.

References

Adachi, B. (2010). *We need women leaders. How do we get them?* Retrieved from http://www.forbes.com/2010/04/09/women-wall-street-gender-discrimination-forbes-women on May 13, 2010.

Burns, J. (1978). *Leadership.* New York: Harper & Row.

Caliper (2005). *Women leaders study: The qualities that distinguish women leaders.* Retrieved from http://www.caliperonline.com/brochures/WomenLeaderWhitePaper.pdf on May 13, 2010.

Chesney, M. (September 2007). *Women in leadership—the ceiling is breaking . . . but watch out for falling glass.* Paper presented at the meeting of the Committee on Women in Psychology Leadership Institute for Women in Psychology: Qualitative Evaluation of Training Needs. Washington, DC.

Chin, J. (2008). Women and leadership. In F. Denmark and M. Paludi (Eds.), *Psychology of women: A handbook of issues and theories* (pp. 701–716). Westport, CT: Praeger.

Denmark, F., Baron, E., Klara, M., Sigal, J., Gibbs, M., and Wnuk, D. (2008). Women as leaders: From the lab to the real world. In M. Paludi (Ed.), *The psychology of women at work: Challenges and solutions for our female workforce* (pp. 35–56). Westport, CT: Praeger.

Doyle, J., and Paludi, M. (1998). *Sex and gender.* New York: McGraw-Hill.

Duff-McCall, K., and Schweinle, W. (2008). Leadership and women. In M. Paludi (Ed.), *The psychology of women at work: Challenges and solutions for our female workforce* (pp. 87–99). Westport, CT: Praeger.

Eagly, A., and Carli, L. (2007) *Through the labyrinth: The truth about how women become leaders.* Boston, MA: Harvard Business School Press.

Eagly, A., and Johannesen-Schmidt, M. (2001). The leadership styles of women and men. *Journal of Social Issues, 57,* 781–797.

Eagly, A., Johannesen-Schmidt, M., and van Engen, M. (2003). Transformation, transactional and laissez-faire leadership styles: A meta-analysis comparing women and men. *Psychological Bulletin, 108,* 233–256.

Eagly, A., and Karau, S. (2002). Role congruity theory of prejudice toward female leaders. *Psychological Review, 109,* 573–598.

Heilman, M., Wallen, A., Fuchs, D., and Tamkins, M. (2004). Penalties for success: Reactions to women who succeed at male gender-typed tasks. *Journal of Applied Psychology, 74,* 935–942.

Jandeska, K., and Kraimer, M. (2005). Women's perceptions of organizational culture, work attitudes, and role-modeling behaviors. *Journal of Managerial Issues, 18,* 461–478.

Oakley, J. (2000). Gender-based barriers to senior management positions: Understanding the scarcity of female CEOs. *Journal of Business Ethics, 27,* 321–334.

Paludi, M., and Fankell-Hauser, J. (1986). An idiographic approach to the study of women's achievement strivings. *Psychology of Women Quarterly, 10,* 89–100.

Powell, G., Butterfield, D., and Bartol, K. (2008). Leader evaluations: A new female advantage? *Gender in Management: An International Journal, 23,* 156–174.

Rodgers-Healey, D. (2003). *12 insights into leadership for women.* Retrieved from www.leadershipforwomen.com.au on May 13, 2010.

Wachs Book, W. (2001). *Why the best man for the job is a woman: The unique female qualities of leadership.* New York: Harper Collins.

Yoder, J. (2001). Strategies for change: Making leadership work more effectively for women. *Journal of Social Issues, 57,* 815–828.

I

Gender, Racial, and Sexual Orientation Microaggressions

Kevin L. Nadal, Katie E. Griffin, and Yinglee Wong

Case Vignette

Bernadette is a 27-year-old Filipina American woman who graduated from law school four years ago. She is currently working for a firm that focuses primarily on criminal law. When she was first hired for the position, she recognized that she was one of the few female attorneys who worked for the company and the only woman of color (besides the female receptionists who work at the front desk). When Bernadette is at work, she often feels uncomfortable when her male coworkers make comments about her clothing or hairstyle. Sometimes the statements seem to be compliments (e.g., her male coworkers often tell her that she looks "pretty" or that she has "beautiful, silky hair"); sometimes they may be well-intended but are a bit degrading (e.g., a male coworker tells her "I like your blouse" as he gazes at her breasts, either subtly or accidentally). She is conflicted because she believes that her male coworkers mostly have good intentions in complimenting her; however, she recognizes that they never comment on other men's appearances, leaving her to feel frustrated that it happens so often and only to her. Many other instances also make Bernadette feel confused. For example, her supervisor (a white male) once told her that she should wear her hair in a ponytail and try to dress more professionally "because of her age." Bernadette was upset by this comment because she knows that she dresses similarly to her older, white, female coworkers. She wonders why everyone is paying attention to her appearance and not to the quality of her work.

Although Bernadette loves her job, she feels distressed about going to the office. She can't help but wonder whether these experiences occur because of her gender, her race, her age, or some combination of them all. She tries to talk to her family about the situation, but because none of them are attorneys or work in similar fields, she doesn't think they can fully understand her. One of her friends from law school suggests that she report the instances to Human Resources. However, Bernadette feels hopeless: she believes that these situations are so subtle that they cannot be classified as sexual harassment or overt discrimination.

Introduction

Since the mid-nineteenth century, women have strived for equality. The women's rights movement has encompassed such events as the first women's rights convention in Seneca Falls in 1848, the passage of the Nineteenth Amendment to the Constitution in 1920, the Equal Pay Act in 1963, Title VII of the Civil Rights Act in 1964, and the founding of the National Organization for Women (NOW) in 1966. Although decades have passed and federal and state laws have been implemented to protect women's civil rights, both overt sexism and subtle discrimination toward women are still widespread (Swim and Cohen, 1997; Swim, Hyers, Cohen, and Ferguson, 2001). For example, in 2009 the Equal Employment Opportunity Commission (EEOC) received 10,665 sexual harassment charges filed by women and 2,031 charges filed by men. Although the U.S. Supreme Court has ruled sexual harassment to be a form of discrimination and policies have been implemented to protect women from sexual harassment, sexism in the workplace still appears to be pervasive in the everyday lives of women.

Several authors have suggested that sexism may be more implicit and difficult to identify (Nadal, 2010; Sue and Capodilupo, 2008; Swim and Cohen, 1997; Swim et al., 2001). Over the past 20 years, a considerable amount of literature has examined the various forms of sexism that exist. However, when general society thinks of sexism, instances of direct and clear forms of sexism may come to mind first. Overt sexism can be defined as verbal or physical sexist actions that are conscious, visible, and observable (Swim and Cohen, 1997). Sexual harassment can usually be categorized as a type of overt sexism, in that the actions and behaviors of an individual are noticed by others, can be labeled as sexist, and can contribute to a hostile environment. Sometimes overt sexism can include instances where an individual may not be conscious of the impacts that one's sexist biases may have. For example, a male associate may openly belittle female employees by saying that women are too emotional or that women don't make good leaders. He may believe he is simply stating an opinion, but the directness of his prejudice may lead individuals who hear such comments to become uncomfortable.

In modern times, sexism in the workplace can also be more hidden and less easy to identify. In fact, several authors have coined terminology to describe the more innocuous forms of sexism that transpire. "Covert sexism" occurs when unequal and harmful actions toward women are committed in a hidden or unconscious manner (Swim and Cohen, 1997). For example, a male professor who grades his male students more leniently than his female students (when the work is similar) may be unconscious of his actions and may not intend to discriminate against his female students. Such a professor may even become defensive if he were challenged and may forthrightly claim that he grades everybody fairly. Similarly, "subtle sexism" is defined as verbal or physical behaviors that are harmful toward women but go unnoticed because they are not perceived to be problematic, or are distinguished as normal behavior (Swim, Mallett, and Stagnor, 2004). For example, when a male patient assumes that a woman working in a hospital is a nurse and not a doctor, he may unconsciously perceive that women are not as intellectual, educated, or capable as men. However, because many in general society may assume this assumption of gender roles to be normal, such an instance may be viewed as an "innocent mistake."

"Objectification theory" assumes that "women are typically acculturated to internalize an observer's perspective as a primary view of their physical selves (Fredickson and Roberts, 1997, p. 173). Simply stated, women are objectified in society on many different levels and in a vast range of situations. Examples can include a woman who is "catcalled" as she walks by a group of men to women who are sexualized in all forms of the media. Objectification can even include much more brutal and malicious actions, like rape or physical abuse (Fredickson and Roberts, 1997). "Benevolent sexism" is defined as "a favorable, chivalrous ideology that offers protection and affection to women who embrace conventional roles" (Glick and Fiske, 2001, p. 109). For example, a man who automatically pays for a woman's dinner or opens doors for her may assume that he is being considerate or a "gentleman." However, he may hold a bias that women are reliant on men or incapable of doing things themselves. So while he may have good intentions, some women may feel that he is promoting the notion that women need to be "taken care of." Finally, "hostile sexism" can be defined as animosity toward women who are seen to minimize men's power (Glick and Fiske, 2001, p. 109). An act of hostile sexism may include a man spreading rumors about his female superior because he feels belittled, undervalued, or threatened by her position of power.

In recent years, a term has been used much more frequently to discuss the subtle forms of discrimination that marginalized or oppressed groups tend to experience: "microaggressions." Microaggressions are defined as "brief and commonplace daily verbal, behavioral, or environmental indignities, whether intentional or unintentional, that communicate hostile, derogatory, or negative racial slights and insults toward members of oppressed groups" (Nadal, 2008, p. 23). Microaggressions can affect a number of target groups, including women; people of color; lesbian, gay, bisexual, and transgender persons; persons with disabilities; religious minorities; and many other groups. Microaggressions are often unconscious, in that the enactor of the microaggression may not recognize the impact that her or his behavior may have on the individual or groups who experience it. Microaggressions are usually interpersonal interactions between two or more individuals, but environments and systems may also have microaggressive qualities. For example, when women are portrayed in the media as being sexual objects or upholding traditional gender roles, an indirect message is sent to audiences that this is what women are expected to be; such environmental microaggressions may lead to unwelcoming or hostile environments and even have effects on women's mental health (Capodilupo, Nadal, Hamit, Corman, Lyons, and Weinberg, 2010).

Subtle discrimination that is specifically aimed toward women has been labeled as gender microaggressions (Capodilupo et al., 2010; Nadal, 2010; Sue and Capodilupo, 2008), which are defined as "brief and commonplace daily verbal, behavioral, and environmental indignities that communicate hostile, derogatory, or negative sexist slights and insults toward women" (Nadal, 2010, p. 155). A taxonomy involving various forms of microaggressions was introduced by Sue and Capodilupo (2008) and includes general themes to be applied to people of color, women, and LGBT persons. Nadal (2010) recently extended the taxonomy by adding two additional themes and focusing explicitly on women's microaggressions experiences. Capodilupo et al. (2010) utilized a qualitative method and directed content analysis to empirically support the proposed taxonomy on gender microaggressions. Findings revealed the various categories of microaggressions experienced by women: *1) Sexual objectification, 2) Invisibility, 3) Assumptions of inferiority, 4) Denial of the reality of sexism, 5) Assumptions of traditional gender roles, 6) Denial of individual sexism, 7) Use of sexist language, and 8) Environmental microaggressions.*

The first category, *Sexual objectification,* consists of behaviors and verbal statements that make women feel like they are sexual objects. Examples may include a woman who is catcalled while walking down the street, a male coworker who glances at his female colleague's breasts, or a male stranger who touches a woman's back or buttocks while exiting an elevator. These messages make women feel that their body is on display and that they are only valued by men physically.

The second category, *Invisibility,* occurs when women are treated as second to men. For example, a woman being overlooked for a promotion even when she produces the same quality of work as a man would signify her invisibility. Moreover, when a conversation at a board meeting is dominated by men, male coworkers may unconsciously believe that women's opinions are unimportant or substandard. These messages imply that women do not deserve the same privileges and opportunities as do men.

The third category, *Assumptions of inferiority,* transpires when men assume that women are incapable of mental and physical activities. For example, when men are asked to lift boxes, move tables/chairs, and/or fix things and women are not, an implicit message is sent that women are physically incapable of certain activities. Another example may include when a male supervisor tells a woman, "I didn't know you had it in you" after she completed a presentation or finished an arduous task. His statement, while being well intentioned, may signify his bias that women are intellectually inferior.

The fourth category, *Denial of reality of sexism*, occurs when a woman is criticized for being sensitive or told that she is overreacting when she complains about sexism. In such an instance, the woman's worldview is being ignored and her experiences with sexism are being dismissed or classified as illogical or untrue.

The fifth category, *Assumptions of traditional gender roles*, presumes that women should conform to gender roles that are prescribed by society. For example, when a female coworker is expected to cook or clean after the office party, she is assumed to perform household chores because of her gender even though she is at work. When women are encouraged to enter more traditionally feminine fields like nursing or teaching instead of engineering or sciences, they are being told indirectly that women are inferior and need to know their place. Finally, when a woman is expected to get married and have children, she is being told that there is only one way to be a woman and that childrearing is the main purpose in a woman's life.

The sixth category, *Denial of individual sexism*, refers to instances where men claim that they are incapable of being sexist. When a woman challenges a man who is sexist and he says, "I have many female friends" or "I have a wife and daughter," he is invalidating her experience and is unable to take ownership of a potentially sexist act he may have committed—whether it was intentional or not. Thus, he sends an indirect message that his perception of a situation is correct and that her experience is untrue or oversensitive.

The seventh category, *Use of sexist language*, occurs when derogatory words are used to belittle women because of their gender. For example, in a workplace setting, if a woman is called "Sexy," "Honey," or other nicknames that are sexist, women may feel that they are being objectified or treated as inferior to men. Overt sexist language is often discouraged in workplace settings, as it can lead to a hostile environment, which could then be classified as sexual harassment. However, there are several ways in which subtle sexist language can occur. For example, when a male doctor is always referred to as "Doctor" but a female doctor is referred to by her first name, a subtle message is sent that women are inferior to men. Moreover, when women are verbally labeled as "overemotional" or "gossipy," unintentional stereotypes about women are communicated in a workplace setting.

Finally, the eighth category, *Environmental microaggressions*, can occur on societal, environmental, and institutional levels. The fact that women get paid less than men for the same exact type of job or that there are few women leaders in government or in the corporate world may send the message that women are inferior or incapable of success. Furthermore, the environmental microaggressions that occur through the media may promote stereotypes of women as sex objects who are subservient to men. Such images can lead to various types of psychological distress for many women—ranging from low self-esteem, poor body image and eating disorders, and depression, as well as everyday emotional reactions like anger, resentment, and frustration.

All of these gender microaggressions can have an alarming effect on the women who are victims to them. Women's experiences with sexism have been found to lower self-esteem; increase feelings of anger and depression; cause sexual dysfunction and eating disorders; create body image issues, and produce other stressors that may impact one's psychological well-being (Fredrickson and Roberts, 1997; Hill and Fischer, 2008; Kozee, Tylka, Augustus-Horvath, and Denchik, 2007; Nadal, 2010; Swim et al., 2001). Research has found that women who suffer from these impacts may find themselves less effective in social and professional settings, and their contributions and accomplishments are often overlooked (Nielsen, 2002; Watkins, Kaplan, Brief, Shull, Dietz, Mansfield, et al., 2006). Finally, experiences with gender microaggressions may also impact one's identity development (Capodilupo et al., 2010), in that they may enable a woman to feel less empowered, more accepting of sexism, or both. Thus, microaggressions may impact one's mental health and, consequently, the achievement of personal and professional goals.

When individuals are the victims or recipients of microaggressions, they often experience a "catch-22": should they react or not? (Nadal, in press; Sue, Capodilupo, Torino, Bucceri, Holder, Nadal, and Esquilin, 2007). If they do choose to respond and confront the enactor of the microaggression, they may put their physical or psychological safety in danger. For example, if a woman is catcalled as she walks down the street and she responds angrily, the enactor may become defensive and react in physically abusive ways. In other settings, the idea of harming one's psychological safety would influence one's decisions. For example, if a woman believes that her male coworkers or supervisors use sexist language, and challenges them, they may become angry with her, leading to a hostile working environment, and potentially even jeopardizing her job or room for advancement. On the contrary, if a victim of a microaggression chooses to not respond, there are physical and psychological consequences: many individuals may perseverate about the incident, and feel psychological distress (e.g., regret, resentment, or frustration in oneself) for not voicing their concern (Nadal, in press). These individuals may regret that they did not say something and may fear that such behavior will continue toward themselves and toward other women and marginalized people. For example, if a male student in the classroom makes subtle sexist remarks, a female student may feel conflicted about whether she wants to say something. Perhaps she does not want to engage in an argument in a public forum, perhaps she does not want to have to represent the voices of all women, or perhaps her personality type is one that is less confrontational and more passive. If she chooses not to say anything (and the professor or no other student does either), she may walk away feeling distressed and thinking about what she could have said. If she is in these situations often and feels unable to say anything, she may feel disempowered and may internalize that she is inferior or weak.

Nadal, Hamit, Lyons, Weinberg, and Corman (in press) discuss the various ways in which women may react to gender microaggressions: emotionally, behaviorally, and cognitively. In their research, women experienced an array of emotions—those that were part of their internalized process (e.g., *guilt, humiliation*, and *discomfort*), and those that they expressed to others and sometimes provoked them to take action (*anger* and *fear*). Female participants discussed the various ways in which they react behaviorally to microaggressions. Some remain passive and choose not to confront the enactor of the microaggression. Others attempt to protect themselves by actively engaging in behaviors that would make them less susceptible (e.g., walking in large groups, being accompanied by male friends, or pretending to be lesbians, so that men won't hit on them). Some women reported avoiding any situations that may lead to microaggressions, while others discussed instances in which they confronted individuals who committed microaggressions. Finally, female participants discussed their cognitive reactions to microaggressions: some said that they have become more resilient, in that they know they have overcome sexism, others learned to just accept that sexism exists and conform to gender roles and expectations, and others have learned to become resistant to sexism and feel empowered to fight against microaggressions when they occur.

Microaggressions can become even more complex when an individual holds intersectional identities. For example, a woman of color may experience both gender and racial microaggressions while a lesbian or bisexual woman may experience both gender and sexual orientation microaggressions. In these cases, it may be difficult for a woman to understand if she is being discriminated against because of her race, sexual orientation, gender, or some combination of all three. This next section will examine the various types of microaggressions that women of color and lesbian or bisexual women may experience as a result of the intersection of their identities.

Racial and Gender Microaggressions toward Women of Color

There has been an array of research on the various types of racial microaggressions that individuals may experience (see Sue, 2010, for a review). Because of the politically correct climate that the United States has embraced, it is less acceptable for people to make racist jokes in public or for people to be overtly discriminatory toward others based on their race. Moreover, with the election of our first African American/biracial president, many people may believe that racism no longer exists. However, racial biases may manifest unconsciously and unintentionally through the form of racial microaggressions. Racial microaggressions have been defined as "brief and commonplace daily verbal, behavioral, or environmental indignities, whether intentional or unintentional, that communicate hostile, derogatory, or negative racial slights and insults to the target person or group" (Sue, Capodilupo, et al., 2007, p. 273). Sometimes, those who commit racial microaggressions may not even be aware of the impact of their behaviors. Yet, the accumulation of racial microaggressions has been found to have a number of psychological impacts (e.g., depression, self-esteem issues, anxiety) for the people of color who experience them (Sue, Bucceri, Lin, Nadal and Torino, 2007; Sue, Nadal, Capodilupo, Lin, Rivera and Torino, 2008).

As with gender microaggressions, several categories of racial microaggressions have been identified. A taxonomy on racial microaggressions describes several categories including: *1) Alien in own land, 2) Ascription of intelligence, 3) Color blindness, 4) Criminality/Assumption of criminal status, 5) Denial of individual racism, 6) Myth of meritocracy,*

7) Pathologizing cultural values/communication styles, 8) Second-Class citizen, and *9) Environmental microaggressions* (Sue, Capodilupo, et al., 2007). *Alien in one's own land* occurs when people of color are assumed to be foreigners, even when they (and their families) have lived in the United States for generations. For example, telling an Asian American that she "speaks good English" can be classified as a microaggression because it sends the message that she is a foreigner or that she was expected to speak broken English because of her race. *Ascription of intelligence* takes place when an individual is assumed to hold a certain intellectual level because of his or her race. For example, assuming that an African American person would be less educated or incapable of solving a mathematical problem sends the message that African Americans are intellectually inferior. On the contrary, if an employer assumes that an Asian American employee is good at math and/or computers, without any reason to think so, the employer sends the message that the Asian is a "model minority." This assumption may appear to be a compliment, but in actuality denies people their individuality and reduces them to a stereotype.

Several types of microaggressions are labeled as invalidations because they negate an individual's true lived experience. *Color blindness* is when an individual claims to not be able to see race. For example, if a white coworker tells a person of color, "I don't see color" or "There is only one race—the human race," she or he is negating the racial reality of a person who knows that racism affects her or his life. Although these comments may be intended to convey egalitarian sentiments, they may elicit negative reactions from the people of color who hear them. This invalidation is similar to the *Myth of meritocracy*, or statements that convey that anyone can succeed if he or she works hard enough, regardless of race, gender, or sexual orientation. This belief suggests that if a person of color is not succeeding at work (e.g., not getting promoted), it must be due to laziness or a lack of effort on that person's part rather than to a systematic lack of social privilege. A final invalidation is the *Denial of racial reality*, in which an individual denies the various forms of racial discrimination a person of color may experience. Telling someone that she or he is being "paranoid" or "oversensitive" or that he or she complains about race too much are all forms of microaggressions.

There are several forms of racial microaggressions that are considered microinsults in that they are often innocuous statements or behaviors that send denigrating messages to the person of color who receives them. *Assumption of criminality* occurs when a person of color is presumed to be violent, unlawful, or dangerous. For example, if a Latino is followed around in a store (while others are not), the storeowner is sending a message that she or he assumes that all people of color are thieves. Microaggressions that *Pathologize cultural values* take place when people of color or ethnic minorities are taught that their ways of doing things are weird, different, or exotic. For example, if someone criticizes a food from a person of color's culture, or makes fun of a tradition that he or she deems as "weird," the enactor is sending a message that the only "correct" or "normal" way to be is that of the white American dominant culture. *Second-Class citizen* racial microaggressions occur when a person of color is treated as inferior to a white person; for example, when a taxicab driver passes by an African American to pick up a white customer, he or she sends an indirect message that the white person is superior and deserving of service before the person of color.

Finally, *Environmental microaggressions* occur when systems and spaces convey a racial hierarchy of the white American dominant culture as superior and people of color as inferior. For example, if one notices in a workplace that the CEO and other executives are only white men, a message is conveyed that whites are better and that people of color are not worthy enough of leadership positions. Similarly, if one steps onto a college campus and notices that all of the buildings are named after white men, a message is sent that the most "important" or "notable" people in the world are white, and that there aren't any people of color who warrant having a building named after them.

Some research has found ways in which women of color are victims of both racial and gender microaggressions. For example, in a study of Asian Americans, the women reported being exoticized by men and being treated as sexual objects because of both their race and their gender (Sue, Bucceri, et al., 2007). These Asian American female participants discussed how they were often told that they had exotic looks, which sent the message that they were different and that being Asian was not considered normal. At the same time, they reported feeling like they were "trophy wives" and how men (particularly white men) expected them to be sexually submissive or passive. Thus, they are being objectified like women of all races are, but are being stereotyped also because of their race. This phenomenon is similar to Rivera, Forquer, and Rangel's

(2010) study on Latina/o Americans, in which female participants reported being sexualized and stereotyped as being "sassy" or "spicy." These stereotypes may lead Latinas to be viewed as hypersexualized and therefore as sexual objects to satisfy men's desires.

Contrarily, African American women have reported experiencing both similar and different types of microaggressions as a result of their intersecting identities. One study found that African American women dealt with microaggressions involving their hair (Sue, Nadal, et al., 2008). For example, African American women were told (explicitly and implicitly) that their hair was "unprofessional" or "unique." Both descriptors can elicit different feelings because of the potential intentions involved. Being told that one's hairstyle is unprofessional conveys that the only acceptable hairstyle in the workplace is that of a white woman and denigrates an African American cultural norm. The intention of the enactor is punitive: the African American woman is being coerced to change her hairstyle. On the other hand, being told that one's hair is "unique" may have a different intention. The individual who makes the statement may believe she or he is sending a compliment; however, an indirect message is being sent that her hair is exotic, different, or not normal.

There are a myriad of ways in which intersectional identities can lead to even more confusion on how to address particular microaggressions. For example, if an African American woman is ignored by the CEO of her company, is it because of her race, her gender, or both? Because of these dual identities, she may feel the burden of having "double minority stress"—or the psychological despair of belonging to two oppressed groups. Moreover, because she belongs to both groups, she may be sensitive about being perceived as an angry black woman. There may be even more of a "catch-22" of whether to respond, as she recognizes that she represents each minority group as well as the combination of both.

Sexual Orientation Microaggressions toward Lesbian and Bisexual Women

Women may also find themselves in situations in which they are discriminated against based on their sexual orientation. Again, although society may be becoming more politically correct, discrimination against lesbians and bisexual women (as well as gay and bisexual men and transgender individuals) may have simply become more subtle in nature, in addition to being blatant or overt. Previous literature has found that lesbian, gay, bisexual, and transgender (LGBT) individuals still experience overt discrimination, such as hate crimes based on sexual orientation, citing that victims of sexual orientation hate crimes report greater levels of psychological distress than their nonbiased counterparts (Herek, Cogan and Gillis, 2002). Sexual orientation hate crimes were shown to display a greater severity of violence as compared to other bias-motivated crimes (Dunbar, 2006). Moreover, sexual orientation hate crimes are more likely to be underreported due to factors such as perceived police bias (Dunbar, 2006; Herek et al., 2002), perceived crime severity (Bernstein and Kostelac, 2002; Herek et al., 2002), and the likelihood that the perpetrator(s) would be punished (Herek et al., 2002). Just as such blatant forms of discrimination can lead to fear, depression, and psychological distress, so too can daily, subtle forms of discrimination.

Sexual orientation microaggressions can be defined as everyday verbal, behavioral, and environmental indignities (whether intentional or unintentional) that communicate hostile, derogatory, or negative heterosexist and homophobic slights and insults toward gay, lesbian, and bisexual individuals (Nadal, Rivera and Corpus, 2010). These microaggressions are often subtle in nature and have a negative impact on the recipient. Similarly, part of the experience of sexual orientation microaggressions involves whether one perceives the interaction to be due to his or her sexual orientation and, if so, whether and/or how to react. This can lead to confusion; and if one reacts to the covert situation, that person may be putting him or herself in a dangerous situation (Nadal et al., 2010). Additionally, the cumulative nature of these daily experiences with subtle sexual orientation microaggressions can lead to a buildup of negative emotions, affect one's interpersonal relationships, and cause subsequent psychological distress (Nadal, Hamit and Issa, in press; Nadal, Issa, Leon, Meterko, Wideman and Wong, under review).

Recent literature has started to explore the various ways in which LGBT individuals can experience sexual orientation microaggressions (Nadal, Issa, et al., under review; Nadal, Skolnik, Wong and Ramos, under review; Nadal, Wong, Issa, Leon, Meterko, and Wideman, under review). An original taxonomy for sexual orientation microaggressions was proposed by Nadal, Rivera, and Corpus (2010), using the taxonomy outlined by Sue and Capodilupo (2008) that includes sexual orientation, race, and gender microaggressions. This taxonomy yielded eight themes: *1) Use of hetero-sexist terminology, 2) Endorsement of heteronormative culture/behaviors, 3) Assumption of universal LGBT experience, 4) Exoticization, 5) Discom-fort/Disapproval of LGBT experience, 6) Denial of societal heterosexism/ transphobia, 7) Assumption of sexual pathology/abnormality*, and *8) Denial of individual heterosexism* (Nadal, Rivera, and Corpus, 2010).

In a qualitative study utilizing focus groups to ask LGB individuals to share their experiences with sexual orientation microaggressions, Nadal, Issa, and colleague (under review) found support for eight themes, grouping together "denial of societal heterosexism/transphobia" and "denial of indi-vidual heterosexism" and adding "assaults and threatening behaviors." The *Use of heterosexist terminology* is characterized by experiences of being called derogatory names or having heterosexist remarks directed toward the LGBT individual. For instance, a lesbian woman may be called a "dyke" or, more subtly, may overhear another individual say "That's so gay," refer-ring to something that is bad or wrong. An *Endorsement of heteronormative culture/behaviors* occurs when a heterosexual conveys a message of hetero-sexuality as normal and homosexuality as abnormal, wrong, or unnatural. An example may be a lesbian being told to dress more like a female, sending the message that not conforming to gender roles goes against the norm, which is immoral or bad. An *Assumption of universal LGBT experience* occurs when a heterosexual assumes that all LGBT individuals are the same. In this case, a heterosexual may assume that all lesbian women are "butch," thus ignoring their individual differences. *Exoticization* is evident when LGBT individuals are viewed as a form of entertainment or are otherwise dehumanized. For example, gay men may be viewed as one's source of comedic entertainment, while lesbian women may be viewed as sexual objects, communicating the message that these roles are the only purpose LGBT individuals serve. A *Discomfort/Disapproval of LGBT experience* is displayed when a heterosexual, whether aware or unaware, shows his/her displeasure of or apprehension toward LGBT individuals. For example, a heterosexual may subconsciously stare at a lesbian couple who are holding hands, while another heterosexual may say, "You're going to hell" to that same couple. In either case, the message being conveyed is that their behav-ior is strange, unusual, and condemnable.

A *Denial of the reality of heterosexism* is evident when individuals deny the occurrence of heterosexism or discrimination based on sexual orientation either within themselves or society. A lesbian may experience this microaggression theme when told by a heterosexual that she is oversensitive or complains too much about her sexual orientation or that heterosexism/discrimination based on sexual orientation no longer exists. Heterosexuals may also deny that they themselves could ever be heterosexist, stating such claims as, "I'm not homophobic, I have a gay friend." Such interactions lead to an invalidation of the individual and her experiences with sexual orientation microaggressions and discrimination. Furthermore, it sends a message to the individual that she cannot confront this person when he or she microaggresses. The *Assumption of sexual pathology/abnormality* is characterized by heterosexuals believing that LGBT individuals are sexually promiscuous or sexually deviant. For instance, a heterosexual may automatically assume that a lesbian would be willing to have or has already had a "threesome." This assumption sends the message that being homosexual is abnormal and deviant. *Assaults and threatening behaviors* can be classified as microassaults, in that they are overt discrimination or assaults in nature; however, the aggressor does not physically harm the individual and may not even have intended to in the first place. For example, in a focus group conducted by Nadal, Issa, and colleagues (under review), a participant reported that she was teased and harassed and had received death threats due to her sexual orientation. While such death threats may be viewed as overt and perhaps even as hate crimes, the harassment and bullying that ensued prior may be viewed as microaggressive.

Nadal, Rivera, and Corpus (2010) cite *Environmental microaggressions* that transpire based on sexual orientation. For example, an LGBT individual who realizes that there is a lack of television shows or movies with plots that revolve around same-sex love stories or relationships is recognizing an environmental microaggression. Such an instance may be viewed as the media's discomfort or disapproval of the LGBT experience. When LGBT characters are portrayed in stereotypical ways, such instances may be categorized as assumptions of a universal LGBT experience or even as exoticization.

Some research has found that LGBT women and LGBT women of color may undergo microaggressions based on their intersectional identities. For example, in Sue, Nadal, et al.'s study (2008) with African American participants, a lesbian woman discussed how one of her coworkers assumed she would not be capable of fixing a computer. She discussed how she was unsure whether the assumption of her inferiority was based on her race, gender, sexual orientation, or some combination of all three. In Nadal, Issa, et al.'s study (under review) with LGBT individuals, some lesbian and bisexual women discussed how men assumed that they would want to engage in group sex with them. Perhaps these women are being objectified because of their gender, their sexual orientation, or some combination of both. Again, as mentioned above, the intersections of two or more identities may lead to a double or triple minority stress, which may then impact an individual's perceptions of workplace climate and perhaps the ability to excel in her or his career.

Microaggressions in the Workplace

Research on microaggressions has focused on how such experiences may manifest in various environments, including the workplace—the space where adult individuals spend the majority of their day. The discrimination that women may face throughout their career can have many adverse effects on their mental health and daily functioning. Previous research on sexual harassment has identified the psychological impact that sexual harassment may have on both women and men (Schneider, Swann, and Fitzgerald, 1997). In order to understand the similarities and differences between microaggressions in the workplace and sexual harassment, it is important to understand the definition of sexual harassment. Sexual harassment can be defined as

> unwelcome sexual advances, requests for sexual favors, and other verbal or physical conduct of a sexual nature . . . when submission to or rejection of this conduct explicitly or implicitly affects an individual's employment, unreasonably interferes with an individual's work performance, or creates an intimidating, hostile or offensive work environment. (U.S. Equal Employment Opportunity Commission, 2009)

Fitzgerald, Gelfand, and Drasgow (1995) have identified three major components as qualifying as sexual harassment in the workplace: gender harassment, unwanted sexual attention, and sexual coercion. Gender harassment is defined as verbal and nonverbal behaviors that convey insulting, hostile, and degrading attitudes about women. Unwanted sexual attention refers to a spectrum of verbal and nonverbal behavior that is offensive, unwanted, and unreciprocated. Finally, sexual coercion includes the extortion of sexual cooperation for job-related considerations. While sexual coercion is a more blatant and intentional form of sexism, the other two categories may have some similarities to gender microaggressions. Gender harassment can be considered a form of a microaggression because the enactor's actions are likely unconscious or unintentional, yet have negative implications for the women who receive them. On the contrary, unwanted sexual attention and sexual coercion are likely to be more conscious processes, in that the individual is persistent in flirting or trying to get the attention of the woman. However, although this is conscious, the intention may not be malicious; therefore, the enactor may continue to behave in this manner. Because of the unconscious and unintentional nature of the experience, both parties may perceive certain behaviors differently, which in turn makes it difficult to address the conflict.

Some microaggressions may be addressed more easily because they may fit the criteria for sexual harassment, while others may be more difficult to attend to because of their subtle nature. For example, Capodilupo et al. (2010) cited a woman participant who discussed how her male coworkers publicly displayed a pin-up poster of a scantily clad woman. This may qualify for sexual harassment as it is objectifying of women in an overtly sexist way. Furthermore, it makes the female employee uncomfortable (thus affecting her performance) and creates a hostile or offensive environment. However, when she asked her coworker to remove the poster, she was told that she was being oversensitive and was led to believe that she complains about sexism too much. This invalidation may be more difficult to qualify as sexual harassment, as it may not appear to be overtly sexist. Although the female employee may be uncomfortable by such an invalidation (which may create a hostile working environment) the subjective nature of the invalidation may complicate the ways in which the situation is handled. Given all of these complexities, some microaggressions in the workplace may fit the criteria of sexual harassment, while some microaggressions may be more difficult to be labeled as such.

Examples of the discrimination that women may face during the hiring process as well as within the workplace can be found under each theme of the gender microaggressions taxonomy previously proposed (Nadal, 2010; Sue and Capodilupo, 2008). Women may experience microaggressions involving sexual objectification or sexist language in a plethora of ways—ranging from male coworkers making sexist jokes to a male employer staring at a female employee's breasts. Invisibility may take place when women are overlooked for promotions or when their ideas at a staff meeting go unnoticed. Microaggressions that assume inferiority may ensue when women are presumed to not be good leaders and are therefore given limited management opportunities. Denial of the reality of sexism transpires when women employees are invalidated when they report to a supervisor the sexist events that they experience. Similarly, when a woman confronts a male coworker on his sexist behavior and he denies her sexism, he is invalidating her experiences and worldview as a woman. An example of women being assumed to uphold traditional gender roles occurs when women are given tasks that may be viewed as conventionally feminine. For example, when a woman is assigned to be in charge of an office party (when men are never asked), a message is sent that women are meant to still serve men, even outside of a home.

Microaggressions may also have an impact on women's career-making decisions. When deciding on a career, women are forced to take into account factors that men may not have to worry about, ranging from social acceptance of peers to minimizing the amount of discrimination or conflicts based on gender role expectations. Women with intersectional identities may encounter even more challenges with their career decision making. For example, women of color may avoid entering fields in which they assume they will be the "only one" and may feel the stress of having to represent all women of color, or all people of color in general. Lesbian and bisexual women may choose their career path with a focus on jobs that they perceive will be the most safe and accepting of their sexual orientation, or perhaps they may choose careers based on conforming to gender roles in order to avoid even more discrimination.

Moreover, microaggressions in the workplace may also have a direct impact on the career development of women with intersectional identities. According to the U.S. Equal Employment Opportunity Commission (2003), women of color make up 14.5 percent of the workplace, which is a significant increase in the past 20 years. However, there is still a relatively smaller number of women of color in management positions, in comparison to white men, white women, and men of color; women in general only account for 14.7 percent of *Fortune* 500 seats, and out of that percentage, only 21 percent are women of color (Catalyst, 2006). Previous literature has cited that women of color may experience discrimination that is based on racism, sexism, and a combination of the two (Catalyst, 2005, 2006; Murrell, 1996; Sanchez-Hucles and Davis, 2010). Some authors cite that sexual harassment toward women of color involves both sex discrimination and race discrimination, which contributes to the difficulty in defining such discrimination and therefore fitting legal standards (Murrell, 1996). Moreover, women of color may be the victims of specific stereotypes, which may impede their advancement in the workplace while also having an impact on their work performance (Catalyst, 2005; Sanchez-Hucles and Davis, 2010). Some have stated that women of color in leadership roles are in "triple jeopardy" because they are scrutinized based on their gender, race, ethnicity, and a combination of all three (Sanchez-Hucles and Sanchez, 2010).

There are a myriad of examples of the types of microaggressions that women of color may experience in the workplace, which align with research focusing on people of color in general. For example, African American and Latinas may be assumed to be intellectually inferior by their employers or coworkers. As a result, it may be common for them to be overlooked for promotions or presumed to not be able to complete an intellectually arduous task. Asian American women may be stereotyped as submissive, so it may be possible for men to treat them as subservient or assume that they would not have leadership or managerial skills. African American women may feel exoticized or denigrated if coworkers make comments about their hair, while Asian American women or Latinas may feel invalidated if someone assumes that a grammatical error they made on a work document was because they don't speak English well and not just a typo.

Lesbian and bisexual women may experience additional barriers in the workplace as a result of their intersectional identities; specific factors at play may include societal stigmas, homophobic attitudes, the perpetuation of negative stereotypes, and others' fears of contracting AIDS through working in the same environment as a LGB individual (Chung, 1995). Research has suggested that when making hiring decisions, sexual minorities, as compared to gender and race variables, are the most likely to be discriminated against, or in this case, not hired (Crow, Fok and Hartman, 1998). Furthermore, one factor associated with such attitudes and subsequent hiring decisions is one's gender role beliefs (Horvath and Ryan,

2003). Consequently, if a potential employer holds rigid gender beliefs, she or he may be more likely to have negative attitudes toward lesbians and therefore be less likely to hire a lesbian. Horvath and Ryan (2003) found that religiosity and beliefs about controllability (i.e., whether or not homosexuality is a choice) were significantly related to attitudes toward lesbian and gay men. These relationships were such that the more religiously involved they were, or the more they believed that homosexuality was a choice, the more negative their attitudes toward lesbians and gay men. The attitudes were, in turn, directly related to hiring decisions, giving light to how discrimination can be faced in the early stages of career development. Day and Schoenrade (1997) found that individuals who were able to come out at work and communicate openly about their homosexuality had increased job satisfaction levels. Paradoxically, research has also reported a relationship between coming out and increased discrimination in the workplace (Ragins and Cornwell, 2001). Additionally, research has found that those who reported higher levels of perceived discrimination reported negative work attitudes and fewer promotions (Ragins and Cornwell, 2001) and those who perceived a higher level of tolerance of heterosexism in the workplace reported increased stress (Waldo, 1999).

Specific examples of the microaggressions that lesbian and bisexual women experience in the workplace may fall in line with the various themes in the taxonomy proposed by Nadal, Rivera, and Corpus (2010). For example, hearing a coworker or potential employer say "That's so gay" in reference to something negative or being called a "dyke" can occur in any stage in one's career development; this is an example of heterosexist terminology, and can result in an unwelcoming, depressing, and even fearful environment for the receiver of such microaggressions. Moreover, an employer who encourages her or his LGBT employees to act more "straight" or to adhere to traditional gender roles may send a microaggressive message to lesbian and bisexual women that heterosexuality and gender-conforming behaviors are normative.

Case Discussion

In order to understand how microaggressions can manifest in the workplace, let's revisit the case of Bernadette, the 27-year-old Filipina American attorney who feels uncomfortable in her office due to subtle comments made about her appearance as well as covert objectification. Her male coworkers consistently tell her how pretty she is, while some glance at her body in subtle ways. Her male supervisor has even commented on Bernadette's appearance, saying that she needs to dress "more professionally." While Bernadette believes that most of her coworkers may have good intentions when they make these statements, she feels as if she is being singled out: such comments are never said to other men, or to the older white women in the office. Bernadette feels distressed about going to work; she feels uncomfortable with her other coworkers and isolated because others don't seem to understand. Her gut instinct is that she is being treated this way because of her gender, race, age, or some combination of the three, but she cognitively knows that these situations are so subtle that they cannot be classified as sexual harassment or overt discrimination.

Bernadette may experience the aforementioned "catch-22" when she considers how to approach this situation. Her current reaction is passive; she does not confront any of her coworkers about the situation, which leads her to feel anxious about coming to work. These feelings may potentially affect her workplace performance and her interpersonal skills, which may have detrimental outcomes on her leadership potential and advancement within her firm. Moreover, because she is a Filipina American, perhaps she may feel she is fulfilling stereotypes of Asian women as being passive and ineffective leaders, which may even increase her distress.

If Bernadette does decide to confront the situation, there are many potential outcomes. If she talks with her male coworkers directly, they may become defensive and assure her that they are not sexist and that she is being oversensitive. If they are not receptive to her feedback, they may become angry with her, potentially leading to an overtly hostile environment. Bernadette may be labeled as the "angry woman" or the "angry minority," which may impact her opportunities for growth in the firm. Moreover, one of the individuals who is making Bernadette feel uncomfortable is her male supervisor (who has made suggestions on how she should dress). If she confronts him, and he is unreceptive to her feedback, the repercussions may range from chastisement, isolation, and possibly even her termination from the company. Thus, Bernadette may feel hesitant in saying anything at all, and instead may passively accept the microaggressions as a normal part of her work experience, not recognizing the impact that these encounters could have on her mental health and performance.

As Bernadette and the other examples given throughout this chapter exemplify, women's careers and workplace experiences have the potential to be significantly impacted by microaggressions. While there are many laws and policies in place to protect against sexual harassment and discrimination, these seemingly innocuous experiences may still occur and be pervasive in many workplace settings. The accumulation of these microaggressions can have an increasing effect on women's mental health and general well-being and on their ability to function and cope on a daily basis. Because these stressors can lead to job dissatisfaction, negative work attitudes and, subsequently, psychological distress and even mental illness, it is imperative that workplaces find ways to address these micro-aggressions in order to improve the lives of women leaders.

References

Bernstein, M., and Kostelac, C. (2002). Lavender and blue: Attitudes about homosexuality and behavior toward lesbians and gay men among police officers. *Journal of Contemporary Criminal Justice, 18*(3), 302–328.

Capodilupo, C. M., Nadal, K. L., Hamit, S., Corman, L., Lyons, O., and Weinberg, A. (2010). The manifestation of gender microaggressions. In D. W. Sue (Ed.), *Microaggressions and marginality: Manifestation, dynamics, and impact* (pp. 193–216). New York: Wiley & Sons.

Catalyst. (2005). *2005 Catalyst Census of Women Board Directors of the Fortune 500.* Retrieved from *http://www.catalyst.org/publication/19/ 2005-catalyst*-census-of-women-board-directors-of-the-fortune-500 on May 31, 2010.

Catalyst. (2006). Connections that count: The informal networks of women of color in the United States. Retrieved from http://www.catalyst.org/ publication/52/connections-that-count-the-informalnetworks-of-women -of-color-in-the-united-states on May 31, 2010.

Chung, Y. B. (1995). Career decision making of lesbian, gay, and bisexual individuals. *The Career Development Quarterly, 44*, 178–190.

Crow, S. M., Fok, L. Y., and Hartman, S. J. (1998). Who is at greatest risk of work-related discrimination—Women, blacks, or homosexuals? *Employee Responsibilities and Rights Journal, 11*(1), 15–26.

Day, N. E., and Schoenrade, P. (1997). Staying in the closet versus coming out: Relationships between communication about sexual orientation and work attitudes. *Personnel Psychology, 50*, 147–163.

Dunbar, E. (2006). Race, gender, and sexual orientation in hate crime victimization: Identity politics or identity risk? *Violence and Victims, 21*(3), 323–337.

Fitzgerald, L. F., Gelfand, M. J., Drasgow, F. (1995). Measuring sexual harassment: Theoretical and psychometric advances. *Basic and Applied Social Psychology, 17*(4), 425–445.

Fredrickson, B.L., and Roberts, T. (1997). Objectification theory: Toward understanding women's lived experiences and mental health risks. *Psychology of Women Quarterly, 21*, 173–206.

Glick, P., and Fiske, S. T. (2001). An ambivalent alliance: Hostile and benevolent sexism as complementary justifications for gender inequality. *The American Psychologist, 56*(2), 109–118.

Herek, G. M., Cogan, J. C. and Gillis, R. J. (2002). Victim experiences in hate crime based on sexual orientation. *Journal of Social Issues, 58*, 319–339.

Hill, M. S., and Fischer, A. R. (2008). Examining objectification theory: Lesbian and heterosexual women's experiences with sexual- and self-objectification. *The Counseling Psychologist, 36*, 745–776.

Horvath, M., and Ryan, A. M. (2003). Antecedents and potential moderators of the relationship between attitudes and hiring discrimination on the basis of sexual orientation. *Sex Roles, 48*(3/4), 115–130.

Kozee, H. B., Tylka, T. L., Augustus-Horvath, C. L., and Denchik, A. (2007). Development of psychometric evaluation of the Interpersonal Sexual Objectification Scale. *Psychology of Women Quarterly, 31*(2), 176–189.

Murrell, A. J. (1996). Sexual harassment and women of color: Issues, challenges, and future directions. In M. S. Stockdale (Ed.), *Sexual harassment in the workplace: Perspectives, frontiers, and response strategies. Women and work: A Research and Policy Series*, Vol. 5 (pp. 51–66). Thousand Oaks CA: Sage.

Nadal, K. L. (2008). Preventing racial, ethnic, gender, sexual minority, disability, and religious microaggressions: Recommendations for promoting positive mental health. *Prevention in Counseling Psychology: Theory, Research, Practice and Training, 2*(1), 22–27.

Nadal, K. L. (2010). Gender microaggressions and women: Implications for mental health. In M. A. Paludi (Ed.), *Feminism and Women's Rights Worldwide, Volume 2: Mental and Physical Health* (pp. 155–175). Westport, CT: Praeger.

Nadal, K. L. (in press). Responding to racial, gender, and sexual orientation Microaggressions in the workplace. In M. Paludi, C. Paludi and E. DeSouza (Eds.), *The Praeger handbook on workplace discrimination: Legal, management, and social science perspectives*. Westport, CT: Praeger.

Nadal, K. L., Hamit, S., and Issa, M. A. (in press). Overcoming gender and sexual orientation microaggression. In M. Paludi and F. Denmark (Eds.), *Victims of sexual assault and abuse: Resources and responses for individuals and families*. Westport, CT: Praeger.

Nadal, K. L., Hamit, S., Lyons, O., Weinberg, A., and Corman, L. (in press). Gender microaggressions: Perceptions, processes, and coping mechanisms of women.

Nadal, K. L., Issa, M. A., Leon, J., Meterko, V., Wideman, M., and Wong, Y. (under review). The manifestation of sexual orientation microaggressions: Perspectives of lesbian, gay, and bisexual people.

Nadal, K. L., Rivera, D. P., and Corpus, M. J. H. (2010). Sexual orientation and transgender microaggressions in everyday life: Experiences of lesbians, gays, bisexuals, and transgender individuals. In D. W. Sue (Ed.), *Microaggressions and marginality: Manifestation, dynamics, and impact* (pp. 217–240). New York: Wiley & Sons.

Nadal, K. L., Skolnik, A., and Wong, Y. (under review). The manifestation of transgender microaggressions: Implications for mental health.

Nadal, K. L., Wong, Y., Issa, M., Leon, J., Meterko, V., and Wideman, M. (under review). Sexual orientation microaggressions: Processes and coping mechanisms for lesbian, gay, and bisexual individuals.

Nielsen, L. B. (2002). Subtle, pervasive, harmful: Racist and sexist remarks in public as hate speech. *Journal of Social Issues, 58*(2), 265–280.

Ragins, B. R., and Cornwell, J. M. (2001). Pink triangles: Antecedents and consequences of perceived workplace discrimination against gay and lesbian employees. *Journal of Applied Psychology, 86*(6), 1244–1261.

Rivera, D. P., Forquer, E. E., and Rangel, R. (2010). Microaggressions and the life experience of Latina/o Americans. In D. W. Sue (Ed.), *Microaggressions and marginalized groups in society: Race, gender, sexual orientation, class and religious manifestations* (pp. 59–83). New York: Wiley and Sons.

Sanchez-Hucles, J. V., and Davis, D. D. (2010). Women and women of color in leadership: Complexity, identity, and intersectionality. *American Psychologist, 65*(3), 171–181.

Schneider, K. T., Swann, S., and Fitzgerald, L. F. (1997). Job-related and psychological effects of sexual harassment in the workplace: Empirical evidence from two organizations. *Journal of Applied Psychology, 82,* 401–415.

Sue, D. W. (2010). *Microaggressions in everyday life: Race, gender, and sexual orientation.* New York: Wiley and Sons.

Sue, D. W., Bucceri, J. M., Lin, A. I., Nadal, K. L., and Torino, G. C. (2007). Racial microaggressions and the Asian American experience. *Cultural Diversity and Ethnic Minority Psychology, 13*(1), 72–81.

Sue, D. W., and Capodilupo, C. M. (2008). Racial, gender, and sexual orientation microaggressions: Implications for counseling and psychotherapy. In D. W. Sue and D. Sue (Eds.), *Counseling the culturally diverse*, 5th ed. (pp. 105–130). New York: John Wiley and Sons.

Sue, D. W., Capodilupo, C. M., Torino, G. C., Bucceri, J. M., Holder, A. M., Nadal, K. L., and Esquilin, M. E. (2007). Racial microaggressions in everyday life: Implications for counseling. *The American Psychologist, 62*(4), 271–286.

Sue, D. W., Nadal, K. L., Capodilupo, C. M., Lin, A. I., Rivera, D. P., and Torino, G. C. (2008). Racial microaggressions against black Americans: Implications for counseling. *Journal of Counseling and Development, 86*(3), 330–338.

Swim, J. K., and Cohen, L. L. (1997). Overt, covert, and subtle sexism: A comparison between the attitudes toward women and modern sexism scales. *Psychology of Women Quarterly, 21*(1), 103–118.

Swim, J. K., Hyers, L. L., Cohen, L. L., and Ferguson, M. J. (2001). Everyday sexism: Evidence for its incidence, nature, and psychological impact from three daily diary studies. *Journal of Social Issues, 57* (1), 31–53.

Swim, J. K., Mallett, R., and Stagnor, C. (2004). Understanding subtle sexism: Detection and use of sexist language. *Sex Roles, 51*(3–4), 117–128.

U.S. Equal Employment Opportunity Commission. (2003). Women of color: Their employment in the private sector. Retrieved from http://archive .eeoc.gov/stats/reports/womenofcolor/womenofcolor.pdf on May 24, 2010.

U.S. Equal Employment Opportunity Commission. (2009). Sexual Harassment. Retrieved from http://www.eeoc.gov/eeoc/statistics/enforcement/ sexual_harassment.cfm on March 18, 2010.

Waldo, C. R. (1999). Working in a majority context: A structural model of heterosexism as minority stress in the workplace. *Journal of Counseling Psychology, 46*(2), 218–232.

Watkins, M. B., Kaplan, S., Brief, A. P., Shull, A., Dietz, J., Mansfield, M., et al. (2006). Does it pay to be a sexist? The relationship between modern sexism and career outcomes. *Journal of Vocational Behavior, 69*, 524–537.

2

Social Stigma Faced by Female Leaders in the Workplace

Whitney Botsford Morgan, Veronica L. Gilrane, Tracy C. McCausland, and Eden B. King

There has been encouraging progress when it comes to the status of women in the American workforce. In 2008, 60 percent of women participated in the labor force; women accounted for 51 percent of all persons employed in management and professional occupations, including traditionally male-dominated roles (e.g., accountants, lawyers) (Bureau of Labor Statistics, 2009). In the past 10 years, limited research suggests that in fact women may be better leaders than males. The Pew Research Center conducted a study of the public's attitudes regarding male and female public leaders (Taylor, Morin, Cohn, Clark, and Wang, 2008). Findings suggested that although women did not rise to the highest positions in public or corporate leadership, when individuals evaluated men and women on eight leadership traits (honest, intelligent, hardworking, decisive, ambitious, compassionate, outgoing, and creative) women were rated higher than men on five of the eight traits. Empirical research supports the notion that women may in fact be effective, or even more effective, leaders than men in certain situations. For example, recent research (Rosette and Tost, 2010) demonstrated a female advantage on both agentic and communal characteristics when success was internally attributed to female top-leaders. Eagly, Johannese-Schmidt, and van Engen's (2003) meta-analysis demonstrated a slight female advantage over men on effective leadership styles (i.e., transformational, contingent reward aspect of transactional style). Additionally, Vecchio (2002) suggested that women may be more effective leaders considering the needs of modern organizations (e.g., person-oriented and honest). Given this evidence, you may ask why women do not advance to positions of leadership. There are several possible responses to this question, but one unanimous explanation is discrimination and prejudice rooted in social stigma (Blau and Kahn, 2006; Kark and Eagly, in press).

Despite progress, there is little debate that gender inequities continue to plague the American workforce (Lyness and Heilman, 2006; Kark and Eagly, in press; Ryan and Haslam, 2007). Discrimination manifests itself in subtle yet pernicious forms (Dovidio and Gaertner, 2004; Hebl, King, Glick, Singletary, and Kazama, 2007) contributing to the underrepresentation of women at the highest levels of the organizational hierarchy (Martell, Lane, and Emrich, 1996). Women only hold 13.5 percent of *Fortune* 500 executive positions and 15.2 percent of corporate board seats. The purpose of this chapter is to identify one of the causes of this phenomenon—social stigma—and to discuss its workplace implications for female leaders.

Social Stigma

Social stigma is a devalued social identity (Crocker, Major, and Steele, 2008) that is socially discrediting and prevents an individual from being fully accepted (Goffman, 1963). Social stigma essentially presents an individual with an unwanted label or set of characteristics that remains with the person. Crocker and colleagues (2003) discussed potential outcomes of stigma that include being the target of negative stereotypes, social rejection, discrimination, and economic disadvantage. Central to the concept of stigma is that discriminatory behavior only occurs under certain situational circumstances. It is important to be clear that we do not suggest that all employed women are stigmatized. Eagly and Carli (2003) specified that women encounter discriminatory behaviors when in situations that are male-dominated and when there are male evaluators. Moreover, a meta-analysis revealed that there was greater gender bias on male-dominated tasks than female-dominated tasks (Swim, Borgida, Maruyama, and Myers, 1989). Similarly, Davison and Burke's (2000) meta-analysis demonstrated that men were preferred over women for male-dominated jobs (d = .34).

Both meta-analyses provide strong evidence that employed women are stigmatized when they participate in stereotypically male-dominated tasks (i.e., leadership). Put simply, context matters. Women are stigmatized in situations where they either are, or act as, leaders, or exert behaviors or characteristics that are representative of leadership. The question that follows such a statement is *why* do female leaders face social stigma in the workplace?

Theoretical Rationale for Social Stigma Faced by Female Leaders

Several theories help build a framework for understanding social stigma faced by female leaders in the workplace. The first, social role theory, suggests that the distribution of men and women into breadwinner and homemaker roles creates stereotypes that support the maintenance of these roles (Eagly, 1987), perpetuating stigma faced by female leaders. A second theory, lack of fit, also explains stigma faced by female leaders (Heilman, 1983). This theory purports that an individual's success in a particular job is determined by a comparison of the perception of the individual's attributes to the perception of the job requirements. Due to social stigma, women are perceived to be incompatible with the demands of leadership. Finally, ambivalent sexism suggests that hostile and benevolent approaches are complementary forms of sexism that maintain the status quo, preventing women from advancing in the workplace (Glick and Fiske, 1996). Together, these theories provide complementary explanations as to how female leaders became a stigmatized subgroup and why this social stigma persists despite evidence of effectiveness of female leaders.

Social Role Theory

According to social role theory of sex differences (Eagly, 1987; Eagly, Wood, and Diekman, 2000), the division in social roles for men and women, particularly in occupational settings, accounts for differences in normative gender behaviors. Eagly and Karau (2002) extended this concept by introducing role congruity theory, which suggests that prejudice may occur to the extent that others perceive a misalignment between stereotypes toward a target group member and characteristics of his or her social role. We propose that women are often devalued or stigmatized as leaders because the discord between their social and occupational roles prevents them from being fully socially accepted (Goffman, 1963). The theoretical foundation of social role theory has been substantiated by empirical findings that support the conclusion that masculine qualities are often associated with male-dominated occupations, particularly those involving managerial roles. For instance, Cejka and Eagly (1999) found that feminine characteristics, such as physical and personality attributes, are viewed as more integral to success in female-dominated occupations, while masculine qualities are viewed as more important to success in male-dominated occupations.

Lack of Fit

Related to role congruity theory, Heilman's (1983) lack-of-fit model contends that individuals perceive that success in a given job is determined by the degree to which the abilities and skills required for a particular occupation correspond to the attributes of an individual. A lack of fit or misalignment between gender and occupational roles may prove especially disadvantageous for women who seek or occupy managerial or leadership positions because of the perception that women's attributes contrast with the qualities of a prototypical leader. Specifically, women are stereotyped as possessing communal attributes, such as warmth, kindness, and a concern for others. Conversely, men are perceived to have agentic attributes, which include confidence, aggressiveness, and dominance. Traditionally, agentic traits have been viewed as characteristic of leader roles (Eagly, 1987; Eagly and Karau, 2002). In reference to gender and leadership roles, research has directly assessed the congruency between gender stereotypes and characteristics of successful managers (Duehr and Bono, 2006; Heilman, Block, Martell, 1989; Schein, 1973, 1975, 2001). Despite evidence from past research demonstrating perceptions that stereotypically masculine attributes align with leader characteristics (Heilman et al., 1989; Schein, 1973, 1975, 2001), more recent findings have illustrated that the traditionally masculine leader prototype may be evolving (Atwater, Brett, Waldman, DiMare, and Hayden, 2004; Duehr and Bono, 2006; Powell, Butterfield, and Parent, 2002; Prime, Carter, and Welbourne, 2009; Johnson, Murphy, Zwedie, and Reichard, 2008). In fact, the literature points to the existence of both masculine and feminine managerial subroles; however, it supports the notion that most successful leader characteristics are perceived as more agentic than communal, and thus more masculine than feminine (Atwater et al., 2004; Powell et al., 2002; Prime et al., 2009).

Implications of Incongruity and Lack of Fit

Researchers have extended the literature on role incongruity and lack-of-fit models by examining how gender stereotypes impact treatment toward women who seek or occupy traditionally masculine positions, such as managerial roles. Drawing from gender discrimination and harassment litigation, Burgess and Brogida (1999) illustrate two ways in which stereotypes about women may lead to discrimination. First, descriptive stereotypes toward women, or perceptions of the attributes that women *do* possess, may engender unfair hiring practices in which women are not selected for male-dominated occupations because they are perceived to possess characteristics that misalign with the role of the job. Second, the prescriptive component of the female stereotype, or beliefs about characteristics that women *should* possess, may lead to unfavorable evaluations of women in masculine type jobs because they are viewed as lacking femininity and violating their gender norms. Often referred to as the double bind, this predicament is especially relevant for women in leadership positions who are viewed as poor leaders for exhibiting feminine behaviors, while those who engage in masculine characteristics that align with managerial attributes are denigrated for lacking femininity (Eagly and Carli, 2007). The latter portion of this double bind has been described as a backlash (Rudman, 1998; Rudman and Glick, 2001) or penalty (Heilman, Wallen, Fuchs, and Tamkins, 2004) that women may experience in the form of discrimination (Rudman and Glick, 1999, 2001), sabotage (Rudman and Fairchild, 2004), or unfavorable evaluations (Heilman et al., 2004).

Additional research testing incongruity theory has illustrated how the interplay between both descriptive and prescriptive stereotypes places women in a double bind. For example, Johnson and colleagues (2008) found that in order for women to be viewed as effective leaders, they had to possess both sensitivity and strength, while male leaders were perceived as effective by possessing only strength. Similarly, Heilman and Okimoto (2007) discovered that without presenting any additional information, male managers were rated as more likeable than female managers; however, when the female managers were presented as communal, they were perceived as more likeable than male managers. These findings suggest that women in male-dominated occupations who balance communal and agentic behaviors may mitigate the negative outcomes of gender and occupational role incongruity. Unfortunately, this strategy to alleviate gender discrimination not only places responsibility on the target but it may also reinforce gender stereotypes.

Ambivalent Sexism

Stereotypes and the underrepresentation of women in leader positions may also be perpetuated through sexism. Sexism may exist in two seemingly unrelated forms. First, hostile sexism refers to the belief that women seek to gain power over men either through their sexuality or feminist principles. This more traditional form of sexism is manifested through overt and destructive actions. Second, benevolent sexism represents the chivalrous idea that women are fragile creatures who should be respected, treasured, and sheltered. Although benevolent sexism seems to be free of malicious intent, it suggests that women lack strength and competence and are most appropriate for stereotypically female social roles (Glick and Fiske, 1997, 2001). For example, a woman may not receive a promotion to a managerial position because her male supervisor wants to protect her from the demanding tasks of a leader.

Although hostile and benevolent sexism seem to occupy polar ends of the sexism spectrum, Glick and Fiske (1996) found that the two types are related and may coexist. For example, one study found that pregnant women were treated in a hostile manner when they engaged in counternormative behaviors by applying for a job, especially if it was stereotypically masculine, and they were treated in benevolent way when they conformed to normative social roles (Hebl et al., 2007). This research demonstrates that individuals may engage in both hostile and benevolent sexist behaviors in order to maintain the status quo. The ambivalent sexism literature is complementary to the social role theory research in explaining the challenges for women seeking to climb the organizational hierarchy. Due to the incongruity between female gender roles and leader social roles, women in leadership positions may be stigmatized or devalued as traditional leaders (Eagly, 1987; Eagly and Karau, 2002). This stigma and lack of acceptance of female leaders may lead others to engage in discriminatory behaviors (Crocker, Major, and Steele, 2003), such as those indicative of benevolent sexism. In other situations, in which women occupy a traditionally feminine social role, the stigma is gone and women may be rewarded not only through more positive evaluations, but also through the seemingly positive behavior indicative of benevolent sexism. In the next sections, we further delineate empirical findings that illustrate the manifestations of stigma faced by female leaders.

Manifestations of Social Stigma

We have thus far reviewed and discussed social stigma and provided theoretical rationale for why female leaders experience stigma. We next present three broad categories (procedural, interpersonal, individual) through which stigma manifests, and in each section discuss the negative consequences of stigma faced by female leaders in the workplace. Procedural manifestations of stigma faced by women leaders encompass a range of experiences focused on the more formalized aspects of the workplace (e.g., work assignments, performance evaluation, promotion). Interpersonal manifestations capture the degree of social interaction (e.g., networking, inclusion) between the female leader and others (e.g., coworker, supervisor) in the workplace. Finally, individual manifestations represent the female leader's felt experiences and resulting desire to advance in the workplace. Each category presents a unique set of challenges that hinders women's success in male-dominated situations (i.e., positions of leadership), ultimately demonstrating the very real consequences of social stigma for female leaders.

Procedural

The procedural manifestations of stigma that women leaders encounter range from subtle differences in work experiences to more formalized disparities in performance evaluations that finally culminate in dramatic discrepancies in promotions to the top tiers of management. Developmental work experiences (DWEs) can be defined as workplace incidents that individuals encounter and learn from, which over time accumulate in the development of job relevant knowledge and skills (Spreitzer, McCall, and

Mahoney, 1997). Both the quantity and quality of these on-the-job experiences are critical components to managerial growth (Morrison, White, and Van Velsor, 1987). Researchers at the Center for Creative Leadership have proposed three critical characteristics of DWE quality: challenge, feedback, and support (Van Velsor, McCauley, and Moxley, 1998). Preliminary empirical evidence suggests that women and men do not differ in the quantity of work experiences provided by employers, but rather in the quality of those experiences (King, Botsford, Hebl, Kazama, Dawson, and Perkins, in press). Specifically, although men and women expressed comparable levels of supervisor support and interest in pursuing challenging experiences and supervisor support, women received less challenging experiences and less negative feedback as compared to their male counterparts. Similarly, anecdotal evidence suggests that mothers returning to the workplace from maternity leave are reassigned to less challenging work (Williams, Manvell, and Bornstein, 2006). Thus, stigma toward female leaders may be manifested in the assignment of qualitatively poorer developmental experiences to women than to men.

Stigma may also be manifested in disparities in performance evaluations, which are an important tool that employers utilize to measure the achievement of their employees. Research suggests that the performance of male leaders may be evaluated more favorably than equally competent female leaders (Eagly, Makhijani, and Klonsky, 1992; Lyness and Heilman, 2006). Success in and of itself is not aberrant for female leaders, but the conditions under which that success is achieved are fundamental to its perception and evaluation by others. Specifically, backlash toward successful women seems to emerge when gender-stereotypic norms have been violated (Cuddy and Fiske, 2004). For example, a meta-analysis found that there was only a slight tendency for individuals to evaluate men in leadership positions more favorably than women in leadership positions; however, this tendency was stronger depending on certain circumstances, including leadership style and organizational context (Eagly, Makhijani, and Klonsky, 1992). Female leaders that engaged in stereotypically masculine leadership styles (i.e., independent, assertive, task-oriented, and autocratic behaviors) were rated less favorably than male leaders. Additionally, female leaders who occupied male-dominated roles experienced this same form of devaluation as compared to their male counterparts. Related research suggests that expanding the criterion space may not be a solution to the problem of stereotyping in evaluations of performance. Since women in leadership positions often occupy male-dominated roles and operate in ambiguous situations, the aforementioned studies provide evidence that female leaders are likely to receive lower performance evaluations than equally competent male leaders. Reinforcing the barrier to upper-level management, Lyness and Heilman (2006) found that promoted women received higher performance evaluations than promoted men. This finding is particularly concerning because it suggests that in addition to women being evaluated more poorly than men, women need to attain higher evaluations in order to be promoted. Stated simply, women need to achieve higher standards if they desire to climb the managerial ladder.

The most visible procedural manifestation of stigma is the discrepancy in promotions at the higher levels of the management hierarchy. Lyness and Judiesch (1999) found that relative to men, women were more likely to be promoted than hired into upper management positions; however, women were less likely to be promoted. In other words, talented women are more likely to attain top leadership positions by ascending the managerial chain (i.e., staying at one organization) as compared to being hired from outside the organization. That being said, even if women decide to pursue the promotional approach to upper-level management, men are still more likely to be promoted than women. Women leaders that do succeed in climbing the management hierarchy often inherit leadership positions that are high risk. Ryan and Haslam (2005) coined the term the "glass cliff" to describe the finding that the appointment of a woman to a board of directors often followed poor organizational performance in the preceding months. Procedural manifestations of stigma toward female leaders, therefore, seem to include situations in which women are set up to fail.

Interpersonal

In contemporary organizations (and society), discrimination presents itself in covert, subtle ways (Dovidio and Gaertner, 2004; Hebl et al., 2007). Interpersonal discrimination is characterized by interpersonal cues (e.g., decreased eye contact and interaction time) that signals liking or collegiality to the individual (Hebl, Foster, Mannix and Dovidio, 2002; Hebl et al., 2007). These interpersonal cues directed toward stigmatized groups (i.e., female leaders) may be a "much more sensitive indicator of hostile biases in occupational contexts" than formalized discrimination (Hebl et al., 2007 p. 1501). The interpersonal manifestations of stigma that women leaders encounter range from subtle differences in perceptions of competence and commitment to more overt disparities including social isolation and even sexual harassment.

Employed women face negative perceptions related to competence and commitment in the workplace. Such negative perceptions are exacerbated when women attempt to assert themselves as leaders in the workplace. Heilman and Haynes (2005) demonstrated that in a group setting, female members were rated as less competent and less likely to play a leadership role than male members. The devalued social identify of female leaders results in outsiders to not only overlook their contributions, but also denigrate their competence when attempting to assert themselves in a group. Lyness and Heilman (2006) confirmed anecdotal evidence that women do indeed have to work harder to prove themselves in the workplace. In order for women to be evaluated as competent, they must unambiguously demonstrate superior performance to their male counterparts (Biernat and Kobrynowicz, 1997; Heilman and Hanyes, 2005). Some argue that because females are often denigrated in the advancement process, women who do achieve positions of leadership are, in fact, more qualified and perform especially well (Biernat, 2005). However, such negative perceptions likely contribute to the underrepresentation of women in positions of leadership.

Interpersonal manifestations extend beyond others' perceptions of capabilities to disparities, including negative affect, social isolation, and even sabotage or sexual harassment. Research suggests that even when men and women are judged equally on competence, female leaders receive more negative nonverbal reactions and affect than do male leaders (Butler and Geis, 1990; Koch, 2005). Consonant with stigma theory, research suggests individuals attempt to avoid stigmatized individuals (Jones, Farina, Hastorf, Markus, Miller and Scott, 1984), potentially preventing women from growing their interpersonal network (Seibert, Kraimer, and Liden, 2001), resisting female authority (Eagly and Karau, 2002; Heilman, 2001), sabotage (Rudman and Fairchild, 2004), and more generally, socially isolating female leaders in the workplace. Stockdale and Bhattacharya (2009) review literature presenting sexual harassment as yet another barrier to women's advancement in male-dominated positions (i.e., leadership). As ambivalent sexism theory suggests, there is also a "softer" side to discrimination. Benevolent sexism suggests that women should be protected and revered; therefore, individuals may use diminutive language (e.g., honey) when interacting with females, creating situations in which women feel devalued. Individuals who view female leaders as competitors may enact such diminutive strategies in an effort to maintain the status quo. Social stigma faced by female leaders, therefore, contributes to negative interpersonal perceptions and interpersonal behaviors that attempt to prevent women from advancing in the organizational hierarchy.

Individual

The individual manifestations of stigma that female leaders encounter largely stem from powerful, and divergent, norms for what it means to be a "woman" and a "leader." Strong familial norms combined with feelings of guilt may result in self-limiting behavior (i.e., lack of career self-efficacy) that ultimately prevents women from further advancement. Social role theory explains the distribution of men and women into bread-winner and homemaker roles, respectively (Eagly, 1987). As a result of these distributions, there is a societal mandate for women to feel they should be responsible for homemaker responsibilities *in addition to* paid work; men, however, feel they should *only* be responsible for paid work. Thus, it is not uncommon for women to participate in paid work, perform the majority of household duties (Hochschild, 2003), and bear the burden of child care responsibilities (Bond, Thompson, Galinsky, and Protas, 2002). This is further complicated by the fact that more senior and prestigious positions place a premium on working long hours and travel. Given the demands of long hours and the expectations to be present on nights and weekends even when unnecessary (Brett and Stroh, 2003), it becomes impossible for women, particularly mothers, to fulfill the ideal roles for both "woman" and "leader." Furthermore, women report greater stress than men from working long hours because women are less likely to be able to lessen the burden of domestic work (Davidson and Fielden, 1999). Thus, these pulls in separate directions may increase the likelihood of conflict in the woman. This may be especially true for employed mothers, as they are juggling both homemaking and caretaking responsibilities. The mother may want to do it all (maintain employment and be an intensive wife/mother), but realize this is not realistic (Johnston and Swanson, 2006), causing discomfort. Furthermore, qualitative research suggests that mothers experienced guilt upon returning to work because they were not able to fully complete the traditionally held role of mother due to their work demands (Seagram and Daniluk, 2002). Family pressure and responsibility does not fully explain the underrepresentation of women in positions of leadership (Kark and Eagly, in press). Discrimination is indeed present and powerful; however, it is important to consider how societal norms hinder the advancement women in the workplace.

Heilman (1983; 2001) discusses how perceived incongruity may lead to outcomes of self-limiting behavior as well as discrimination. As discussed throughout this chapter, outcomes of social stigma include discrimination. However, we have not yet considered the self-limiting nature of stigma faced by female leaders and its consequences. Self-limiting behaviors may include the devaluing of one's contributions, lack of self-promotion, or anxiety over advancement. This generalized lack of career self-efficacy may stem from a questioning of women's decisions regarding their roles in work and family or self-limiting thoughts regarding their capabilities in a male-dominated environment. Low career self-efficacy may link back to the lack of task mastery (Bandura, 1977) that female leaders encounter due to procedural manifestations of stigma. Regardless of the source, this lack of career self-efficacy may result in increased distraction from work (Kanfer and Ackerman, 1996), lack of persistence (Bandura, 1997), and ultimately dissatisfaction in their job. A similar phenomenon—stereotype threat—suggests that sheer awareness of the stereotype results in the stereotypic, lower performance. Davies, Spencer, and Steele (2005) revealed that when participants in groups viewed stereotypical portrayals, the women (and not the men) exhibited less interest in becoming the leader. Thus, female leaders' own awareness of their social stigma creates yet another, albeit self-limiting, challenge to advancement.

"Double" Stigma

Thus far we have addressed social stigma faced by female leaders and the procedural, interpersonal, and individual consequences. This next section discusses "double" stigma, or situations that likely heighten the already devalued social indentify of female leaders. Employees of contemporary organizations often have multiple intersecting identities that create an opportunity to denigrate women for more than their position of leadership or attempts toward advancement. We briefly review the literature on tokens, race and ethnicity, as well as mothers and lesbians, and discuss how an additional stigma may exacerbate perceived negativity toward female leaders.

Tokens are individuals who are subject to negative treatment because their social category (e.g., women) is numerically underrepresented in certain contexts (e.g., senior leadership) (Yoder, 1991). Kanter's (1977) original theory on tokenism outlined this process, suggesting that tokens received enhanced visibility and therefore pressure to perform, and their differences become exaggerated, creating social isolation and rejection from peers and the organizations. Empirical research confirms female tokens do indeed receive negative treatment (Goldenhar, Swanson, Hurrel, Ruder, and Deddens, 1998; King, Hebl, George, and Matusik, 2010). Given the numerical underrepresentation of women in senior leadership positions both in the public and private sector, tokenism theory suggests that these women may be particularly susceptible to negativity due to their female and token status. It is likely that this double stigma (female and token) heightens others' negative attitudinal and behavioral responses, exaggerating the previously discussed consequences of stigma.

Society currently maintains negative stereotypes for several nonwhite categories, resulting in disadvantage status for these subgroups. For example, African American women report social isolation in the workplace (Bell and Nkomo, 2001) and greater resistance to their authority than did white women (Bell and Nkomo, 2001). Empirical data supports the notion that discrimination is more prevalent toward African American and Hispanic than white employees (Avery, McKay, Wilson, and Tonidandel, 2007). Given that gender and race are visible stigmas, we can see just how many women have reached some of the highest positions of leadership. Although we have three examples from modern society—Condoleezza Rice (first female, African American secretary of state), Sonia Sotomayor (first female, Hispanic Supreme Court justice), and Ursula Burns (first female, African American *Fortune* 500 CEO)—women who hold positions of leadership tend to be white. In fact, recent statistics show that 29 percent of senior managers are white women, as opposed to 3 percent who are African American women (EEOC, 2009). Furthermore, the median weekly earnings of African American women are $554; white women earn $654 (Bureau of Labor Statistics, 2009). As difficult as it may be for women to rise to positions of leadership, women of color have a double disadvantage due to their gender and race.

Stigma theory discusses both visible and invisible stigmas, noting unique challenges (i.e., disclosure) for individuals with invisible stigmas (e.g., pregnant women, lesbians). Pregnant women represent the epitome of womanhood, as they are fulfilling expectations of their role as a woman. However, this function is incongruent with their role as a worker (Ridgeway and Correll, 2004), and even to a larger extent their role as a leader. In fact, King and Botsford's (2009) theoretical work presented pregnancy as stigma and addressed challenges for disclosing this invisible stigma. Furthermore, Cuddy, Fiske and Glick (2004) demonstrated that when women become mothers, they are perceived to have lost competence and gained warmth. Heilman and Okimoto (2008) confirmed this finding that mothers are indeed perceived to lack competence. Again, we propose that being female and a mother opens these individuals up to being doubly stigmatized, and they therefore become targets of enhanced negativity.

Finally, being lesbian, gay, bisexual, or transgendered (LGBT) is yet another invisible stigmatized characteristic (Ragins, Cornwell, and Miller, 2003). Day and Greene (2008) purport that if both small and large organizations wish to be successful, inclusivity of LGBT workers is, in fact, a requirement. Recent examples demonstrate progress in this area. For example, there is discussion in the United States of repealing the military's "Don't Ask, Don't Tell" policy; while Houston elected its first female, openly gay mayor; and the European Union's Employment Equality Directive (2000) made it unlawful to discriminate against LGB individuals. Even so, Colgan, Wright, Creegan, and McKearney (2006) discussed that persistent challenges exist. Despite this progress, research suggests that gay and lesbian employees who disclose their sexual orientation perceive discrimination and lack of advancement (Ragins and Cornwell, 2001), stereotyping, and even sexual harassment (Giuffre, Dellinger, and Williams, 2008). In conclusion, the increasing number of women with multiple identities in the workplace presents these individuals with the difficult situation of being subject to multiple stigmas and therefore exaggerated negativity and discrimination.

Strategies for Remediation

Given the plethora of information reviewed in this chapter identifying negativity toward female leaders in the workplace, it is difficult to avoid asking what action can be taken to remediate this discrimination. Lyness and Heilman (2006) called for research to learn more about the strategies women have used to gain entry to, and demonstrate success in, strongly male positions. Research points to limited strategies that female leaders may enact to reduce negativity directed toward them. We discuss several, recognizing that each unduly places the burden on the woman herself, arguably adding yet another challenge on the path to attaining positions of senior leadership.

First, Johnson et al.'s (2009) research suggested that female leaders must demonstrate strength and sensitivity in order to be evaluated as effective. Thus, female leaders who are aware of their leadership style may be able to adjust their style to demonstrate both strength and sensitivity, and prevent discrimination. For example, a female leader who exhibits a more masculine leadership style may be able to reduce negativity by enacting behaviors that are perceived to be sensitive (e.g., demonstrating consideration for subordinates). Similarly, Heilman and Haynes (2005) demonstrated that unless there is clear evidence of women's competence, their success is attributed to men and therefore they are less likely to be the leader. Therefore, female leaders may make an effort to credential themselves and protect against discrimination by demonstrating extreme and consistent competence. When female leaders demonstrate competence in their chosen career, the denigration of women becomes more difficult, thus mitigating roadblocks to the advancement of women to positions of leadership. Both the "strong and sensitive" and the "competence" approach require the woman to essentially credential herself against negativity from others by overachieving and making it undeniable that she should advance in the workplace.

A second remediation strategy is for women to build social capital by developing relationships with key stakeholders. For example, Allen, Eby, Poteet, Lentz, and Lima (2004) demonstrated that mentoring relationships tend to enhance career progress by providing both career and psychosocial mentoring. Furthermore, formal mentoring programs that take into consideration the mentor–protégé match and training quality influence the effectiveness of mentoring (Allen, Eby, and Lentz, 2006). Women who aspire to positions of leadership can therefore hopefully align themselves with a mentor who provides both career and psychosocial support, helping to pave their way to climbing the organizational ladder. Similarly, women who are able to network within their organization and career field may be able to better position themselves for positions of leadership. However, Forret and Dougherty (2004) found that men received a boost for increasing visibility whereas this was not always the case for women. The authors propose that this may be because women are typically involved with less-prestigious assignments or because others may perceive that women are trying to compensate for their current position by engaging in such behaviors. Although this presents a double bind for women (i.e., they network, but don't appear to make a conscious effort), those who are able to successfully network and build social capital may enhance their likelihood of advancement. Linehan and Scullion (2008) conducted a series of interviews with 50 female managers that revealed that women reported barriers to networks, and also reported that women felt that access to such formal and informal networks would provide career advantages. Women who take the time to build their network may develop alliances and effectively reduce the number of individuals who attempt to denigrate their success, while simultaneously increasing the number of individuals who may act as advocates for their advancement.

Conclusion

Despite progress in the American workforce, gender inequities persist that prevent women from achieving positions of leadership. This chapter identified social stigma as the root of such stereotyping and discrimination and presented the procedural, interpersonal, and individual manifestations of stigma and its negative consequences for female leaders. We also discussed situations of double stigma, whereby certain individuals are subject to discrimination based upon their status as a female leader as well as a second, stigmatized social group (e.g., race). Finally, we presented proposed strategies to remediate perceived discrimination and attempt to rectify inequities faced by female leaders. This summary of the literature should serve as a call to researchers and practitioners alike to not only explore the forces that suppress women in counterstereotypic positions, such as leadership, but to also investigate procedural and interpersonal methods for alleviating the negative effects of the stigma that many women in positions of leadership face.

References

Allen, T. D., Eby, L. T., O'Brien, K. E., and Lentz, E. (2006). The state of mentoring research: A qualitative review of the current research methods and future research implications. *Journal of Vocational Behavior, 73*, 343–357.

Allen, T. D., Eby, L. T., Poteet, M. L., Lentz, E., and Lima, L. (2004). Career benefits associated with mentoring for protégés: A meta-analysis. *Journal of Applied Psychology, 89*, 127–136.

Atwater, L. E., Brett, J. F., Waldman, D., DiMare, L., and Hayden, M. V. (2004). Men's and women's perceptions of the gender typing of management subroles. *Sex Roles, 50*, 191–199.

Avery, D. R., McKay, P. F., Wilson, D. C., Tonidandel, S. (2007). Unequal attendance: The relationships between race, organizational diversity cures, and absenteeism. *Personnel Psychology, 60*, 875–902.

Bandura, A. (1991). Social cognitive theory of self-regulation. *Organizational Behavior and Human Decision Processes, 50*, 248–287.

Bell, E. J. E., and Nkomo, S. M. (2001). *Our separate ways: Black and white woman and the struggle for professional identity.* Boston: Harvard Business School Press.

Biernat, M. (2005). *Standards and expectancies: Contrast and assimilation in judgments of self and others.* New York: Psychology Press.

Biernat, M., and Kobrynowicz, D. (1997). Gender- and raced-based standards of competence: Lower minimum standards but higher ability standards for devalued groups. *Journal of Personality and Social Psychology, 72*, 544–557.

Blau, F. D., and Kahn, L. M. (2006). The gender pay gap: Going, going . . . but not gone. In F. D. Blau, M. C. Brinton, and D. B. Grusky (Eds.), *The declining significance of gender?* (pp. 37–66). New York: Russell Sage Foundation.

Bond, J. T., Thompson, C., Galinsky, E., and Protas, D. (2002). *The 2002 national study of the changing workforce.* New York: Families and Work Institute.

Botsford Morgan, W. and King, E. B. (in press). Clarifying the career decisions of mothers by exploring the content of work experiences. In G. Baugh and S. Sullivan (Eds.), *Finding balance: Research in careers* (Vol. 3). New York: Wiley.

Brett, J. M., and Stroh, L. K. (2003). Working 61 hours a week: Why do managers do it? *Journal of Applied Psychology, 88,* 67–78.

Burgess, D., and Borgida, E. (1999). Who women are, who women should be: Descriptive and prescriptive gender stereotyping in sex discrimination. *Psychology, Public Policy and Law, 5,* 655–692.

Butler, D., and Geis, F. L. (1990). Nonverbal affect responses to male and female leaders: Implications for leadership evaluations. *Journal of Personality and Social Psychology, 58,* 48–59.

Cejka, M. A., and Eagly, A. H. (1999). Gender-stereotypic images of occupations correspond to the sex segregation of employment. *Personality and Social Psychology Bulletin, 25,* 413–423.

Colgan, F., Wright, T., Creegan, C., and McKearney, A. (2009). Equality and diversity in public services: Moving forward on lesbian, gay and bisexual equality? *Human Resource Management Journal, 19*(3), 280–301.

Crocker, J., Major, B., and Steele, C. (1998). Social stigma. In D. T. Gilbert and S. T. Fiske (Eds.), *Handbook of social psychology,* 4th ed. (pp. 504–553). New York: McGraw-Hill.

Cuddy, A. J. C., and Fiske, S. T. (2004). When professionals become mothers, warmth, doesn't cut the ice. *Journal of Social Issues, 60,* 701–718.

Davidson, M. J., and Fielden, S. (1999). Stress and the working women. In G. N. Powell (Ed.), *Handbook of gender and work* (pp. 413–426). Thousand Oaks, CA: Sage.

Davies, P. G., Spencer, S. J., and Steele, C. M. (2005). Clearing the air: Identity safety moderates the effects of stereotype threat on women's leadership aspirations. *Journal of Personality and Social Psychology, 88,* 276–287.

Davison, H. K., and Burke, M. J. (2000). Sex discrimination in simulated employment contexts: A meta-analytic investigation. *Journal of Vocational Behavior, 56*, 225–248.

Day, N. E., and Greene, P. G. (2008). A case for sexual orientation diversity management in small and large organizations. *Human Resource Management, 47*, 637–654.

Dovidio, J. F., and Gaertner, S. L. (2004). Aversive racism. In M. P. Zanna (Ed.), *Advances in experimental social psychology*, Vol. 36 (pp. 1–52). San Diego, CA: Elsevier Academic Press.

Duehr, E. E., and Bono, J. E. (2006). Men, women, and managers: Are stereotypes finally changing? *Personnel Psychology, 59*, 815–846.

Eagly, A. H. (1987). *Sex differences in social behavior: A social role interpretation.* Hillsdale, NJ: Erlbaum.

Eagly, A. H., and Carli, L. L. (2003). The female leadership advantage: An evaluation of the evidence. *The Leadership Quarterly, 14*, 807–834.

Eagly, A. H., and Carli, L. L. (2007). *Through the labyrinth: The truth about how women become leaders.* Boston: Harvard Business School Press.

Eagly, A. H., Johannesen-Schmidt, M. C., and van Engen, M. L. (2003). Transformational, transactional, and laissez-faire leadership styles: A meta-analysis comparing women and men. *Psychological Bulletin, 129*, 569–591.

Eagly, A. H., and Karau, S. J. (2002). Role congruity theory of prejudice toward female leaders. *Psychological Review, 109*, 573–598.

Eagly, A. H., Makhijani, M. G., and Klonsky, B. G. (1992). Gender and the evaluation of leaders: A meta-analysis. *Psychological Bulletin, 111*, 3–22.

Eagly, A. H., Wood, W., and Diekman, A. B. (2000). Social role theory of sex differences and similarities: A current appraisal. In T. Eckes and H. M. Traunter (Eds.), *The developmental social psychology of gender* (pp. 123–174). Mahwah, NJ: Erlbaum.

Forret, M. L., and Dougherty, T. W. (2004). Networking behaviors and career outcomes: Differences for men and women? *Journal of Organizational Behavior, 25*, 419–437.

Giuffre, P., Dellinger, K., and Williams, C. L. (2008). 'No retribution for being gay?': Inequality in gay-friendly workplaces. *Sociological Spectrum, 28*, 254–27.

Glick, P., Fiske, S. T. (1996). The ambivalent sexism inventory: Differentiating hostile and benevolent sexism. *Journal of Personality and Social Psychology, 70*, 491–512.

Glick, P. and Fiske, S. T. (1997). Hostile and benevolent sexism: Measuring ambivalent sexist attitudes toward women. *Psychology of Women Quarterly, 21*, 119–135.

Glick, P., and Fiske, S. T. (2001). An ambivalent alliance: Hostile and benevolent sexism as complementary justifications for gender inequality. *American Psychologist, 56*, 109–118.

Goffman, E. (1963). *Stigma: Notes on the management of spoiled identity.* New York: Simon and Schuster, Inc.

Goldenhar, L. M., Swanson, N. G., Hurrell, J. J., Ruder, A., and Deddens, J. (1998). Stressors and adverse outcomes for female construction workers. *Journal of Occupational Health Psychology, 3*, 19–32.

Hebl, M. R., King, E. B., Glick, P., Kazama, S., and Singletary, S. (2007). Hostile and benevolent reactions toward pregnant women: Complementary interpersonal punishments and rewards that maintain traditional roles. *Journal of Applied Psychology, 92*, 1499–1511.

Hebl, M. R., Mannix, L., and Dovidio, J. (2002). Formal and interpersonal discrimination: A field study of bias toward homosexual job applicants. *Personality and Social Psychology Bulletin, 28*, 815–825.

Heilman, M. E. (1983). Sex bias in work settings: The Lack of Fit model. *Research in Organizational Behavior, 5*, 269–298.

Heilman, M. E., Block, C. J., Martell, R. F., Simon, M. C. (1989). Has anything changed? Current characterizations of men, women, and managers. *The Journal of Applied Psychology, 74*, 935–942.

Heilman, M. E., and Haynes, M. C. (2005). No credit where credit is due: Attributional rationalization of women's success in male-female teams. *Journal of Applied Psychology, 90*, 905–916.

Heilman, M. E., and Okimoto, T. G. (2008). Motherhood: A potential source of bias in employment decisions. *Journal of Applied Psychology, 93*, 189–198.

Heilman, M. E., Wallen, A. S., Fuchs, D., and Tamkins, M. M. (2004). Penalties for success: Reactions to women who succeed at male gender-typed tasks. *Journal of Applied Psychology, 89*, 416–427.

Hochschild, A., and Machung, A. (2003). *The second shift: Working parents and the revolution at home.* New York: Viking-Penguin.

Johnston, D. D., and Swanson, D. H. (2006). Constructing the "good mother": The experience of mothering ideologies by work status. *Sex Roles, 54*, 509–51.

Johnson, S. K., Murphy, S. E., Zewdie, S., and Reichard, R. J. (2008). The strong, sensitive type: Effects of gender stereotypes and leadership prototypes on the evaluation of male and female leaders. *Organizational Behavior and Human Decision Processes, 106*, 39–60.

Jones, E. E., Farina, A., Hastorf, A. H., Markus, H., Miller, D. T., and Scott, R. A. (1984). *Social stigma: The psychology of marked relationships.* New York: Freeman.

Kanfer, R., Ackerman, P. L. (1996). Self-regulatory skills perspective to reducing cognitive interference. In I. Sarason, G. Pierce, and B. Sarason (Eds.), *Cognitive interference: Theories, methods, and findings* (pp. 153–171). Hillsdale, NJ, and England: Lawrence Erlbaum Associates, Inc.

Kanter, R. M. (1977). *Men and women of the corporation.* New York: Basic Books.

Kark, R., and Eagly, A. (in press). Gender and leadership: Negotiating the labyrinth. In J. C. Chrisler and D. R. McCreary (Eds.), *Handbook of gender research in Psychology.* New York: Springer.

King, E. B., Hebl, M. R., George, J. M., and Matusik, S. F. (2010). Understanding tokenism: Negative consequences of perceived gender discrimination in male-dominated organizations. *Journal of Management, 36*, 537–554.

King, E. B., Botsford, W., Hebl, M. R., Kazama, S., Dawson, J. F., and Perkins, A. (in press). Benevolent sexism at work: Gender differences in the distribution of challenging work experiences. *Journal of Management.*

Koch, S. C. (2005). Evaluative affect display toward male and female leaders of task- oriented groups. *Small Group Research, 36*, 678–703.

Linehan, M. and Scullion, H. (2008). The development of female global managers: The role of mentoring and networking. *Journal of Business Ethics, 83*, 29–40.

Lyness, K. A., and Heilman, M. E. (2006). When fit is fundamental: Performance evaluations and promotions of upper-level female and male managers. *Journal of Applied Psychology, 91*, 777–785.

Lyness, K. S., and Judiesch, M. K. (1999). Are women more likely to be hired or promoted into management positions? *Journal of Vocational Behavior, 54*, 158–173.

Martell, R. F., Lane, D. M., and Emrich, C. (1996). Male-female differences: A computer simulation. *American Psychologist, 51*, 157–158.

Morrison, A. M., White, R. P., and Van Velsor, E. (1987). *Breaking the glass ceiling: Can women reach the top of America's largest corporations?* Reading, MA: Addison-Wesley.

Powell, G. N., Butterfield, D. A., and Parent, J. D. (2002). Gender and managerial stereotypes: Have the times changed? *Journal of Management, 28*, 177–193.

Prime, J. L., Carter, N. M., and Welbourne, T. M. (2009). Women "take care," men "take charge": Managers' stereotypic perceptions of women and men leaders. *The Psychologist-Manager Journal, 12*, 25–49.

Ragins, B. R., and Cornwell, J. M. (2001). Pink triangles: Antecedents and consequences of perceived workplace discrimination against gay and lesbian employees. *Journal of Applied Psychology, 86*, 1244–1261.

Ragins, B. R., Cornwell, J. M., and Miller, J. S. (2003). Heterosexism in the workplace: Do race and gender matter? *Group and Organization Management, 28*, 45–74.

Ridgeway, C. L., and Correll, S. J. (2004). Motherhood as a status characteristic. *Journal of Social Issues, 60*, 638–700.

Rosette, A. S., and Tost, L. P. (2010). Agentic women and communal leadership: How role prescriptions confer advantage to top women leaders. *Journal of Applied Psychology, 95,* 221–235.

Rudman, L. A. (1998). Self-promotion as a risk factor for women: The costs and benefits of counterstereotypical impression management. *Journal of Personality and Social Psychology, 74,* 629–645.

Rudman, L. A., and Fairchild, K. (2004). Reactions to counterstereotypic behavior: The role of backlash in cultural stereotype maintenance. *Journal of Personality and Social Psychology, 87,* 157–176.

Rudman, L. A., and Glick, P. (2001). Prescriptive gender stereotypes and backlash toward agentic women. *Journal of Social Issues, 57,* 743–762.

Ryan, M. K. and Haslam, S. A. (2005). The glass cliff: Evidence that women are over-represented in precarious leadership positions. *British Journal of Management, 16,* 81–90.

Schein, V. E. (1973). The relationship between sex role stereotypes and requisite management characteristics. *Journal of Applied Psychology, 57,* 95–100.

Schein, V. E. (1975). Relationships between sex role stereotypes and requisite management characteristics among female managers. *Journal of Applied Psychology, 60,* 340–344.

Schein, V. E. (2001). A global look at psychological barriers to women's progress in management. *Journal of Social Issues, 57,* 675–688.

Seagram, S., and Daniluk, J. C. (2002). "It goes with the territory": The meaning and experience of maternal guilt for mothers of pre-adolescent children. *Women and Therapy, 25,* 61–88.

Seibert, S. E., Kraimer, M. L., and Liden, R. C. (2001). A social capital theory of career success. *Academy of Management Journal, 44,* 219–237.

Speitzer, G. M., McCall, M. W., and Mahoney, J. D. (1997). Early identification of international executive potential. *Journal of Applied Psychology, 82,* 6–29.

Stockdale, M. S., and Bhattacharya, G. (2009). Sexual harassment and the glass ceiling. In M. Barreto, M. K. Ryan, and M. T. Schmitt (Eds.), *The glass ceiling in the 21st century: Understanding barriers to gender inequality* (pp. 171–199). Washington, DC: APA Books.

Swim, J., Borgida, E., Maruyama, G., and Myers, D. G. (1989). McKay, Joan versus McKay, John. Do gender stereotypes bias evaluations? *Psychological Bulletin, 105*, 409–429.

Taylor, P., Morin, R., Cohn, D.V., Clark, C., and Wang, W. (2008). *A paradox in public attitudes: Men or women: Who's the better leader?* Washington, DC: Pew Research Center.

Van Velsor, E., McCauley, C. D., and Moxley, R. S. (1998). Introduction: Our view of leadership development. *Handbook of leadership development* (pp. 1–28). San Francisco: Jossey-Bass Publishers.

Vecchio, R. P. (2002). Leadership and gender advantage. *Leadership Quarterly, 13*, 643–671.

Williams, J. C., Manvell, J., and Bornstein, S. (2006). "Opt out" or pushed out?: How the press covers work/family conflict—The untold story of why women leave the workplace. The Center for WorkLife Law.

Yoder, J. D. (1991). Rethinking tokenism: Looking beyond the numbers. *Gender and Society, 5*, 178–192.

3

Evaluation of Female Leaders: Stereotypes, Prejudice, and Discrimination in the Workplace

Susan A. Basow

In 1982, Ann Hopkins was denied partnership at Price Waterhouse, one of the top accounting firms in the United States, despite her stellar record, which included having produced more billable hours than any other candidate up for partnership that year. Out of 88 candidates proposed for partner, she was the only woman; in fact, out of a total of 662 company partners, only 7 were women. Hopkins sued on the basis of sex discrimination and won at every level, including the Supreme Court (*Price Waterhouse v. Hopkins*, 1989). The sex discrimination argument rested on evidence that Hopkins had been denigrated for behavior that would have merited praise had it been evidenced by a man: she was evaluated as tough, aggressive, no-nonsense, and driven. One evaluator had suggested she could improve her chances of making partner if she would "walk more femininely, talk more femininely, dress more femininely, wear make-up ... " (Fiske, Bersoff, Borgida, Deaux, and Heilman, 1991, p. 1050). This landmark case relied heavily on the *amicus curiae* brief submitted by the American Psychological Association (APA) that documented how women being evaluated for leadership positions are frequently in a double bind: if they engage in the same behaviors as their male counterparts, they may be perceived negatively; if they don't engage in the same behaviors as their male counterparts, they also may be perceived negatively.

As other chapters have noted, women are underrepresented in leadership positions despite evidence that they can be effective leaders (Eagly, 2007). Due to gender stereotypes, however, women leaders are often not thought of or perceived as effective. Cultural expectations of women (to be nurturant, sensitive, kind) only partially overlap with cultural expectations of leaders (to be assertive, dominant, competent); in contrast, cultural expectations of men overlap nearly completely with expectations of leaders. Women who display the traits expected of leaders are at risk for being considered unfeminine (Kanter's (1993) "Iron Maiden" role); this appears to be what happened to Ann Hopkins at Price Waterhouse. Yet women who display the traits expected of women are at risk for not being perceived as leader-like (Kanter's Pet, Seductress, or Mother roles). Thus, to be seen positively as a leader, women must walk a fine line (the area of overlap): being assertive but not overly so; being dominant but still interpersonally sensitive; being competent but still likeable. As Catalyst (2007), the nonprofit organization working to build inclusive workplaces, so aptly described the results of its research on executives' perception of women leaders, women in leadership positions are in a double bind: "damned if you do [conform to female or leader stereotypes], doomed if you don't."

This chapter will focus on examining this double bind faced by women leaders, and on how gender stereotypes can lead to prejudicial attitudes and discriminatory behavior. We'll first explore the dimensions on which leaders can be evaluated and then focus on the many factors affecting evaluations of female leaders: gender-typed behaviors, interests, and traits; the maternal "penalty"; contextual factors; and rater factors.

Evaluating Leaders

Evaluations of leaders are built upon basic psychological processes of interpersonal perception, interpretation, and judgments. As social psychologists have long demonstrated, what we perceive is based substantially on what we expect to perceive. If we expect someone to be kind to us and instead that person reminds us of something we haven't yet done, we may get offended and perceive that person as overly critical. However, if we expect a person to be a stern taskmaster and that person reminds us of the same unfinished task, we are likely to have a less negative reaction; indeed, we may even appreciate the reminder. Same behavior, different reactions based on our expectations.

Gender (as well as other) stereotypes can be viewed as a set of expectations about how each gender does or should act. Stereotypes also serve as cognitive filters through which we perceive behavior. A strongly worded statement issued by a man might be viewed as a sign of his authority, confidence, or power. The same statement issued by a woman might be viewed as a sign of her high-handedness, demandingness, or coldness.

Because gender is confounded by status differences, with men as a group viewed as higher in status than women as a group, women leaders have to contend with perceptions of role incongruity based not only on gender but also on status. As role incongruity theory (Eagly and Karau, 2002; Eagly and Koenig, 2008) suggests, people whose behaviors or traits match expectations (based on roles or status) tend to be perceived more positively than people whose behaviors or traits contradict expectations. High-status individual (e.g., men) are assumed to be competent; thus it is harder for men to demonstrate incompetence than it is for a woman (Foschi, 2000). Conversely, because lower-status individuals (e.g., women) are expected not to be competent, it is harder for them to demonstrate excellence or competence than it is for higher-status individuals. For example, if a male leader makes an error of judgment, he's likely to be given the benefit of the doubt (e.g., "perhaps he was too busy to give the matter sufficient attention"). The same error by a female leader is likely to be viewed as confirmation that she is not a good leader. In contrast, an effective decision made by a male leader is likely to confirm his competence, whereas the same decision may be viewed as "lucky" if made by a female leader.

Indeed, recent research confirms that white male trainees who make performance-related mistakes are less likely to have these noted in a formal performance log than are the same mistakes made by white female trainees (Biernat, Fuegen, and Kobrynowicz, 2010). The explanation is that since white men are expected to be competent, when they make mistakes, the mistakes are likely to be noted but not taken as signs of incompetence. However, because women (and blacks) are expected to be incompetent, when they make mistakes, the mistakes are taken as confirmation of their lower level of ability. Thus, it is easier for women leaders to be viewed as incompetent than it is for their male counterparts.

As these findings suggest, evaluators tend to use different standards when judging women and men (Biernat, 2003; Biernat et al., 2010). Because men leaders are the norm, their behaviors and styles set the standard. Employees who have a male supervisor typically talk about their "boss"; employees who have a female supervisor typically talk about their "female boss." Not surprisingly, then, when women leaders are evaluated, their gender is usually salient, and their behavior is judged against what is expected "for a woman."

Overall, women leaders often must work harder to be perceived as equally competent as their male counterparts, and it is far easier for them to "fall from grace" than their male counterparts, as well. This is exactly what the Catalyst (2007) study found regarding women executives: they are judged by higher competency standards than are men while receiving lower rewards and having to repeatedly prove themselves.

Two of the major dimensions that people use in evaluating others are competency and likeability/warmth. Gender stereotypes are directly related to these dimensions, with men in general being viewed as more competent than women, and women in general being viewed as more warm and likeable than men (Cikara and Fiske, 2009; Eagly and Mladinic, 1993; Fiske, Cuddy, Glick, and Xu, 2002). Although these dimensions are orthogonal to each other (one can be high, or low, on both dimensions at the same time), gender stereotypes operate to make them seem like opposites. That is, when women are perceived as competent, they often are perceived as less likeable than when they are perceived as less competent. The reverse is true for men: when they are perceived as less competent, they are less liked. The Catalyst (2007) study found strong evidence of this pattern: women leaders could be perceived as competent or likeable, but they rarely were perceived as both.

Overall, although male leaders certainly can be evaluated negatively, they at least start from a position of role congruence in their leader role. In contrast, female leaders typically start from a position of incongruence. As we will see in the next section, additional factors related to role incongruence can further affect evaluations of women leaders.

Factors Affecting Evaluations of Women Leaders

There are many factors that affect evaluations of women leaders: gender-typed behaviors, interests, and traits; the maternal "penalty"; contextual factors; and rater factors.

Gender-Typed Attributes

As Ann Hopkins found out, women are expected to exhibit such "feminine" behaviors as nurturance, compassion, sensitivity, and "niceness"; that is, to be communal—interpersonally oriented and interpersonally skilled. Yet, leaders are expected to exhibit such "masculine" behaviors as dominance, agency, and competitiveness; that is, to be agentic—task-oriented and focused. Numerous research studies (and cases like *Price Waterhouse v. Hopkins*) have documented that women who display agentic behaviors may be denigrated unless they also show evidence of the expected communal behaviors (Eagly and Carli, 2007; Eagly, Makhijani, and Klonsky, 1992; Heilman and Okimoto, 2007; Rudman, 1998; Rudman and Fairchild, 2004). For example, although women who display strong agentic traits may be rated as highly competent, they also may be rated as socially deficient; as a consequence, such women are less likely to be hired or promoted than their male counterparts.

In addition to this backlash effect, women also may have to deal with shifting evaluative criteria. For example, although a strong female job applicant may be rated more favorably than a similarly qualified man, he still may be more likely to be hired for an executive position (Biernat and Kobrynowicz, 1997). It appears that raters tend to evaluate a woman against others of her gender (e.g., "she's really assertive *for a woman*"), whereas a man tends be judged against a more absolute standard ("he's really assertive"). For hiring decisions, the absolute standard is more likely to be relied upon.

Another form of shifting evaluative criteria also occurs. As Phelan and colleagues (2008) found, women who display agentic qualities not only may be rated lower in social skills than an identically described man, but such ratings of women's (lower) social skills figure more prominently in decisions to hire the woman for a leadership position than the man. Thus, agentic women may be "doubly disadvantaged": they may be perceived as socially unskilled, *and* their competence may be deemphasized when employment-related decisions are made. Presenting oneself as primarily communal, however, won't necessarily help; women with a strong communal focus also are perceived as less competent than their more agentic sisters. This is the double bind for professional women: whether they are agentic or communal, they are less likely to be hired for a leadership position than their male counterpart.

Because women are expected to be kinder than men, the expression of anger, in particular, may be a challenge for women professionals. Brescoll and Uhlmann (2008) conducted a series of studies and found that when a male professional (e.g., a CEO) expressed anger in a videotaped job interview, raters evaluated his status and his competence more highly (or the same), mainly because his anger typically was attributed to the situation (e.g., "his colleagues' behavior caused his anger"). In contrast, when a female professional expressed anger, her status and perceived competence decreased, mainly because raters attributed her emotional reactions to her personality (e.g., "she's an angry person"). Thus, women leaders need to take pains to provide objective external reasons for their negative emotions; otherwise they run the risk of being perceived as a "witch."

Because of the backlash effect and the shifting standards of evaluation of female leaders, it is perhaps not surprising that women leaders often use different leadership styles than men leaders. In particular, compared to their male counterparts, women leaders are more likely to use a transformational leadership style (one in which the leader supports and empowers her followers, inspiring them to reach their potential) as well as provide contingent rewards for a subordinate's satisfactory performance (Eagly, Johannesen-Schmidt, and van Engen, 2003; Yoder, 2001). This transformational leadership style, combining both agentic and communal qualities, appears to fit the narrow area of overlap. Fortunately, this leadership style typically has been found to be very effective for both men and women (Eagly et al., 2003; Eagly, 2007), although perhaps more so for women (Ayman, Korabik, and Morris, 2009).

From the research literature, we can conclude that to be effective and evaluated positively, women leaders need to find a good way to balance authority and friendliness; that is, to demonstrate both strong agentic and communal qualities (Ayman and Korabik, 2010; Basow, Phelan, and Capotosto, 2006; Carli. LaFleur, and Loeber, 1995; Eagly and Carli,

2007; Friedman and Yorio, 2006; Heilman and Okimoto, 2007; Rudman and Glick, 2001). This is not an easy thing to do, because women who smile too much or who display too much emotion may also be seen as not leadership material (Friedman and Yorio, 2006; Phelan et al., 2008).

Overall, women leaders are evaluated through the lens of gender stereotypes. Although many women have found ways to be effective leaders, having to find the "right" balance represents an extra burden on women that men who aspire to, or who are in, leadership positions do not have.

Maternal Penalty

An additional factor that affects women leaders is motherhood. Besides the very real challenges of balancing work and family life for employed women who still typically carry the predominant burden of child care responsibilities, are the stereotypic perceptions of mothers. As research has documented (Correll, Benard, and Paik, 2007; Cuddy, Fiske, and Glick, 2004), when raters are asked to evaluate male and female managers or consultants who are equally qualified, a woman who also is portrayed as a mother is perceived as less competent and less promotable, and is paid less, than the same woman who is not a mother. For men, not only is being a parent not a strike against them, but in some cases they actually are paid more than their nonparent male counterpart. Indeed, the pay gap between mothers and nonmothers is larger than the pay gap between women and men (Avellar and Smock, 2003; Crittenden, 2001).

The explanation for this "motherhood penalty" rests on two related factors: the stereotypes of mothers as not being committed workers (Correll et al., 2007); and the lower status attributed to "mothers" compared to "employees" (Ridgeway and Correll, 2004). For men, being a father does not signal a negative change in status; indeed, fathers may be viewed as even more responsible and committed to the job than their nonparent counterparts. Because of their lower status, employees who are mothers appear to be judged by a harsher standard than are employees who are nonmothers (Correll et al., 2007). This dynamic is identical to the harsher standard applied to women as a group compared to men as a group, as described above. In many ways, the difference in standards is more pronounced when based on employee parental status than it is when based on employee gender.

Pregnancy itself can also be a discriminatory cue, since it reminds observers of women's traditional child-rearing role. Glick and Fiske (2007) review research that documents that women are more likely to be patronized and viewed as incompetent when pregnant than when not pregnant. They are particularly unlikely to be viewed as suited for a management position.

Given the above, it is perhaps not surprising that female executives are less likely to be married and/or to have children than are their male counterparts (Lyness and Thompson, 1997). Even when they are married or are mothers, women executives often take pains to keep their personal and professional identities separate.

In general, cues that trigger traditional female stereotypes (such as pregnancy and motherhood) are associated with more discriminatory evaluations of professional women since communal traits in women are seen as antithetical to the agentic traits expected in leadership positions.

Contextual Factors

As noted earlier, just by being in a leadership position, women are viewed as role incongruent and likely to be evaluated negatively. Two additional contextual factors affect evaluations as well: how gender-typical (or atypical) is the field, and how many other women are present in the organization's leadership positions.

Not surprisingly, most discrimination (including use of shifting criteria) occurs against individuals who are in contexts viewed as nontraditional for their gender (Basow, 1995, 1998; Eagly and Carli, 2007; Glick and Fiske, 2007). Eagly's (2007) review of the research on female leadership found that favorable attitudes toward women as leaders have increased over the last 50 years except for workplace environments that are male dominated or are traditionally masculine, such as the military or high-status political office. It is only in such contexts that women's leadership effectiveness is actually rated lower than men's, probably because these environments are most inconsistent with stereotypes of women.

A related contextual factor is how isolated a particular woman leader is in her organization. When fewer than 20 percent of leadership positions are held by a woman (as is typically the case in the top positions in business, education, and politics), her gender becomes a salient characteristic

(Fiske et al., 1991; Glick and Fiske, 2007; Kanter, 1993; Yoder, 2001). Recall that at the time of Ann Hopkins' review for partner at Price Waterhouse, she was the sole woman being considered in an organization in which only about 10 percent of the partners were women. As a result, gender-related characteristics, and male resistance to women's "intrusion" into a male-dominated domain, were made more salient.

Rosabeth Moss Kanter's (1993) study of women in corporations found that gender stereotyping is most likely to occur when women are so numerically in the minority that they are viewed as "token" hires. In such cases, coworkers and supervisors, who are unused to working with women in positions of authority, are likely to try to typecast the woman into one of four female stereotypes: the Pet (liked but incompetent; child-like; naïve); the Mom (nurturant but not viewed as competent); the Seductress (the sex-object; desirable but not competent); or the Iron Maiden (competent but unfeeling and unlikeable). None of these roles facilitate positive leadership evaluations. These reactions to women aspiring to traditionally male positions were evident in the 2009 U.S. presidential campaign. Hillary Clinton, a contender for the Democratic nomination, was typically typecast as the Iron Maiden, and criticized for wearing pantsuits and lack of warmth. Sarah Palin, the Republican vice presidential candidate, was typically typecast variously in the other three roles: the Pet (cute but not very smart), the Seductress (emphasis on her beauty pageant experience and looks), or the Mom (emphasis on her family role and children). Gender stereotyping thus affected evaluations of women leaders for these traditionally masculine positions in politics, positions never held by a woman.

Another contextual factor relevant for evaluations of women leaders is the "glass cliff" phenomenon (Ryan and Haslam, 2005; Ryan, Haslam, and Kulich, 2010). Archival research of 100 major corporations in the U.K. documented that women were most likely to attain leadership positions (in this case, be appointed a member of the board of directors) when the organization had already been experiencing declining performance in the preceding five months. In contrast, when an organization was doing very well, women were less likely to be put in leadership positions than were men. A similar pattern has been found in politics. Women are more likely to be put forward as political candidates when the contest is viewed as risky, while men are more likely to be candidates for contests that are viewed as safe. Such risky, high-profile positions put women leaders under more scrutiny and more stress, and it's likely that they subsequently get more blame for "failure" (e.g., not being able to reverse a company's declining performance; losing an election) than their male counterparts.

Overall, gender stereotyping and negative evaluations of women leaders are most marked in traditionally male or masculine contexts. Furthermore, women leaders are more likely than men to be in risky leadership positions that may further intensify how they get evaluated.

Rater Characteristics

There are several rater characteristics that contribute to an individual's likelihood of discriminating against women leaders: rater gender and rater attitudes toward women and gender roles. These, of course, are related, since men compared to women tend to hold more traditional attitudes toward women and gender roles, and to ascribe to higher levels of hostile sexism (Glick and Fiske, 2007; Twenge, 1997). Because men tend to hold more *prescriptive* stereotypes regarding what women *should and should not* do than do women, men are more likely to commit many forms of hostile discrimination, including sexual harassment. Although many studies find that both men and women discriminate against women (Glick and Fiske, 2007), male raters appear to be particularly likely to use gender stereotypes when rating female professionals (Carli, 2001; Eagly and Karau, 2002; Eagly, 2007). Men also appear to be particularly sensitive to the previously described variables that affect leadership evaluation: gender-related attributes of the leader, and the gendered aspects of the work context. In other words, men are particularly likely to discriminate against women leaders who do not display traditionally feminine qualities, especially when the work environment is traditionally male/masculine. This is what occurred in the *Price Waterhouse v. Hopkins* case.

Male subordinates may have a particularly challenging time when they receive a negative evaluation from a female superior (Sinclair and Kunda, 2000). Although no one likes to receive a negative evaluation, men who do so from a woman tend to devalue her competence significantly more than they do from a man who provides the identical evaluation. The reasons for this pattern are likely to be twofold: the woman supervisor is violating gender stereotypes of being nurturant and kind; she also is demonstrating power and status over the man, thereby violating her ascribed lower status.

His devaluation of her is one way for him to regain some power and control.

Not only might men be more likely than woman to apply gender stereotypes to women leaders who are nontraditional in some way, but their views can affect those of others, even when the form this discrimination takes is very subtle. As Glick and Fiske (2001) documented, sexism can take two forms: *hostile sexism,* which reflects negative attitudes toward women who challenge traditional gender norms; and *benevolent sexism*, which reflects a paternalistic view of women as "wonderful but weak." These attitudes are correlated with each other, although many people have difficulty recognizing benevolent sexism as a form of discrimination against women since it seems to be associated with "positive" views of women. Its discriminatory aspect is mainly apparent when women step out of traditional female roles and behaviors.

Good and Rudman (2010) recently found that when a female job applicant for a traditionally male position (a managerial job at a large warehouse-style retail store that required "masculine" skills and behaviors, such as locking up late at night) was interviewed by a male interviewer, the ratings of evaluators who read the interview transcript were strongly affected by the interviewer's sexist attitudes as well as their own. In particular, when the male interviewer displayed either hostile sexism (e.g., stating that most women are not qualified for such a job) or benevolent sexism (e.g., stating that male coworkers could help the "nice young lady"), the female job applicant's competence was evaluated negatively and she was less likely to be hired than if the interviewer was nonsexist, at least when the male interviewer himself was viewed favorably. Because benevolent sexism is often unrecognized as such, male interviewers who exhibited such behaviors often were viewed quite favorably. This meant that the female job applicant who had a benevolently sexist interviewer was very likely to be rated poorly, especially when the evaluators themselves scored high in hostile sexism. It appears that the kind of protective paternalism exhibited by the interviewer's benevolent sexism "unleashed" the evaluator's own negative attitudes toward aspiring career women. Thus, both kinds of sexism can negatively affect women leaders either directly or indirectly.

As suggested by the previous findings, evaluators' attitudes toward women and gender roles may be a key factor in evaluating women leaders, more important than evaluator gender per se. Thus, women with traditional attitudes toward women and gender roles also tend to show negative attitudes toward women leaders, especially if such leaders are nontraditional (i.e., have strong agentic qualities, or are in a field that is traditionally masculine) (Cooper, 1997; Forsyth, Heiney, and Wright, 1997). Other rater attitudes that may contribute to negative evaluations of women leaders are high social dominance orientation, as well as strong beliefs in a just world (Oldmeadow and Fiske, 2007). People who are high in these two beliefs, both of which serve to justify social inequalities, are more likely to link low-status groups (such as women) with incompetence than are people who are low in such beliefs. Thus, it may be harder for individuals with such attitudes toward inequality to evaluate women leaders positively.

Overall, evaluators with traditional attitudes toward gender roles, who are most likely to be men, are most likely to negatively evaluate women leaders, especially if the leader appears nontraditional.

Summary

Women in leadership position face unique obstacles due to gender stereotypes. First, they are placed in a double bind due to their perceived role incongruence: if they conform to expectations of femininity, they are unlikely to be viewed as leadership material; however, if they conform to expectations of (agentic) leaders, they are likely to be viewed as unfeminine. In either case, they may be perceived negatively. Women leaders must walk a fine line, combining both communal and agentic behaviors, warmth and competence, in strategic ways, in order to be perceived positively.

Some women leaders face more obstacles than others when it comes to being evaluated fairly. Women who are nontraditional in some way (personal style, traits, appearance), or who are in positions not traditionally held by women, face added scrutiny. Such women leaders are likely to experience backlash, whereby their competence is both underrecognized and devalued. They may be held to higher standards, as well as put in riskier leadership positions, than their male counterparts. Any behavior that signals traditional female roles, such as pregnancy and motherhood, increases the likelihood of negative ratings of competence and leadership. Those most likely to engage in such discriminatory evaluations are those with traditional attitudes toward women and gender roles, as well as those with a strong belief in the need for social hierarchies and a just world. Women and men both can possess such beliefs, but men tend to do so more than women.

The Catalyst (2007) study of executives' attitudes toward women leaders also explored how women executives coped with some of the challenges. Four main strategies were employed, representing a wide range of styles: confronting the inequitable situation quickly and directly; demonstrating overtly that they have the skills and competence needed for the job; utilizing clear and effective communication; and minimizing the salience of gender. Of course, organizational strategies are needed as well, to ensure gender equity in the workplace.

Although the factors affecting evaluations of women leaders discussed in this chapter clearly are challenging, there is room for optimism. As more women attain positions of leadership, their "token" status will be eliminated and the salience of gender stereotypes will be reduced. Furthermore, the most negative attitudes toward women leaders are expressed by those who have not actually had a woman supervisor. Employees who have actual experience with women leaders tend to rate them similarly to men leaders (Eagly, 2007). Thus, as more people have experience with women in positions of power, some of the negative expectancies should be modified. Finally, women leaders have been found to be as effective as (or even more effective than) their male counterparts. As our understanding of effective leadership expands to include transformational leadership, expectations of leaders will come to include empowerment and communication skills, and, hopefully, expectations of women will come to include competence. Indeed, favorable attitudes toward women as leaders have increased over the last 50 years; it is likely that this trend will continue. Given the strength of gender stereotypes, however, it is unlikely that gender will ever be a nonissue.

References

Avellar, S., and Smock, P. J. (2003). Has the price of motherhood declined over time? A cross-cohort comparison of the motherhood wage penalty. *Journal of Marriage and Family, 65*, 597–607.

Ayman, R., and Korabik, K. (2010). Leadership: Why gender and culture matter. *American Psychologist, 65*, 157–170.

Ayman, R., Korabik, K., and Morris, S. (2009). Is transformational leadership always perceived as effective? Male subordinates' devaluation of female transformational leaders. *Journal of Applied Social Psychology, 39*, 852–879.

Basow, S. A. (1995). Student evaluations of college professors: When gender matters. *Journal of Educational Psychology, 87*, 656–665.

Basow, S. A. (1998). Student evaluations: The role of gender bias and teaching styles. In L. H. Collins, J. C. Chrisler, and K. Quina (Eds.), *Career strategies for women in academe: Arming Athena* (pp. 135–156). Thousand Oaks, CA: Sage.

Basow, S. A., Phelan, J., and Capotosto, L. (2006). Gender patterns in college students' choices of their best and worst professors. *Psychology of Women Quarterly, 30*, 25–35.

Biernat, M. (2003). Toward a broader view of social stereotyping. *American Psychologist, 58*, 1019–1027.

Biernat, M., Fuegen, K., and Kobrynowicz, D. (2010). Shifting standards and the inference of incompetence: Effects of formal and informal evaluation tools. *Personality and Social Psychology Bulletin, 36*, 855–868.

Biernat, M., and Kobrynowicz, D. (1997). Gender- and race-based standards of competence: Lower minimum standards but higher ability standards for devalued groups. *Journal of Personality & Social Psychology, 72*, 544–557.

Brescoll, V. L., and Uhlmann, E. L. (2008). Can an angry woman get ahead? Status conferral, gender, and expression of emotion in the workplace. *Psychological Science, 19*, 268–275.

Carli, L. L. (2001). Gender and social influence. *Journal of Social Issues, 57*, 725–741.

Carli, L. L., LaFleur, S. J., and Loeber, C. C. (1995). Nonverbal behavior, gender, and influence. *Journal of Personality and Social Psychology, 68*, 1030–1041.

Catalyst. (2007). *The double-bind dilemma for women in leadership: Damned if you do, doomed if you don't.* New York: Author.

Cikara, M., and Fiske, S. T. (2009). Warmth, competence, and ambivalent sexism: Vertical assault and collateral damage. In M. Barreto, M. K.

Ryan, and M. T. Schmitt (Eds.), *The glass ceiling in the 21st century: Understanding barriers to gender equality* (pp. 73–96). Washington, DC: American Psychological Association.

Cooper, V. W. (1997). Homophily or the Queen Bee Syndrome: Female evaluation of female leadership. *Small Group Research, 28*, 483–499.

Correll, S. J., Benard, S., and Paik, I. (2007). Getting a job: Is there a motherhood penalty? *American Journal of Sociology, 112*, 1297–1338.

Crittenden, A. (2001). *The price of motherhood.* New York: Henry Holt and Co.

Cuddy, A. J. C., Fiske, S. T., and Glick, P. (2004). When professionals become mothers, warmth doesn't cut the ice. *Journal of Social Issues, 60*, 701–718.

Eagly, A. H. (2007). Female leadership advantage and disadvantage: Resolving the contradictions. *Psychology of Women Quarterly, 31*, 1–12.

Eagly, A. H., and Carli, L. L. (2007). *Through the labyrinth: The truth about how women become leaders.* Boston, MA: Harvard Business School.

Eagly, A. H., Johannesen-Schmidt, M. C., and van Engen, M. L. (2003). Transformational, transactional, and laissez-faire leadership styles: A meta-analysis comparing women and men. *Psychological Bulletin, 129*, 569–591.

Eagly, A. H., and Karau, S. J. (2002). Role congruity theory of prejudice toward female leaders. *Psychological Bulletin, 108*, 233–256.

Eagly, A. H., and Koenig, A. M. (2008). Gender prejudice: On the risks of occupying incongruent roles. In E. Borgida and S. T. Fiske (Eds.), *Beyond common sense: Psychological science in the courtroom* (pp. 63–81). Malden: Blackwell Publishing.

Eagly, A. H., Makhijani, M. G., and Klonsky, B. G. (1992). Gender and the evaluation of leaders: A meta-analysis. *Psychological Bulletin, 111*, 3–22.

Eagly, A. H., and Mladinic, A. (1993). Are people prejudiced against women? Some answers from research on attitudes, gender stereotypes and judgments of competence. In W. Stroebe and M. Hewstone (Eds.), *European review of social psychology,* Vol. 5 (pp. 1–35). New York: Wiley.

Fiske, S. T., Bersoff, D. N., Borgida, E., Deaux, K. and Heilman, M. E. (1991). Social science research on trial: Use of sex stereotyping research in *Price Waterhouse v. Hopkins. American Psychologist, 46*, 1049–1060.

Fiske, S. T., Cuddy, A. J., Glick, P., and Xu, J. (2002). A model of (often mixed) stereotype content: Competence and warmth respectively follow from perceived status and competition. *Journal of Personality and Social Psychology, 82*, 878–902.

Forsyth, D. R., Heiney, M. M., and Wright, S. S. (1997). Biases in appraisals of women leaders. *Group Dynamics: Theory, Research, and Practice, 1*, 98–103.

Foschi, M. (2000). Double standards for competence: Theory and research. *Annual Review of Sociology, 26*, 21–42.

Friedman, C., and Yorio, K. (2006). *The girl's guide to being a boss (without being a bitch).* New York: Morgan Road Books.

Glick, P., and Fiske, S. T. (2001). An ambivalent alliance: Hostile and benevolent sexism as complementary justifications for gender inequality. *American Psychologist, 56*, 109–118.

Glick, P., and Fiske, S. (2007). Sex discrimination: The psychological approach. In F. Crosby (Ed.), *Sex discrimination in the workplace: Multidisciplinary perspectives* (pp. 155–187). Malden, MA: Blackwell.

Good, J. J., and Rudman, L. A. (2010). When female applicants meet sexist interviewers: The cost of being a target of benevolent sexism. *Sex Roles, 62*, 481–493.

Heilman, M. E. (2001). Description and prescription: How gender stereotypes prevent women's ascent up the organizational ladder. *Journal of Social Issues, 57*, 657–674.

Heilman, M. E., and Okimoto, T. G. (2007). Why are women penalized for success at male tasks? The implied communality deficit. *Journal of Applied Psychology, 92*, 81–92.

Kanter, R. M. (1993). *Men and women of the corporation*, 2nd ed. New York: Basic Books.

Lyness, K. S., and Thompson, D. E. (1997). Above the glass ceiling? A comparison of matched samples of male and male executives. *Journal of Applied Psychology, 82*, 359–375.

Oldmeadow, J., and Fiske, S. T. (2007). System-justifying ideologies moderate status = competence stereotypes: Roles for belief in a just world and social dominance orientation. *European Journal of Social Psychology, 37*, 1135–1148.

Phelan, J. E., Moss-Racusin, C. A., and Rudman, L. A. (2008). Competent yet out in the cold: Shifting criteria for hiring reflect backlash toward agentic women. *Psychology of Women Quarterly, 32*, 406–413.

Ridgeway, C. L., and Correll, S. J. (2004). Motherhood as a status characteristic. *Journal of Social Issues, 60*, 683–700.

Rudman, L. A. (1998). Self-promotion as a risk factor for women: The costs and benefits of counterstereotypical impression management. *Journal of Personality and Social Psychology, 74*, 629–645.

Rudman, L. A., and Fairchild, K. (2004). Reactions to counterstereotypic behavior: The role of backlash. *Journal of Personality and Social Psychology, 87*, 157–176.

Rudman, L. A., and Glick, P. (1999). Feminized management and backlash toward agentic women: The hidden costs to women of a kinder, gentler image of middle managers. *Journal of Personality and Social Psychology, 77*, 1004–1010.

Ryan, M. K., and Haslam, S. (2005). The Glass Cliff: Evidence that women are over-represented in precarious leadership positions. *British Journal of Management, 16*(2), 81–90.

Ryan, M. K., Haslam, S. A., and Kulich, C. (2010). Politics and the glass cliff: Evidence that women are preferentially selected to contest hard-to-win seats. *Psychology of Women Quarterly, 34*, 56–64.

Sinclair, L., and Kunda, Z. (2000). Motivated stereotyping of women: She's fine if she praised me but incompetent if she criticized me. *Personality and Social Psychology Bulletin, 26*, 1329–1342.

Twenge, J. M. (1997). Attitudes toward women, 1970–1995: A meta-analysis. *Psychology of Women Quarterly, 21*, 35–51.

Yoder, J. (2001). Making leadership work more effectively for women. *Journal of Social Issues, 57*, 815–828.

4

The Advancement of Women at Work: The Continued Struggle to Break the Glass Ceiling

Jennica Webster, Terry A. Beehr, and Tina C. Elacqua

Introduction

As we embark on the twenty-first century, some women have certainly made inroads into powerful positions in society, including political leaders, clergy, and corporate leaders, all of which are spheres long dominated by men. Based on this improvement, some people have gone as far as to suggest that the glass ceiling has been "broken" (Pelosi, 2007). Despite the progress women have made into some powerful roles, however, their scarcity continues to be a widespread problem across many domains. Several phrases have been offered to reflect the experience of women in high-level positions in organizations in specific occupations. The phrase the *political glass ceiling* (Palmer and Simon, 2001) was coined to explain the underrepresentation of women in Congress, who account for only 17 percent of all representatives. The *stained glass ceiling* (Fisher, 2000) was introduced to depict the experience of women in church leadership positions, who only make up 17 percent of the clergy (Bureau of Labor Statistics, 2009). The *glass ceiling* metaphor was first brought forth to describe the experiences of women within the workplace (Hymowitz and Schellhardt, 1986), where, as in Congress and the clergy, few women have made it to top-ranking positions. Of *Fortune* 500 companies, women only represent 3 percent of CEOs and 15 percent of the board of directors (Catalyst, 2009). In the top publicly traded companies around the world, women represent only 14 percent of corporate executives (Catalyst, 2010).

These raw statistics reinforce the struggle that women continue to face in their quest to reach equality with men at the highest levels of organizational hierarchies. The glass ceiling metaphor emerged in the 1980s to describe the experience of women in the workplace, and it refers to a phenomenon whereby subtle and invisible barriers impede the advancement of women into upper-management positions regardless of their qualifications (Morrison, White, and Van Velsor, 1987). The term "glass" implies that these barriers are invisible or transparent, which can give the false illusion that top-level positions are accessible to women. The concept began to receive attention from both the general public (Pogrebin, 1988) and academic scholars in the 1980s (Laser, 1988). Based on this attention, the notion of a glass ceiling was recognized by public policy makers to the extent that in 1991, the U.S. Department of Labor established the Glass Ceiling Commission, whose main focus was to identify those invisible barriers for women's advancement and then report the findings with recommendations on how to break it. Thus for 20 years, the U.S. government has voiced concern over and has sought ways to eliminate the inequality women face at work.

Since the introduction of the *glass ceiling*, many scholars and practitioners have offered new metaphors and phrases to help describe and explain the dearth of women in top positions. For instance, the *glass slipper* suggests that women are less likely to pursue positions of power (Rudman and Heppen, 2003), and that part of the reason more women are not in these positions may be that they have not pursued these positions vigorously, or that they don't want them. *Sticky floors* reflects self-imposed hurdles that keep women stuck on the middle rungs of the career ladder (Shambaugh, 2008). The *glass cliff* describes the precariousness of leadership positions held by women, meaning that when women do reach top positions, it tends to be in organizations that are likely to fail (and the women in charge will get the blame; Ryan and Haslam, 2005). *Labyrinth* was introduced to replace the *glass ceiling* metaphor in order to reflect the changing times (Eagly and Carli, 2007a). *Labyrinth* implies that although women face barriers, they can ultimately overcome them if they persist and make their way through a series of choices and efforts.

Although there are subtle differences between these various metaphors, they all acknowledge that women are underrepresented in top-ranking jobs. The most widely known term and the one codified in law is the term *glass ceiling*. Therefore, in order to avoid confusion, it is the term we use throughout this chapter.

Scholarship over the last several decades has provided us with substantial advances in our understanding of the barriers that prohibit the advancement of women in organizations. Given the substantive body of literature specifically on gender bias, we focus on it as a primary factor in the glass ceiling's existence. To structure our discussion of the theoretical and empirical developments in the glass ceiling literature, we offer a model as a guide. Our goal is to take a deep look at gender bias with the intent to highlight those societal and interpersonal forces that severely challenge and at times prevent women from advancing to top-ranking positions. Thus, the purpose of this chapter is to provide a synopsis of the literature on the current state of women in their fight to reach the top echelons of corporate America. We will begin by providing the basic theoretical framework for the model, and then review the theoretical and empirical evidence for each link while keeping this framework in mind. The chapter concludes with a discussion of the various strategies to break the glass ceiling.

Theoretical Framework Underlying the Model

Before describing the model, we should first consider the issues of gender and gender bias. Gender, in contrast to sex, is more than a biological characteristic; rather, it is a multifaceted system that represents the assumptions and beliefs a society holds about men and women (Ferree, Lorber, and Hess, 1999; Ridgeway and Correll, 2004). Historically, men have been the dominant gender in most societies; this has hindered women in many spheres, including the workplace (Bell and Nkomo, 2001). *Bias* is a complex term that reflects a collection of reactions including stereotypes, prejudice, and discrimination about a group of people (Cuddy, Fiske, and Glick, 2007; Fiske, 1998). The purpose of this chapter is to explore the ways in which a gender-biased system shapes women's experiences as they move through the hierarchy of their work organization.

To help understand bias, we call upon Fiske's (2004) social bias framework, which suggests that four basic motives or needs underlie the root source of all social bias. The first of these, *understanding*, refers to the idea that people need to make sense of their environment. To do this, people tend to use categories, schemas, and expectations to simplify and process information about other people. The second of these, *belonging*, reflects people's need to feel a part of a group, often resulting in prejudice, or in-group favoritism. The third motive, *controlling*, refers to people's basic desire to want to control their environments. People want to be able to avoid any danger that could harm them. One way people do this is by ostracizing those who act as potential threats. The last motive regarding social bias, *enhancing self*, represents the notion that people need to feel good about themselves, and therefore use different types of tactics to make sure the self is protected. They may do this by openly debasing out-group members. Taken together, each of these motives is reinforced indirectly through stereotypes, prejudice, and discrimination, which lay the theoretical foundation for the model.

Before moving on, we want to address the issue of blatant versus subtle bias (Fiske, 2004). The four motives of bias, as described above, result in one of two forms of bias: blatant or subtle. On the one hand, blatant bias is more overt and relatively easy to identify. Blatant forms of gender bias include being openly hostile and discriminatory to an out-group; for example, openly rejecting an applicant for a job due to her gender or race. Legislation has been designed to eradicate many kinds of blatant forms of bias in many countries. In the United States, for example, the Equal Pay Act (1963) and subsequent Civil Rights legislation (e.g., Civil Rights Acts of 1964 and 1991) made it illegal to base employment decisions, such as salary determinations and hiring decisions, on gender. On the face of it, these legal developments can help give the illusion that gender inequity is a thing of the past or that it is easy to overcome through legislation and litigation. However, neither of these conclusions is true.

On the other hand, the biases that women face today often take on the subtle form, which is less easily recognizable. It is automatic, unconscious, and unintentional (Fiske, 2002, 2004). Subtle forms of bias include withholding the expression of positive feelings such as warmth, compassion, or respect toward members of an out-group (Fiske, 2002); withholding actions—which amounts to no action, something that is hard to observe (i.e., one can't easily observe something that isn't present). These forms of bias are embedded in our expectations and attitudes and manifest themselves in our thoughts and behaviors. They permeate organizations and are part of their structure, culture, and practices. They can defy even our best intentions. Because of this, they are not easy to overcome. Indeed, Meyerson and Fletcher (2000) go as far as to say "... most of the barriers that persist today are insidious—a revolution couldn't find them to blast away" (p. 127).

Model: Sources of the Glass Ceiling

There are subtle yet consequential barriers that prevent or severely challenge women from reaching the top-level positions in their organizations. These barriers are represented by the effects that stereotypes and prejudice have on discrimination by others and on women's own choices; a large portion of these effects are driven by people's need to understand, belong, control, and enhance. Thus, the proposed model and review are consistent with the social bias framework. In a sequential and causal way, the model proposes that societal constraints and interpersonal constraints can influence the woman's own internal constraints and/or the differential treatment she receives in the workplace. The following sections discuss the components of the proposed model.

Societal Constraints

The societal constraints or cultural stereotypes faced by women can influence them to conform to gender stereotypes on their own, and they also can influence others to treat women differently from men. Societal constraints include the expectations and beliefs a society holds for men and women. Sex, like age and ethnicity, is an observable attribute that is often used as a heuristic to infer and generalize information about people (Gawronski, 2003). As a society, we share certain beliefs and expectations about how men and women will behave, which perpetuate gender stereotypes. Stereotypes are simple, overgeneralized, widely shared *ideas* about a particular group of people (Heilman, 2001). People use social stereotypes to help reduce the amount of information processing needed to engage in social interactions. In other words, they are a "cognitive shortcut" used to make assumptions about others, reducing the need for people to seek information about every person individually. Gender stereotypes can often lead people to infer inaccurate and misleading information about others, however, because people are rarely exact representations of their group's stereotype (Fiske, 2004).

Stereotypes are formed through the social customs, traditions, and norms of society, and because organizations operate within the larger society, those same stereotypes occur in organizations. That is, society's stereotypes are reflected in the kinds of beliefs and expectations we have for organizational members (Eagly and Karau, 2002). These culturally shared gender stereotypes are beliefs about both how a group actually is (*descriptive*) and how it should be (*prescriptive*) (Heilman, 2001). For example, a descriptive stereotype is the belief that women are emotional and needy, whereas a prescriptive stereotype is the belief that women should behave in ways that are consistent with being emotional and needy. When people hold a stereotype about a group of people, they expect them to have certain attributes as well as behave in ways that reinforce those attributes.

Drawing from Fiske's (2004) social bias framework, stereotypes are driven by the need to understand, to belong, to control, and to self-enhance. For the first of these, *the need to understand*, stereotypes help satisfy people's need to make sense of the situations in which they find themselves. That allows us to make assumptions about people's roles within a particular setting, such as the workplace. Stereotypes thus help us interact with and understand other people by referencing the expectations we have about them. For example, in a U.S. health care setting, it is likely that people would assume that the men are doctors and the women are nurses. The second need that drives stereotype formation and use, the *need to belong*, suggests that stereotypes can facilitate the promotion of in-groups and out-groups. They promote cohesion and group unity among group members as well as perceptions of dominance on the part of members of the in-group over the out-group, usually by encouraging the cognition that the in-group is superior in one or more important ways. For example, male managers might view women as not having the right characteristics to make good upper-level managers, and therefore they would not advocate their promotions.

As for the third need, *the need to control*, stereotypes give people direction and guidance in unfamiliar situations. People are usually uncomfortable in new or ambiguous situations, and thus stereotypes, when they evoke familiar associations, can create a sense of control over possible external threats from the out-group (Fiske and Berdahl, 2007). For example, groups who have more power can influence the reputation of the out-group. Lastly, stereotypes can serve to enhance one's self-image. They reinforce one's own identity and promote feelings of uniqueness, and, in doing so, help protect and reinforce the self-image. Thus, if I belong to a small group of high-ranking women in the military, I can identify with that group and believe that I have whatever set of positive traits I perceive the group has.

If these four needs drive stereotypes, how are they used in making employment decisions, and what are the stereotypes that people associate with women, and, more importantly, with women in leadership roles? As we subsequently show, people often rely on gender to infer suitability for particular roles. This discussion will be followed by a review of two widely held gender stereotypes that reinforce the glass ceiling.

Use of Gender Stereotypes to Evaluate Compatibility

Society expects women to engage in a certain set of descriptive behaviors, and men to engage in others. People typically associate women with communal behaviors and men with agentic behaviors (Eagly and Sczesny, 2009). Communal behaviors are associated with kindness, empathy, helpfulness, and sensitivity. In contrast, agentic behaviors are characterized by confidence, aggressiveness, ambition, and competitiveness. The qualities most often ascribed to effective leaders are also those associated with men (i.e., agentic behaviors; Eagly and Johannesen-Schmidt, 2001; Willemsen, 2002). This is no surprise, because the role of leader in most societies has been predominately occupied by men. The phrase, "think leader–think male" was coined nearly 40 years ago (Schien, 1973) and can still be applied to people's beliefs today (Powell, Butterfield, and Parent, 2002). The incongruence between the attributes ascribed to women and ascribed to effective leaders puts women in a conundrum (Eagly and Karau, 2002; Heilman, 2001; Lyness and Heilman, 2006). Because of the *lack of fit* between assumed women's qualities and the qualities associated with leaders, women are often found unsuitable for leadership roles (Gorman and Kmec, 2009). The assumption that there is a lack of fit negatively biases evaluations made about women (Heilman, 2001). That is, society views women as not having "the right stuff" (Eagly and Carli, 2007b). Therefore, few women ever get the opportunity to access these positions.

There is empirical evidence to support the lack-of-fit model (Pichler, Simpson, and Stroh, 2008). For example, in a study examining the performance ratings and promotability of middle and senior managers over a two-year time period, women in senior positions were found to have a significant disadvantage compared to women in middle-management positions and men in both middle and senior positions (Lyness and Heilman, 2006). Specifically, women in senior positions, which were perceived to be a better fit for men, were given less favorable performance ratings than men. In addition, women who were promoted to senior level positions had previously received significantly higher performance ratings than men who were promoted to the same position, thus implying that women were held to higher standards than men in order to achieve their current rank. The historically masculine qualities associated with high-ranking roles forces women to perform a balancing act between expressing communal and agentic characteristics. Women who demonstrate agentic characteristics are criticized for lacking femininity, whereas women who show characteristics of communality are criticized for lacking in the qualities needed to be an effective leader (Eagly and Carli, 2004, 2007a). A very public example of this occurred during the 2008 presidential election. Hillary Clinton was criticized and ridiculed for being "too austere" or "too angry." However, when she cried during an interview she was disparaged for being "too emotional" (Kornblut, 2009).

Use of Gender Stereotypes to Evaluate Competence and Warmth

People use gender as a proxy for inferring a person's level of competence. Competence is abstract, not observable, and thus people have to use other indicators to gauge a person's level of competence when making employment decisions. Because higher-level positions are characterized by having more power, greater decision-making ability, and higher social status, competence is viewed as a critical indicator of success for these positions (Gorman and Kmec, 2009). In a perfectly merit-based world, employment decisions would be based on valid predictors of ability and performance. However, as we discussed earlier, stereotypes, biases, expectations, and prejudices affect the evaluations of others. A common gender stereotype is that women are less competent compared to men especially when women deviate from their stereotypic female roles (Fiske, Cuddy, Glick, and Xu, 2002). There is a large body of literature supporting this claim (Eagly, Wood, and Diekman, 2000). In one such study, successful women were not only rated as less competent compared to equally successful men, but they were also less liked and received much harsher evaluations of performance (Heilman, Wallen, Fuchs, and Tamkins, 2004). This was only the case, however, when women were working in characteristically male-type roles. Another interesting finding showed that when information was provided about the level of previous success the women had, their competence ratings increased, possibly indicating that making facts about women's past success more salient can reduce biases. However, women who received higher competence ratings were also more strongly disliked (Heilman et al., 2004).

On the other side of this spectrum are women who pursue more traditional roles centered on family or work, for example women as mothers or secretaries. Because these are traditionally female-gendered roles, society attributes much more socially desirable traits to women in these roles (Cikara and Fiske, 2009), such as mothers being warm and caring, and secretaries being friendly and service-oriented. Unfortunately, although these socially desirable traits are attributed to mothers and secretaries, a number of negative traits are also attributed to these roles, including weakness and incompetence (Cuddy, Fiske, and Glick, 2004). Taken together, this implies that women are faced with a paradox. On the one hand, if women are successful in nontraditional roles, they are faced with the possibility of being rejected and disliked by others (because they are deviating from a stereotypic female role). On the other hand, if women are successful in traditionally female roles, they are faced with the possibility of being seen as inept and powerless.

Use of Gender Stereotypes to Evaluate the Ability of Mothers

An important stereotype that negatively impacts the advancement of women at work includes those traits associated with motherhood. Research shows that having children is associated with greater career success for men, but less for women (Kirchmeyer, 2006). Let us try to understand why this may be the case. As we have already mentioned, being a

woman uncovers unconscious stereotypes that people have about acceptable ways in which women are expected to behave. Unfortunately, these
behaviors are incongruent with the behaviors deemed desirable for a successful leader of adults (Heilman, 2001). This lack-of-fit perception is
suggested to be exacerbated by women who are mothers (Heilman and
Okimoto, 2008). That is, gender stereotypes are heightened and more
salient for working mothers because mothers are the prototype of womanhood and femininity in our society (Cuddy et al., 2004). This implies that
mothers are perceived as being even more deficient, compared to childless
women, of the attributes believed to be necessary for leadership roles. The
assumed discrepancy between mothers' traits and leaders' traits creates a
gap in fit perceptions; the greater the gap the more damaging the effects
are. Having children imparts expectations on women as professionals
and mothers. It is assumed that women in our society are primarily
devoted to or are responsible for child-rearing and caregiving roles;
unfortunately, these roles are largely undervalued in organizations and
are in conflict with the stereotype of an effective leader.

The stereotype of caregiver denotes the assumption that women are less
dedicated and less committed to their careers (Liff and Ward, 2001) and
more likely to experience family–work conflict (Hoobler, Wayne, and
Lemmon, 2009) than men. This is a faulty assumption, however, for a
number of reasons. First, women and men take on several roles in their
lifetime that they are able to successfully fulfill. To assume that women
devote all of their time, energy, and resources to being a mother over their
entire life span is obviously erroneous. The commitment invested in caring for children is typically greatest during the first few years of the child's
life, and therefore does not last an entire career. Second, men and women
share the responsibility of caring for children. Thus, both working mothers
and fathers should have similar levels of work interfering with family and
family interfering with work. Empirical evidence supports this claim. In
fact, a meta-analysis revealed that gender had a near-zero relationship
with work–family conflict and only a weak relationship with family–work
conflict (Byron, 2005).

There are also perceptions about mothers' being disadvantaged in other
ways. Heilman and Okimoto (2008) conducted an experiment to examine
whether respondents showed bias toward mothers in their ratings of perceived competence and promotion screening-recommendations. In line

with predictions, mothers were expected to be less competent and were less likely to be recommended for further consideration for advancement to high-ranking positions compared to working fathers and childless women. In a similar study, Cuddy et al. (2004) found that compared to working fathers and childless women, mothers were anticipated to be less competent, and respondents were less interested in hiring, promoting, and educating them. Relatedly, Hoobler et al. (2009) found that managers often make assumptions about their employees' level of family–work conflict. The study examined whether managers perceived that women have a more difficult time balancing their work roles and their family roles, while controlling for actual family responsibilities and women's reports of their family–work conflict. As expected, managers did have this perception. Consequentially, these perceptions were related to fewer promotions and ratings of promotability for women.

Interpersonal Constraints

According to the model, interpersonal constraints or prejudices can eventually result in women choosing different career paths (internal constraints), or others' treating women differentially from men in the workplace. Mentorships and social networks are two types of developmental relationships that are valuable resources and that can help employees progress and succeed in their careers (Belliveau, 2005; Eby, Allen, Evans, Ng, and Dubois, 2008; Wanberg, Welsh, and Hezlett, 2003). Developmental relationships have several benefits for employees, including an increase in employee visibility, a chance to become more skilled, and a means to learn about promotional opportunities. Some scholars have suggested that these relationships can help women guard against certain barriers such as stereotypes (Pini, Brown, and Ryan, 2004) and discrimination (Bierema, 2005). Unfortunately, however, women are found to either be excluded or get less return from these developmental relationships than men (Ibarra, 1995; Ibarra, Kilduff, and Tsai, 2005). To clarify the latter point, women tend to have relationships with those who hold low-ranking positions (Lin, 1999); consequently, those individuals have lower status and less authority over organizational resources compared to those in high-ranking positions.

Accordingly, women may be excluded from the benefits of high-quality, high-status developmental relationships. To understand why this may be the case, we turn to social identity theory and the social bias framework to provide insight. In keeping with social identity theory (Turner, Brown, and Tajfel, 1979) people identify with and derive their self-images from subjectively meaningful social groups and their perceived social status. Moreover, people make relative comparisons between groups with which they identify (in-groups) and with which they do not (out-groups). The creation of in-groups and out-groups cause people to differentiate between *us* and *them*. Those individuals who are categorized as *us* are usually better liked and preferred over those who are categorized as *them* (Otten and Wentura, 2001), resulting in prejudice (Fiske, 2004). Although prejudice can entail "enhanced in-group positivity, enhanced out-group negativity, or both," it usually involves enhanced in-group positivity even in the absence of out-group negativity (Brewer, 2007, p. 730). Therefore, the prejudice that occurs is often subtle and difficult to detect. Further, this process of categorization and subsequent prejudice occurs automatically, before realization, and thus can give the illusion of honesty and impartiality (Otten and Moskowitz, 2000).

In view of the social bias framework, the formation of in-groups and out-groups and the subsequent prejudice toward out-groups that follows is partly driven by the motives of belonging and self-enhancing (Fiske, 2004). Regarding the former, people need to affiliate with others and feel socially accepted in a group (Baumeister and Leary, 1995). People strive to build meaningful and stable relationships. The need to belong encourages people who employ a number of tactics to enhance group solidarity (Baumeister and Leary, 1995). For instance, a strategy to enhance group solidarity is to show favoritism for in-group members (Fiske, 2004). As noted above, favoring one's in-group over an out-group is the foundation of prejudice. Therefore, in-group members are often shown preferential treatment over out-group members. The second underlying motive for being prejudiced against out-group members is the need to enhance the self. People evaluate their value partly by their affiliated group membership. Consequently, in order for people to have a positive view of the self, they attribute positive qualities to the in-group (Baumeister and Leary, 1995).

Taken together, the social bias framework and social identify theory help us understand why women have fewer developmental relationships with people of high status and power. Because—according to social identity theory—men predominately hold leadership roles in organizations, they are more likely to coach, support, and mentor others who are members of their in-group (other men). Men are likely to protect their group's values and status by bolstering other men into positions of power, thus maintaining superiority over women. This indeed is a form of prejudice reinforcing a gender hierarchy that is in favor of men. In-group favoritism or prejudice is more likely to be prevalent among those fighting to obtain high-status leadership positions (Gorman and Kmec, 2009). These high-level jobs are by nature characterized as having greater control and power over other people and resources. Therefore, people are motivated to secure those positions for members of the in-group. An example of this can be seen in the old boys' networks, which are informal networks of men who develop business relationships at various locations (e.g., golf courses) where women are traditionally excluded. Men may not purposefully prevent women from joining, but regardless of intent, women are still disadvantaged.

Empirical evidence has shown that women tend either to be excluded from developmental relationships altogether (e.g., Dreher and Cox, 1996; Lyness and Thompson, 2000; Ragins and Cotton, 1991) or to receive fewer benefits from them (e.g., Dreher and Cox, 2000; Lyness and Thompson, 2000). In a study comparing men and women executives, women reported that they were overlooked by people in informal networks that are helpful for getting promoted (Lyness and Thompson, 2000). This is consistent with the notion of an old boys' network, in which women are typically excluded. Research has also shown that women tend to receive fewer benefits when they do have developmental relationships. A longitudinal study examining the career progression of men and women over a period of four years showed that having a mentor was more beneficial for men than for women, such that men received higher compensation (Kirchmeyer, 2002). Along these same lines, Forret and Dougherty (2004) found that men received more promotions and higher financial returns when they engaged in network behaviors than women.

Internal Constraints

The component of internal constraints (pressure to conform) in the proposed model reflects the impact that bias—and, in particular, stereotypes—can have on women's career choices and interests. These pressures influence the life choices women make, the attitudes they have, and the ways in which they behave (Klein and Snyder, 2003), and they can result in the glass ceiling effect of fewer women in top roles in the workplace. As previously discussed, people form expectations both about what men and women are like (*descriptive*) and how they should behave (*prescriptive*), and assume that women (or men) will have similar interests and skill sets as other women (or men). Together, these expectations and assumptions about men and women lead to the development of gender stereotypes. Starting at a young age, these stereotypes are learned, reinforced, and internalized (Fitzgerald and Harmon, 2001). People are pressured to conform to these stereotypes (Eagly and Wood, 1999) and therefore try to live up to them (Lippa, 2005). So, women who decide on careers with limited advancement opportunity or choose to stay home to be full-time mothers do so because they have learned to love these roles or because this is what society expects of them. There is research to suggest that gender stereotypes can indeed affect individuals' career decisions and leadership aspirations. For example, women who were exposed to subtly primed stereotypes reported lower aspirations for power and status (Davies, Spencer, and Steele, 2005). More specifically, people automatically and unconsciously conformed to gender stereotypical behaviors after viewing TV commercials that depicted gender stereotypes. In a similar study, after viewing gender stereotypical commercials, women had less interest in pursuing educational programs that required high levels of math (Davies, Spencer, Quinn, and Gerhardstein, 2002).

Gender stereotypes influence individuals' career decisions through processes of socialization and stereotype threat (Zhang, Schmader, and Forbes, 2009). The first of these, gender socialization, is the process by which children learn the norms and expectations for men and women (Ward, 2003). Children learn directly from parents (McHale, Crouter, and Whiteman, 2003) and peers (Witt, 2000), and indirectly through mass media (Hurst and Brown, 2008; Signorielli, 1993). These agents socialize women (or men) against behaving in ways that are stereotypically masculine (or feminine) and send strong messages about what characteristics are most valued about girls and boys. As noted earlier, society places a high value on communal behaviors for girls, whereas agentic behaviors are most valued for boys (Eagly and Sczesny, 2009). Accordingly, women are confronted with messages that suggest women and leadership roles are incompatible; thus women who are choosing a career track may not seek to hold powerful positions because they do not see themselves as fitting that role.

This is also the case for certain areas of expertise. For example, research shows that gender socialization drives girls away from mathematical and scientific fields (Crombie et al., 2005). Therefore, these messages influence a person's identify and concept of the self (Zhang et al., 2009). People internalize these stereotypical gender beliefs through the socialization process to the point that it influences their interests (Eddleston, Veiga, and Powell, 2006). For example, in a meta-analysis, men's and women's job attribute preferences were consistent with gender stereotypes (Konrad, Ritchie, Lieb, and Corrigall, 2000). Specifically, women reported that interpersonal relationships such as friendships, interaction with coworkers, and opportunities to make friends were important aspects of the job more than men did, whereas men reported that status attainment such as power, influence, and leadership duties were important more than women did.

Research suggests that people classify occupations as being either masculine or feminine (Hartung, Porfeli, and Vondracek, 2005), and that because of gender stereotypes, people are encouraged to choose gender-appropriate occupations (Fitzgerald and Harmon, 2001). Furthermore, those occupations dominated by men tend to have greater power and more control over resources than those dominated by women (Eagly and Wood, 1999). Some women are constrained by gender stereotypes and gravitate toward roles with less prestige (family roles, less distinguishable careers) (Cejka and Eagly, 1999). If women break the rules, moving away from society's expectations and performing outside their gendered scripts, they are punished socially. For example, feminists are considered unattractive and unlikable (Haddock and Zanna, 1994). Also, as already mentioned, women who exhibit masculine qualities such as aggression and assertiveness tend to be disliked by others (Heilman et al., 2004).

The second process through which gender stereotypes influence individuals' career decisions is stereotype threat, which occurs when an individual is in a situation for which a negative stereotype about their groups applies (Steele, 1997; Steele and Aronson, 1995). The fear of being judged or treated stereotypically can cause people to perform poorly. This is especially the case for women who are performing stereotypically male activities such as math and science. For example, in an experiment that manipulated the instructions of a math test, women did as well as men when they were told beforehand that performance on the test did not vary by gender; however, when no such information was given, women performed worse than men (Spencer, Steele, and Quinn, 1999). A similar study examining stereotype threat found that women who were tested in a room with other men test takers performed worse than if they were tested only with other women in the room (Inzlicht and Ben-Zeev, 2003). To be successful in high-level positions, successful completion of cognitive tests is often necessary, and when women receive lower test scores, it may seem they are less qualified for the job (Zhang et al., 2009). Not only do lower test scores influence the perceptions of others, but they can also influence the perceptions that women have about their own ability. Thus stereotype threat increases frustration, anxiety, and self-deprecation, which are likely to steer women away from male-dominated domains (Zhang et al., 2009). That is, women may self-select out of careers that have distinguished career ladders leading to top levels of organizations.

Differential Treatment

Differential treatment (discrimination) of women in the workplace is often one of the first causes we think of when considering the glass ceiling. The subtle, yet detrimental, ways in which men and women are treated differently at work has damaging effects for the representation of women in high-ranking positions. Denying people equality based on one's own stereotypes or prejudice is discrimination, and oftentimes is so subtle that "... the target is unlikely to comprehend fully what is going on, and the perceiver can deny—to self and other alike—that the interaction was biased" (Fiske, 2004, p. 421). Regardless of intention, subtle discrimination can have debilitating effects on the advancement of women. Even small differences in promotion rates can eventually leave large differences in ratios of men and women at the top of the hierarchy in organizations (Agars, 2004). Organizations are responsible for offering developmental opportunities to prepare employees for advancement. Opportunities such as promotions, transfers, and challenging assignments are examples of methods used for employees to develop the needed skill set to be effective leaders. However, women are not extended these same opportunities, which generate a skill gap, and ultimately men ascend to higher level positions more quickly than women (Gorman and Kmec, 2009). A great deal of attention in employment research has been given to differential treatment, for example, in industrial–organizational psychology and human resources management literatures. An abundant amount of empirical evidence supports the claim that women are discriminated against in the workplace. For example, research has shown that women receive lower performance evaluations from male subordinates (Lyness and Heilman, 2006), are less likely to receive overseas assignments (Lyness and Thompson, 2000), and are awarded fewer promotions (Blau and Devardo, 2007; Kirchmeyer, 2002).

Legislation as well as research has focused on differential treatment. Many countries have laws requiring equal treatment of the sexes in the workplace. These laws thus apply directly to the differential treatment facet of the glass ceiling model. Because there are other powerful factors at work (i.e., societal constraints, interpersonal constraints, and internal constraints), however, these laws are not completely effective in destroying the glass ceiling. In fact, some of the other factors in the model, especially societal constraints and interpersonal constraints, are primary causes in the sense that they come before and influence differential treatment. By the time differential treatment in organizations occurs, these other factors have already wielded their negative influences. That is what makes it so hard to fully remove glass ceiling effects through legislation regarding the point of differential treatment decisions.

Conclusion

The development of the model and the review of the literature that follows from it provide an up-to-date and in-depth examination of factors that serve to create and perpetuate the glass ceiling. Over the last few decades, strides have been taken to protect women's rights, usually in the form of antidiscrimination laws and policies that have helped eradicate blatant gender inequality in the workplace. However, despite this progress, there remains a deeply embedded societal gender bias that is unlikely to be resolved solely through public policy. In fact, the bias that remains in organizations today is now more subtle and complex than it was in the past. The model presented in this chapter does not intend to place blame on any particular group. For the most part, this modern form of gender bias is unintentional and therefore difficult for both the bias holder and recipient to see. To end with a glimpse of optimism, we do believe that there are solutions to this problem, and with the help of the bias holder, bias recipient, and organization, the glass ceiling effect will one day be a metaphor of the past.

References

Agars, M. D. (2004). Reconsidering the impact of gender stereotypes on the advancement of women in organizations. *Psychology of Women Quarterly, 28*, 103–111.

Baumeister, R., and Leary, M. R. (1995). The need to belong: Desire for interpersonal attachments as a fundamental human motivation. *Psychological Bulletin, 117*, 497–529.

Bell, E. L., and Nkomo, S. M. (2001). *Our separate ways: Black and white women and the struggle for professional identity.* Boston, MA: Harvard Business Review.

Belliveau, M. A. (2005). Blind ambition? The effects of social networks and institutional sex composition on the job search outcomes of elite coeducational and women's college graduates. *Organizational Science, 16*, 134–150.

Bierema, L. L. (2005). Women executives' concerns related to implementing and sustaining a women's network in a corporate context. *Organization Development Journal, 23*, 8–20.

Blau, F. D., and Devardo, J. (2007). New evidence on gender differences in promotion rates: An empirical analysis of a sample of new hires. *Industrial Relations: A Journal of Economy and Society, 46*, 511–550.

Brewer, M. B. (2007). The importance of being we: Human nature and intergroup relations. *American Psychologist, 62*, 728–738.

Bureau of Labor Statistics. (2009). *Household data annual averages.* Retrieved from http://www.bls.gov/cps/cpsaat11.pdf on February 18, 2010.

Byron, K. (2005). A meta-analytic review of work–family conflict and its antecedents. *Journal Vocational Behavior, 67*, 169–198.

Catalyst. (2009). *Women in U.S. management.* Retrieved from http://www.catalyst.org/file/308/qt_women_in_us_management.pdf on March 7, 2010.

Catalyst. (2010). *2010 Women in Business in Australia, Canada, South Africa, and United States.* Retrieved from http://www.catalyst.org/file/347/qt_australia_canada_south_africa_us.pdf on March 8, 2010.

Cejka, M. A., and Eagly, A. H. (1999). Gender-stereotypic images of occupations correspond to the sex segregation of employment. *Personality and Social Psychology Bulletin, 25*, 413–423.

Cikara, M., and Fiske, S. T. (2009). Warmth, competence, and ambivalent sexism: Vertical assault and collateral damage. In M. Barreto, M. K. Ryan, and M. Schmitt (Eds.), *The glass ceiling in the 21st century: Understanding barriers to gender equality* (pp. 73–96). Washington, DC: American Psychological Association.

Crombie, G., Sinclair, M., Silverthorn, N., Byrne, B. M., DuBois, D. L., and Trinneer, A. (2005). Predictors of young adolescents' math grades and course enrollment intentions: Gender similarities and differences. *Sex Roles, 52*, 351–367.

Cuddy, A. J., Fiske, S. T., and Glick, P. (2004). When professionals become mothers, warmth doesn't cut the ice. *Journal of Social Issues, 60*, 701–718.

Cuddy, A. J., Fiske, S. T., and Glick, P. (2007). The BIAS map: Behaviors from intergroup affect and stereotypes. *Journal of Personality and Social Psychology, 92*, 631–648.

Davies, P. G., Spencer, S. J., Quinn, D. M., and Gerhardstein, R. (2002). Consuming images: How television commercials that elicit stereotype threat can restrain women academically and professionally. *Personality and Social Psychology Bulletin, 28*, 1615–1628.

Davies, P. G., Spencer, S. J., and Steele, C. M. (2005). Clearing the air: Identity safety moderates the effects of stereotype threat on women's leadership aspirations. *Journal of Personality and Social Psychology, 88*, 267–287.

Dreher, G. F, and Cox, T. H. (1996). Race, gender and opportunity: A study of compensation attainment and the establishment of mentoring relationships. *Journal of Applied Psychology, 81*, 297–308.

Dreher, G. F., and Cox, T. H. (2000). Labor market mobility and cash compensation: The moderating effects of race and gender. *Academy of Management Journal, 43,* 890–900.

Eagly, A. H., and Carli, L. L. (2004). Women and men as leaders. In J. Antonakis, A. Cianciolo, and R. J. Sternberg (Eds.), *The nature of leadership* (pp. 279–301). Thousand Oaks, CA: Sage Publications.

Eagly, A. H., and Carli, L. L. (2007a). *Through the labyrinth.* Boston, MA: Harvard Business School Press.

Eagly, A. H., and Carli, L. L. (2007b). Women and the labyrinth of leadership. *Harvard Business Review, 85,* 63–71.

Eagly, A. H., and Johannesen-Schmidt, M. C. (2001). The leadership styles of women and men. *Journal of Social Issues, 57,* 781–797.

Eagly, A. H., and Karau, S. J. (2002). Role congruity theory of prejudice toward female leaders. *Psychological Review, 109,* 573–598.

Eagly, A. H., and Sczesny, S. (2009). Stereotypes about women, men, and leaders: Have times changed? In M. Barreto, M. K. Ryan, and M. Schmitt (Eds.), *The glass ceiling in the 21st century: Understanding barriers to gender equality* (pp. 21–47). Washington, DC: American Psychological Association.

Eagly, A. H., and Wood, W. (1999). The origins of sex differences in human behavior: Evolved dispositions versus social roles. *American Psychologist, 54,* 408–423.

Eagly, A. H., Wood, W., and Diekman, A. B. (2000). Social role theory of sex differences and similarities: A current appraisal. In T. Eckes, and H. M. Trautner (Eds.), *The developmental social psychology of gender* (pp. 123–174). Mahwah, NJ: Lawrence Erlbaum.

Eby, L. T., Allen, T. D., Evans, S. C., Ng, T., Dubois, D. L. (2008). Does mentoring matter? A multidisciplinary meta-analysis comparing mentored and non-mentored individuals. *Journal of Vocational Behavior, 72,* 254–267.

Eddleston, K. A., Veiga, J. F., and Powell, G. N. (2006). Explaining sex differences in managerial career satisfier preferences: The role of gender self-schema. *Journal of Applied Psychology, 91,* 437–445.

Ferree, M., Lorber, J., and Hess, B. (1999). *Revisioning gender.* Thousand Oaks, CA: Sage Publications.

Fisher, L. (2000, July 17). The stained glass ceiling. *Time, 156.*

Fiske, S. T. (1998). Stereotyping, prejudice, and discrimination. In D. T. Gilbert, S. T. Fiske, and L. Gardner (Eds.), *The handbook of social psychology,* 4th ed. (pp. 357–411). New York, NY: McGraw-Hill.

Fiske, S. T. (2002). What we know now about bias and intergroup conflict, problem of the century. *Current Directions in Psychological Science, 11,* 123–128.

Fiske, S. T. (2004). Stereotyping, prejudice, and discrimination: Social biases. In S. T. Fiske (Ed.), *Social beings: A core motives approach to social psychology* (pp. 397–457). New Jersey: Wiley.

Fiske, S. T., and Berdahl, J. (2007). Social power. In A. E. Kruglanski, and E. T. Higgins (Eds.), *Social psychology: Handbook of basic principles,* 2nd ed. (pp. 678–692). New York, NY: Guilford Press.

Fiske, S. T., Cuddy, A. J., Glick, P., and Xu, J. (2002). A model of (often mixed) stereotype content: Competence and warmth respectively follow from perceived status and competition. *Journal of Personality and Social Psychology, 82,* 878–902.

Fitzgerald, L. F., and Harmon, L. W. (2001). Women's career development: A postmodern update. In F. T. Leong, and A. Barak (Eds.), *Contemporary models in vocational psychology: A volume in honor of Samuel H. Osipow* (pp. 207–230). Mahwah, NJ: Lawrence Erlbaum Associates.

Forret, M. L., and Dougherty, T. W. (2004). Networking behaviors and career outcomes: Differences for men and women? *Journal of Organizational Behavior, 251,* 419–437.

Gawronski, B. (2003). On difficult questions and evident answers: Dispositional inference from role-constrained behavior. *Personality and Social Psychology Bulletin, 29,* 1459–1475.

Gorman, E. H., and Kmec, J. A. (2009). Hierarchical rank and women's organizational mobility: Glass ceilings in corporate law firms. *American Journal of Sociology, 114,* 1428–1474.

Haddock, G., and Zanna, M. P. (1994). Preferring "housewives" to "feminists": Categorization and the favorability of attitudes toward men. *Psychology of Women Quarterly, 18*, 25–52.

Hartung, P. J., Porfeli, E. J., and Vondracek, F. W. (2005). Child vocational development: A review and reconsideration. *Journal of Vocational Behavior, 66*, 385–419.

Heilman, M. E. (2001). Description and prescription: How gender stereotypes prevent women's ascent up the organizational ladder. *Journal of Social Issues, 57*, 657–674.

Heilman, M. E., and Okimoto, T. G. (2008). Motherhood: A potential source of bias in employment decisions. *Journal of Applied Psychology, 93*, 189–198.

Heilman, M. E., Wallen, A. S., Fuchs, D., and Tamkins, M. M. (2004). Penalties for success: Reactions to women who succeed at male tasks. *Journal of Applied Psychology, 89*, 416–427.

Hoobler, J., Wayne, S., and Lemmon, G. (2009). Bosses' perceptions of family–work conflict and women's promotability: Glass ceiling effects. *Academy of Management Journal, 52*, 939–957.

Hurst, S. J., and Brown, J. D. (2008). Gender, media use, and effects. In S. Calvert and B. Wilson (Eds.), *The handbook of children, media, and development* (pp. 98–120). Malden, MA: Blackwell Publishing.

Hymowitz, C., and Schellhardt, T. (1986, March 24). The glass ceiling: Why women can't seem to break the invisible barrier that blocks them from the top jobs. *The Wall Street Journal*.

Ibarra, H. (1995). Race, opportunity, and diversity of social circles in managerial networks. *Academy of Management Journal, 38*, 673–703.

Ibarra, H., Kilduff, M., and Tsai, W. (2005). Zooming in and out: Connecting individuals and collectivities at the frontiers of organizational network research. *Organizational Science, 16*, 359–371.

Inzlicht, M., and Ben-Zeev, T. (2003). Do high-achieving female students underperform in private? The implications of threatening environments on intellectual processing. *Journal of Educational Psychology, 95*, 796–805.

Kirchmeyer, C. (2002). Change and stability in managers' gender roles. *Journal of Applied Psychology, 87*, 929–939.

Kirchmeyer, C. (2006). The different effects of family on objective career success across gender: A test of alternative explanations. *Journal of Vocational Behavior, 68*, 323–346.

Klein, O., and Snyder, M. (2003). Stereotypes and behavioral confirmation: From interpersonal to intergroup perspectives. In M. Zanna (Ed.), *Advances in experimental social psychology*, Vol. 35 (pp. 153–234). San Diego, CA: Elsevier Academic Press.

Konrad, A. M., Ritchie, E. J., Lieb, P., and Corrigall, E. (2000). Sex differences and similarities in job attribute preferences: A meta-analysis. *Psychological Bulletin, 126*, 593–641.

Kornblut, A. (2009). *Notes from a cracked glass ceiling. Hillary Clinton, Sarah Palin, and what it will take for a woman to win.* New York, NY: Crown Publishing.

Laser, S. A. (1988). Breaking the glass ceiling: Can women reach the top of America's largest corporations? *Personnel Psychology, 41*, 637–641.

Liff, S., and Ward, K. (2001). Distorted views through the glass ceiling: The construction of women's understandings of promotion and senior management positions. *Gender, Work and Organization, 8*, 19–36.

Lin, N. (1999). Building a theory of social capital. *Connection, 22*, 28–51.

Lippa, R. A. (2005). *Gender, nature, and nurture.* Mahwah, NJ: Lawrence Erlbaum Associates.

Lyness, K. S., and Heilman, M. E. (2006). When fit is fundamental: Performance evaluations and promotions of upper-level female and male managers. *Journal of Applied Psychology, 91*, 777–785.

Lyness, K. S., and Thompson, D. E. (2000). Climbing the corporate ladder: Do female and male executives follow the same route? *Journal of Applied Psychology, 85*, 86–101.

McHale, S. M., Crouter, A. C., and Whiteman, S. D. (2003). The family contexts of gender development in childhood and adolescence. *Social Development, 12*, 125–148.

Meyerson, D. E., and Fletcher, J. K. (2000). A modest manifesto for shattering the glass ceiling, *Harvard Business Review, 78*, 157–161.

Morrison, A. M., White, R., and Von Velsor, M. A., and the Center for Creative Leadership. (1987). *Breaking the glass ceiling: Can women reach the top of America's largest corporations?* Reading, MA: Addison-Wesley.

Otten, S., and Moskowitz, G. B. (2000). Evidence for implicit evaluative in-group bias: Affect-biased spontaneous trait inference in a minimal group paradigm. *Journal of Experimental Social Psychology, 36,* 77–89.

Otten, S., and Wentura, D. (2001). Self-anchoring and ingroup favoritism: An individual-profiles analysis. *Journal of Experimental Social Psychology, 37,* 525–532.

Palmer, B., and Simon, D. (2001). *The political glass ceiling: Gender, strategy and incumbency in U.S. House elections 1978–1998. The Institute for Women's Policy Research.* Retrieved from http://iwpr.org/pdf/Wmns_Rep_0200.pdf on February 18, 2010.

Pelosi, N. (2007, January 4). *Pelosi calls for a new America built on the values that made our country great.* Retrieved from http://www.speaker.gov/newsroom/speeches?id=0006 on March 7, 2010.

Pichler, S., Simpson, P., and Stroh, L. K. (2008). The glass ceiling in human resources: Exploring the link between women's representation in management and the practices of strategic human resource management and employee involvement. *Human Resource Management, 47,* 463–479.

Pini, B., Brown, K., and Ryan, C. (2004). Women-only networks as a strategy for change? A case study from local government. *Women in Management Review, 19,* 286–292.

Pogrebin, R. (1988, August 14). Ways to rise above the "glass ceiling." *New York Times.*

Powell, G. N., Butterfield, D. A., and Parent, J. D. (2002). Gender and managerial stereotypes: Have the times changed? *Journal of Management, 28,* 177–193.

Ragins, B. R., and Cotton, J. L. (1991). Easier said than done: Gender differences in perceived barriers to gaining a mentor. *Academy of Management Journal, 34,* 939–951.

Ridgeway, C., and Correll, S. J. (2004). Unpacking the gender system: A theoretical perspectives on gender beliefs and social relations. *Gender and Society, 18,* 510–531.

Rudman, L. A., and Heppen, J. (2003). Implicit romantic fantasies and women's interest in personal power: A glass slipper effect? *Personality and Social Psychology Bulletin, 29,* 1357–1370.

Ryan, M. K., and Haslam, S. A. (2005). The glass cliff: Evidence that women are over-represented in precarious leadership positions. *British Journal of Management, 16,* 81–90.

Shambaugh, R. (2008). *It's not a glass ceiling, it's a sticky floor.* New York, NY: McGraw Hill.

Schein, V. E. (1973). The relationship between sex-role stereotypes and requisite management characteristics. *Journal of Applied Psychology, 57,* 95–100.

Signorielli, N. (1993). Television, the portrayal of women, and children's attitudes. In G. L. Berry, and J. K. Asamen (Eds.), *Children and television: Images in a changing sociocultural world* (pp. 229–242). Thousand Oaks, CA: Sage.

Spencer, S. J., Steele, C. M., and Quinn, D. M. (1999). Stereotype threat and women's math performance. *Journal of Experimental Social Psychology, 35,* 4–28.

Steele, C. M. (1997). A threat in the air: How stereotypes shape intellectual identity and performance. *American Psychologist, 69,* 797–811.

Steele, C. M., and Aronson, J. (1995). Stereotype threat and the intellectual test performance of African Americans. *Journal of Personality and Social Psychology, 52,* 613–629.

Turner, J. C., Brown, R. J., and Tajfel, H. (1979). Social comparison and group interest in ingroup favourtism. *European Journal of Social Psychology, 9,* 187–204.

U.S. Department of Labor. (1991). *A report on the glass ceiling initiative* (Publication No. DOC L1.2:G46). Washington, DC: U.S. Government Printing Office.

Wanberg, C. R., Welsh, E. T., and Hezlett, S. A. (2003). Mentoring research. *Research in Personnel and Human Resources Management, 22,* 39–124.

Ward, L. M. (2003). Understanding the role of entertainment media in the sexual socialization of American youth: A review of empirical research. *Developmental Review, 23*, 347–388.

Willemsen, T. M. (2002). Gender typing of the successful manager: A stereotype reconsidered. *Sex Roles, 46*, 385–391.

Witt, S. D. (2000). The influence of peers on children's socialization to gender roles. *Early Child Development and Care, 162*, 1–7.

Zhang, S., Schmader, T., and Forbes, C. (2009). The effects of gender stereotypes on women's career choice: Opening the glass door. In M. Barreto, M. K. Ryan, and M. Schmitt (Eds.). *The glass ceiling in the 21st century: Understanding barriers to gender equality* (pp. 125–150). Washington, DC: American Psychological Association.

5

Leadership: Perspectives and Experiences of a Minority Woman

Josephine C. H. Tan

The term "leadership" is often associated with the ability to command from lead positions in a political, corporate, or institutional unit. However, leadership occurs in other contexts, such as in academic committees where the form of governance is more collegial based, or in informal groups of young people (e.g., teenagers, university students) with similar interests and identification. Some leaders are formally voted, acclaimed, or appointed into designated roles that have titles and clearly defined duties. Other leaders are identified through more informal means that rely not on the number of votes received but on the degree of high influence that they have on members of the group. Regardless of the context, a leader is an individual who has the formal authority/power or the respect of others to influence their thinking and/or to mobilize them into actions (Yukl, 2009). Sitkins (2009) has a more tongue in cheek, albeit not totally inaccurate, definition: "Turn around and see if anyone is following you!" (p. 12).

There is an abundance of writing on leadership (e.g., Barling, Christie, and Hoption, 2011; Hollander, 2009). Different kinds of leadership styles have been identified, a variety of leadership theories have been developed and tested, and the contemporary focus in the research area now includes diversity (e.g., Ayman and Korabik, 2010). Readers who wish to learn more about the theoretical and empirical aspects of leadership are encouraged to seek out the literature. This chapter, however, takes an experiential approach in which I share my views and experiences on leadership as a minority woman. I have served in formal as well informal leadership capacity in student organizations, ad hoc and formal academic committees within and outside of my university, and on professional regulatory and psychological organizations on provincial and national levels. Looking back at my life in order to write this chapter, I am truly surprised by the degree of my participation. Leadership roles were never a part of my life ambitions.

The reader is probably asking at this point with some degree of skepticism, how then did I find myself taking on leadership roles? Leadership has taught me a great of self-reflection, and using that self-reflection now, I must say that I was asked, persuaded, requested, or compelled out of a sense of duty to do something *for* the program, the society, the organization, the group, and so on. The core reason was *service to the collective.*

Leadership and Management

Leaders have the capacity to influence the group or the collective and to set the vision and culture of the system. Duties of a manager typically consist of attending to the daily operations of a system or organization, in part through task delegation and supervision of individuals or teams assigned to the tasks. Yet for both leaders and managers, the interpersonal skills to work with people and to manage teams or the entire group are critical. In a system that has a hierarchical top-down form of governance, the leader and managers are more easily identifiable because of their formal titles and delineated roles. Moreover, the vision and goals of the system are typically defined or guided by the leader, and the implementation of most tasks to achieve those goals are normally performed by the manager and the rest of the system.

However, in contexts where the form of governance is more collegial, such as in a university setting where the members have similar credentials, it becomes tricky to differentiate the manager from the leader. How does the chair of an academic committee whose membership is voluntary in nature "command" a colleague to undertake a task? We know that that is not possible, so we do it in the form of request. If the colleague turns down the request for some reason, then what is the next step? Perhaps we might ask for a different volunteer to take on the task. How does an academic leader approach a colleague in the same department who is not doing his or her part on the team and is affecting team morale and task progress? In such cases, I have found it necessary to put on my manager hat and utilize whatever interpersonal skills I have to address the problem.

As can be seen, the distinction between a leader and a manager can be blurred because it depends on the context, the formality of the roles, the demands of the task, and the expectations placed on the individual. Perhaps such a distinction is not possible, because at critical times, a leader might have to adopt a more managerial role. Similarly, a manager might have to exhibit some leadership qualities when a leadership vacuum exists and the group cohesion breaks down.

Leadership Qualities

I have had the opportunity to work with a number of men and women leaders, and have observed their style and learned from them. Some are charismatic, highly self-promoting, and rely on others to do the work. Others are quietly effective with little fanfare. Some simply do everything themselves and occasionally inform the group. Some leaders are ineffectual in that they are "laissez-faire ... in which the leader avoids making decisions, abdicates responsibility, and does not use their authority" (Antonakis, Avolio, and Sivasubramaniam, 2003, p. 265). A few are destructive, as defined by the ill-consequences of their leadership.

I view effective leaders to be those who can accomplish group goals with the support and efforts of a group. Almost invariably, such leaders possess emotional intelligence. These individuals are cognizant of their inner states and motives, are skilled in reading the same in others (empathy), employ effective social skills that engage others, and are able to create team cohesion and resolve problems. Research has shown that emotional intelligence predicts who becomes a leader (Goleman, 1995).

Effective leaders are also skilled in communicating with others. They listen well and try to hear what others have to say with an open mind. Their ability to read others helps them understand the explicit and implied meanings in messages that are conveyed to them. They have strong persuasive powers and can appeal to others on a logical, empirical, and emotional level. Their written and verbal communications are clear and well organized, and their points are well argued, with an end goal in mind.

Their excellent communication skills lend well to team building, building a following, resolving problems, and developing a vision or strategic plans.

Another characteristic that I have observed in effective leaders is their thorough knowledge of the group that they serve from a historical, current, and future perspective. Knowing the history of the group, such as its origins, allows one to track its developmental trajectory to the present day, and appreciate the forces—obstacles and resources—that influenced its evolution. An understanding of the group from the inside, such as its different parts and their interrelations, is critical. An understanding of how the group maps onto the greater system at large and about the types of external influences and pressures on the group that can potentially impact on its functioning and future development is equally important. Additionally, familiarity with the short- and long-term directions of the group, along with its current focus, opportunities, and challenges, allows one to lead it in the desired direction and to reach progressive milestones. In the absence of such information, a leader has the opportunity to work collaboratively with group members to develop a vision and strategic plan.

Another attribute that I particularly admire in effective leadership is the value with which the leaders regard individual group members. Individual followers are often considered to be their most valuable resource. Enthusiastic and energetic group members contribute to team cohesion and harmony, a common identity, increased productivity, the sharing of creative and innovative ideas, and the renewal and sustainability of the group. These leaders engage in what Bass (1985) calls intellectual stimulation— they encourage curiosity and stimulate the individuals to develop creative and innovative ways of problem solving and moving forward.

Several effective leaders also have the capacity to instill confidence and optimism in others, which is valuable, especially in times of crisis. This might be what some researchers refer to as charisma, which helps "facilitate the followers' emotional attachment and psychological identification" (Mitchell and Boyle, 2009, p. 459). Many effective leaders are also flexible and capable of adapting to the needs of the group and rising to meet the internal and external forces on the group.

Unfortunately, I have also seen destructive leaders at work. Their characteristics include authoritarianism, defensiveness, a dismissal of feedback, the promotion of self-interests at the expense of the collective, a dehumanization of individuals by treating them as a drain or a gain on the budget, retaliation against individuals by taking away resources that diminish their status within the system and interfere with their productivity, a failure to communicate or disclose fully or honestly, a failure to consult or to consult adequately, blaming the individuals in the group instead of taking some responsibility when failure occurs, forcing changes on the system against the will of the collective, etc. The members under the destructive leadership become demoralized, apathetic, insecure, and depressed and complain that they lack direction or information from their leaders. The information gap strengthens the rumor mill, where gossip is unfortunately treated as the truth when it mostly reflects the pessimism and fears experienced by the collective. Whatever form of transgression the destructive leadership might make, the end result is reduced group morale, decreased productivity, and failure to meet goals.

Gender and Leadership

Are there gender differences in leadership style? This question has received considerable scrutiny and studies on gender differences in different components of leadership styles have been carried out (e.g., Eagly and Johannesen-Schmidt, 2001; Eagly, Johannesen-Schmidt, and van Engen, 2003). My experience is that generally, men leaders tend to be more hierarchical and agentic and women leaders to be more facilitative and communal. These characteristics can be discerned from the manner in which the leaders run meetings, communicate with others, and resolve problems. The men are more likely to express their opinions with greater ease and in a clear, direct fashion; the women present their ideas in a tentative, mitigated fashion, sometimes in the form of a question. Men also seem to have less difficulty disagreeing or even arguing with others and standing their ground. Women, on the other hand, acknowledge discrepant views and in rebuttal, might reiterate their own views in a tentative, inquiring manner. Differences in interpersonal behaviors are also evident. Men show more dominant cues (rapid speech, no hesitation) that are associated with competence; women show more warmth cues (smiling, head nodding) that reflect communality. Women are also more ready than the men to provide others with positive reinforcement and offers of assistance.

I see both the agentic and communal styles as being congruent with effective leadership, as long as the leader has the flexibility to utilize both in the appropriate way and at the right time. For instance, the agentic style can be helpful in shepherding the group to arrive at a decision, while the communal style can enhance the discussion process by encouraging diverse viewpoints, facilitating consensus building, and reducing the risk of conflicts. Each style, when taken to the extreme, can potentially lead to a breakdown of the group. The agentic style can turn authoritarian leading to anger and conflicts, while the communal style can lead to a loss of focus and indecisiveness.

Despite general gender differences in leadership styles, it is not possible to stereotype individual men and women leaders. The leaders I have worked with often incorporate both leadership styles, with a proclivity toward one particular style. For the most part, they are sufficiently flexible to modify their mannerisms and actions when the situation calls for it to keep the group process on track.

There is, however, one difference between men and women leaders that I often see. After a decision has been made, the men delegate the tasks to others (usually a subordinate) for implementation and maintain a relatively hands-off approach. The subordinate is responsible for keeping the leader posted and for troubleshooting to make sure the task is accomplished. Women leaders operate differently. They supervise the tasks in greater detail, are more heavily involved in their accomplishment, and sometimes take on the tasks themselves to ensure quality or timeliness. As a result, women leaders have a heavier burden and a higher risk of burnout. Women attribute their deeper involvement to a sense of responsibility and commitment to the task and a grave concern for adverse consequences to the group should the tasks not be done well or on time. Of course, there are exceptions to this observation.

Challenges in Leadership Roles for Women

The role of leadership is often perceived as incongruent with the female gender role, which can result in prejudicial evaluations and reactions toward women leaders (Eagly and Johannesen-Schmidt, 2001). The reactions that I have received in leadership roles are mixed. I tend to receive more support and cooperation from younger individuals, regardless of their gender. Their interpersonal demeanor is equally respectful. As for reactions from other leaders, women leaders generally adopt a more communal style with me. The reactions of men leaders who are sensitive to diversity issues tend to be highly positive and supportive. Those who have less sensitivity tend to be pompous and condescending in both tone and behavior, and a couple of them have been outright dismissive toward me, such as repeatedly ignoring my communications to them and choosing to respond to me only at their whim and fancy.

Several of the women leaders with whom I have worked have noted the challenges of working on a team basis. Their stories share common threads, and I can identify with some. Taking on a greater workload than other committee members and feeling underappreciated for their efforts is a frequent comment. Another common experience is that other members on a committee unfairly take credit for the work carried out by the women. The women also complain that some committee members do not do their share of the work and express their growing concern of adverse consequences for the group unless they themselves take up the slack. Yet they are aware that this might put them into an undesirable situation, in which their efforts are unfairly credited to someone else. The term "badge of status" has been used to refer to an individual occupying a high position and taking credit for the work associated with that role when in fact the work is carried out by others.

Women also reported having the strong impression that men are automatically regarded by others as more competent and knowledgeable solely on the basis of their gender. Women mentioned that their contributions to discussions and their attempts to wield influence are often ignored and that they are interrupted more frequently than men in meetings. Some of the women resented being treated like a "gopher" (someone who does menial things for others) despite occupying a lead role. Very often, they noted that their communal style of leading is misunderstood as reflecting inadequacy, ineffectiveness, a failure to act decisively, and a lack of confidence, all of which reduces their credibility as a leader.

The women also mentioned suffering from the loss of a support network when they move from a peer to a lead position within their system. The system accommodates the change by redefining the relationship that the women had with their ex-peers. The informality and spontaneity of the previous peer relationships give way to greater formality and more rigid boundaries that delineate the status difference. Unless the women can seek out other sources of support, they are likely to remain isolated and lonely in their leadership positions. A woman's transition to a leadership position is less stressful when the group to which she belongs includes several women. The tendency for women to be communal despite status differential is likely a protective factor.

The women who change their interpersonal style to reflect more agency and more of a "take command and control" approach reported facing fewer problems in leadership positions as a result, even though they might have felt some misgivings about the need to change. Anecdotal evidence shows that some women can in fact become more agentic, dominating, demanding, competitive, and authoritarian than men. In effect, the leadership role changed the women. These women are disliked unless they incorporate some facilitative and communal characteristics into their leadership style, such as expressing warmth and support for others (Carli, 2001).

Culture and Leadership

The need to consider culture in leadership is gaining increasing recognition (Chin, 2010; Sanchez-Hucles and Davis, 2010). The intersection of gender and culture sometimes increases the challenge for minority women in leadership positions. In my case, I grew up in a traditional Asian society; my with parents were schooled in the traditional Chinese educational system, which is influenced by Confucianism. This meant that I was socialized heavily into the traditional female gender role, which is antithetical to leadership aspirations. It also meant that I was not exposed to women leader role models when growing up. The Confucian values of dedicated work ethics, group harmony, and personal sacrifice for the collective good as well as the principle that those in the highest position of authority carry the greatest responsibility to the collective were also ingrained into me. I attended university in Canada; there, I was exposed to and adopted a more individualistic way of being, which made the thought of a leadership role more acceptable. I reconciled my leadership roles with the cultural forces present in me by interpreting leadership positions as a duty to contribute and serve the collective, instead of promoting self-interests.

Cultural and gender influences doubly reinforced my communal and facilitative leadership style, which occasionally contributed to others' devaluing my abilities and effectiveness. My discomfort with group disharmony interfered with my ability to disagree or challenge when I needed to.

I had a dominant "personal sacrifice" work ethic: It led to overwork, burn-out, and my realization that the inequality in my workload might well in part be the product of my own work ethic. Furthermore, I grew to realize that I unfairly expected others who were not from my cultural background to share my work ethic.

Self-reflection and insight led me to modify my behavior and thinking in order to achieve a more realistic and balanced perspective. I aim to combine dominant and communal cues in my interpersonal style to increase my credibility and effectiveness. I have reined in my belief in self-sacrifice for the collective, I have limited my urge to jump in and take up the slack for others, and my respect for others' need and desire to have a work–life balance has grown. It also helps that as I gain more experience and recognition in leadership work, any explicit or undercurrent bias against me as a minority woman leader becomes increasingly diminished.

Conclusion

Women can as effective as men in leadership roles. However, they experience problems in these roles, such as reduced credibility on the basis of their gender, an increased workload, less recognition for their efforts, and compromised social support. Their tendency to use a communal form of leadership style is sometimes mistaken for inadequacy and ineffectiveness. The intersection of culture and gender can produce increased challenges for minority women leaders.

Suggestions for Women Seeking Leadership Positions

I have several suggestions for women who are interested in leadership positions. Be aware of why you desire the role and ask what you can offer or contribute to the group you wish to lead. Observe and learn from other women and men leaders, acquire different leadership skills, and be flexible and intelligent in their employment. Be aware of your physical and emotional limits in the role without incurring burnout. Avoid dual relationships, maintain professional boundaries, and do not allow social disapproval to deter you from performing effectively (one cannot please everyone at the same time). Additionally, develop strong social skills and communication skills. The presence of a strong support network can weather you through the leadership challenges that come your way. Be insightful of yourself and others, and know the forces within and without yourself that shape you and your leadership performance. Be careful about seeking a high-level leadership position immediately because it helps to begin by gaining experience at a lower level. Become familiar with the structure, function, and dynamics of the group you wish to lead before stepping into a leadership role. Leadership is a developmental process with no endpoint, for there is no such thing as a perfect leader. However, it can be highly intrinsically rewarding for one who chooses to serve.

References

Antonakis, J., Avolio, B. J., and Sivasubramaniam, N. (2003). Context and leadership: An examination of the nine-factor full-range leadership theory using the Multifactor Leadership Questionnaire. *The Leadership Quarterly, 14*, 261–295. doi:10.1016/S1048-9843(03)00030-4.

Ayman, R., and Korabik, K. (2010). Leadership. Why gender and culture matter. *American Psychologist, 65*(3), 157–170. doi: 10.1037/a0018806.

Barling, J., Christie, A., and Hoption, C. (2011). Leadership. In S. Zedeck (Ed.), *APA handbook of industrial and organizational psychology: Vol 1. Building and developing the organization* (pp. 183–240). Washington, DC: American Psychological Association.

Bass, B.M. (1985). Leadership: Good, better, best. *Organizational Dynamics, 13*(3), 26–40.

Carli, L. L. (2001). Gender and social influence. *Journal of Social Issues, 57*(4), 725–741.

Chin, J. L. (2010). Introduction to the special issue on diversity and leadership. *American Psychologist, 65*(3), 150–156. doi: 10.1037/a0018716.

Eagly, A. H., and Johannesen-Schmidt, M. C. (2001). The leadership styles of women and men. *Journal of Social Issues, 57*(4), 781–797.

Eagly, A. H., Johannesen-Schmidt, M. C., and van Engen, M. L. (2003). Transformational, transactional, and laissez-faire leadership styles:

A meta-analysis comparing women and men. *Psychological Bulletin, 129* (4), 569–591. doi: 10.1037/0033-2909.129.4.569.

Goleman, D. (1995). *Emotional intelligence: Why it can matter more than IQ.* New York, NY: Bantam Books.

Hollander, E. P. (2009). *Inclusive leadership. The essential leader–follower relationship.* New York, NY: Routledge.

Mitchell, R. J., and Boyle, B. (2009). A theoretical model of transformational leadership's role in diverse teams. *Leadership and Organization Development Journal, 30*(5), 455–474. doi: 10.1108/01437730 910968714.

Sanchez-Hucles, J. V., and Davis, D. D. (2010). Women and women of color in leadership. *American Psychologist, 65*(3), 171–181. doi: 10.1037/a0017459.

Sitkins, R. (2009). *Rough notes, 152*(7), 12–15.

Yukl, G. (2009). *Leadership in organizations,* 6th ed. Upper Saddle River, NJ: Prentice Hall.

6

Women, Leadership, and the Glass Ceiling in the Nonprofit Sector

Susan Strauss

Women's grassroots activism has long been the foundation for social justice and public interest efforts such as abolitionism, suffrage, and political reform, among others (Davidson, 2003). The reshaping of public policy, child welfare, social services, and the arts in the nineteenth and twentieth centuries was led by women (O'Neil, 1994), even though most charitable organizations from the seventeenth century to the early twentieth century were led by men.

Throughout history, women were pivotal in societal reform over a century of American chronicles (Shimmel, n.d.). These women include Lucretia Mott and Elizabeth Cady Stanton, leaders for women's rights; Emma Hart Willard, founder of Emma Willard School, which trained women as teachers and opened up higher education to them; Mary McLeod Bethune, who opened a school for black girls and served as a minority affairs advisor to President Roosevelt; and Margaret Sanger, who revolutionized women's birth control by organizing the International Planned Parenthood Federation.

Jane Addams is well known for her activism for the rights of women, children, the working class, and the poor; in recognition of her work, she was the first woman to be awarded the Nobel Peace Prize. Addams's Hull House, the first of hundreds of settlement houses throughout the

United States, served as a place for educated women to congregate to discuss and investigate the ominous aspects of society (Shimmel, n.d.). Shimmel asserted that "these women, through their lobbying, advocacy, and charitable works, tackled controversial issues including child labor laws, fair labor standards, city sanitation, health care, and women's suffrage" (p. 2). The settlement houses, of which there were 400 by the beginning of the twentieth century, catalyzed thousands of women to eventually serve in public office.

Philanthropic women's organizations were credited with bringing together a *sisterhood* to support the women's movement, and in rebellion of society's oppression of women (McCarthy, 1994). As a result, feminist scholars attribute the genesis of the nonprofit sector (NPS) to the women's movement.

Historically, women have worked collaboratively in groups, clubs, councils, and committees (Hayes, 1999). Women's groups have had remarkable clout in early social reform. For example, in 1830, the Female Moral Reform Society of New York passed laws and ordinances against prostitution, gambling, alcoholism, and profanity (Hayes, 1999), and inspired an early mutiny against men's oppression of women (McCarthy, 1994). Even though women at that time did not have the right to vote, they worked unceasingly to ensure that those politicians supportive of their cause were elected. Women lobbied for specific laws and funding for their organizations, as well as protested for their rights as women. Women paved the way for the current welfare state by utilizing the nonprofit sector, seen as less corrupt and less selfish than the government, to cultivate the passage of social legislation.

Once women gained the right to vote in 1920, they gained some political leverage by demonstrating that they would not vote for male gentry who were not sympathetic to women's convictions (Muncy, 1991). There was a substantial number of women serving as social reform activists; feminism is said to have developed from their struggle to develop the social reform movement (Katz, 1986). Women's more recent accomplishments in the nonprofit sector are found in the peace movement, environmentalism, children's rights, the rights of minorities, consumer protection, classism, and the continuing fight for equal rights for women (O'Neil, 1994).

The irony is that from the early social reform movement to the present time, once nonprofit programs were created by women and gained some element of notoriety, men took control, relegating the women to volunteer positions in contrast to paid positions (Burbridge, 1994). Passage of the 1964 Civil Rights Act, Title VII, resulted in a tripling of the number of women in nonprofit managerial jobs. The NPS was one of the few venues in which women attained power and distinction. From 1969–1991, opportunities for management positions for women in the nonprofit sector increased (Preston, 1994).

Classism and racism continued to prevail in the NPS, functioning as a microcosm of the dominant groups in society. Despite their ongoing travails and involvement in the NPS, the research literature provides scant recognition of the contributions by women of color. (Odendahl and Youmans, 1994). The patriarchal ideology of nonprofits consists of white upper-class female workers with white men at the helm. Militant feminists and others continued to discriminate based on racism and classism. These *isms,* with accompanying hostility and society's patriarchy, served as a catalyst for people of color to form their own social service agencies, many of which were lead by women.

Little is known about the roles of Native American and Asian American women in the NPS. The government and nonprofit sectors offered the majority of opportunities for managerial women and blacks; however, black women's opportunities were diminished compared to white women (Preston, 1994). Though 1991 brought more equity to occupational levels of both men and women, the same could not be said about racial equality for black women. The gaps between black and white women's achievement and salary heightened between 1969–1991, with black women earning lower wages and employment in less prestigious work.

Women in the NPS earned significantly more in wages than women in government employment by 1991 (Preston, 1994). Interestingly, from 1973 to 1991 women and men earned roughly the same amount of money; this was partially attributed to gender differentiation across the array of occupations. Women managers were paid 22 percent less than their male colleagues, which was theorized to reflect men's greater responsibility and prestige. Steinberg and Jacobs (1994) concluded that the debased perception of low wages in the NPS reflect the deprecated view of women's work in the sector.

Definition of Nonprofit Sector

Nonprofit is both a legal and a formal construct (Lott, 1994). A nonprofit organization is one that serves a public purpose by advancing scientific initiatives; education and health; social welfare; and freedom of thought, word, and deed (Salamon, 1999). As organizations, they are required to be tax-exempt under the Internal Revenue Code tax exemption 501(c)(3) (Lott, 1994; Shaiko, 1996; Wellford and Gallagher, 1988) and 501(c)(4), which include welfare and employee associations (Lott, 1994; Shaiko, 1996) and usually state agencies (O'Neil, 1994). Lott (1994) identified a nonprofit as an obscure concept, such as nonwhite, perhaps understood more by what it is not, such as a corporation, rather than what it is. These organizations exert their influence on Washington, D.C., federal policy making and are also referred to as *public interest groups* (PIG) (Berry, 1977). Berry defined PIGs as organizations that "seek a collective good, the achievement of which will not selectively or materially benefit the membership or activists of the organization (p. 7).

Types of organizations within the nonprofit sector are diverse and include such organizations as the Teachers Insurance and Annuity Association, the NFL, NY Stock Exchange, an association that preserves rare butterflies (O'Neil, 1994), libraries, museums, art galleries, zoos (Preston, 1994), as well as scientific, philanthropy, literary, and civil leagues (Lott, 1994). Other examples include the American Civil Liberties Union, Children's Defense Fund, Mothers Against Drunk Driving, the National Council of Senior Citizens, and the National Rifle Association (Berry, 1977). Churches, arts and advocacy groups, fraternal organizations, professional and political associations, and unincorporated affiliations such as self-help groups are examples of nonprofits. The NPS has the distinction of being perceived as the seat for social reform and purporting equal power, which is often the antithesis of what government and for-profit organizations are noted for (Lott, 1994). Excluding the unincorporated organizations, it is estimated that there are approximately 1.4 million nonprofit organizations in the United States (Berry, 1977).

Charitable works and mutual assistance, social change and advocacy, and creating legitimate institutions make up the three aspects of the non-profit sector (Lott, 1994). Charity work and assistance best depicts the nonprofit organization from private and government institutions. The three largest employment groups are health, education, and social welfare/ human services (O, Neil, 1994), with women accounting for between 66 percent and 75 percent of employees (Preston, 1990).

Gender and Nonprofits

In countries where women have achieved some equitable power to men, such as the United States, women are more likely to volunteer and be members of nonprofit organizations (Themudo, 2009). In contrast, in countries where women are not empowered to partake in societal issues, men are the more likely nonprofit member and volunteer. A woman's role and status in society, then, plays a role in her activity in the NPS.

Odendahl and Youmans (1994) stipulated that gender is a foundational precept in societies around the globe. Steinberg and Jacobs (1994) agreed and saw gender as the foundation on which our society not only begets differences among symbols, people, and concepts, but uses them to create hierarchy, domination, value, and power.

> Gender is not a passive or fixed entity. It is created and maintained both by everyday social interaction and by past practices and policies that represent the culmination of previous decisions and compromises, much of it gender neutral in appearance. Indeed, the appearance of neutrality gives the policies and practices much of their force. (p. 93)

Odendahl and Youmans (1994) discussed the oppression of women within the NPS as potentially the underlying factor for a lack of funding and heavy reliance on volunteers. The authors estimate that more than 5 million women are employed by nonprofits and 50 million women are volunteers. The U.S. culture's viewpoint on money is that volunteer work is somehow less valuable—perhaps because it is carried out primarily by women.

In 1990, more than half of the 90 million NPS volunteers were women (Hodgkinson, Weitzman, Toppe, and Noga, 1992). The accomplishments of the NPS are often considered subordinate to those of the corporation, perhaps due to its having females as its primary workers (Steinberg and Jacobs, 1994). The authors proposed that the NPS is gendered in four dimensions: (a) The worker's gender with females as the predominant worker; (b) types of occupations and the characteristics of the jobs with obvious divisions of labor based on gender; (c) the strata of power with predominantly men at the helm; and (d) the overall stereotypical beliefs about the NPS illustrating, according to Kanter (1977), those roles and responsibilities associated with the *feminine*, such as the overall well-being, health, education, and welfare of society and the individual (Odendahl and Youmans, 1994). Roper (1994) asserted that because non-profits provide these typical female tasks, men devalue and subordinate women and their work.

The nonprofit sector creates a venue in which women are more likely to hold professional and managerial roles than they do in for-profit or government organizations (O'Neil, 1994). Women are often likely to gain desirable skills with less repetition in their NPS work than in for-profit work (Gibelman, 2000). The nonprofit labor pool consists of 75 percent women compared with a total workforce of 50 percent women (Preston, 1990, 1994). Women hold 50 percent of the professional and managerial positions in the NPS compared to 21 percent in government and less than 10 percent in the for-profit sector (Shackett and Trapani, 1987). Despite the high percentage of women in professional and managerial jobs, men still dominate in governance positions of board members and executive directors (Gibelman, 2000; Odendahl and Youmans, 1994). Take health care, for example, where most physicians are male and most nurses are female.

Women's organizations have more difficulty raising funds for programs that specifically target women and girls, though there have been some successes and improvements since 1997 (Davidson, 2003). Women's philanthropic organizations provide an avenue of funding, however, that give credence and viability to female specific concerns. Furthermore, women's organizations reach out to a broader pool of potential donors based on ethnicity, class, and other backgrounds, thereby discerning them from the typical funds. The existence of women's funds has proven successful in furthering women and girls' philanthropic donors to benefit female-focused agendas.

The Glass Ceiling and Gender Discrimination

It has been argued that the occupations of the NPS are dispensed based on gender, with the male establishment heading up a largely female work force (O'Neil, 1994). Sadly, it appears that women's potency in the NPS does not match their membership. While women are found in staffing positions, they hold disproportionately few positions of power such as executive directors and board members (Shaiko, 1996). In a study by Grey and Katz (1996), only 16 percent of chief executives were female and their median salary was approximately $30,000 less than their male counterparts' salary.

Few studies have paid attention to female trustees, donors, and policy makers within male lead organizations (McCarthy, 1994). A nonprofit culture is one of the dominant cultures and is therefore not as likely to modulate itself to meet the needs of minority women (Hernandez, 1994). In their attempts to become accepted members of a nonprofit, minority women have faced the same hurdles that they experience in society. Latinas are perched on the lowest rung of the hierarchical ladder. The literature is scant on Asian American and Native American women (Burbridge, 1994). Both women and men must take on the role of responsible leadership to search for, solicit, and incorporate minority candidates into nonprofit organizations (Roper, 1994).

Lott (1994) posited that a lack of research on the nonprofit is a further reflection of women's low status—that research has not explored or documented women's rich historical and current involvement in philanthropy and volunteerism within the nonprofit realm. With rare exception (Gibelman, 1995), research investigating the glass ceiling in the nonprofit sector is nonexistent; rather, studies focusing on the corporate milieu, government, and professional groups are the standard (Gibelman, 2000). Even the Glass Ceiling Act of 1991 refers only to the corporate workplace (U. S. Department of Labor, 1991). The Glass Ceiling Commission (1995) found that "a glass ceiling exists and that it operates substantially to exclude minorities and women from the top levels of management" (p. 7). According to Gibelman (2000), the "glass ceiling" refers to the following:

> . . . transparent but real barriers, based on discriminatory attitudes or organizational bias, that impede or prevent qualified individuals, including (but not limited to) women, racial and ethnic minorities, and disabled persons, from advancing into management positions. The majority of "glass ceiling" research has ignored the nonprofit sector. (p. 251)

Despite the fact that women account for 68 percent of employees in the overall nonprofit sector (Hodgkinson,Weitzman, Abrahams, Crutchfield, and Stevenson, 1996), and for 75 percent in health and human services (Burbridge, 1994), management positions—chiefly senior management—are disproportionately held by men, and men earn higher salaries than women at all levels of the organization (Gibelman, 2000; Guy, 1993). That said, as a result of women disproportionately staffing the NPS, they are sometimes at an advantage for promotions than their sisters in the for-profit or government organizations, for several reasons (Shaiko, 1996). First, the NPS continues to grow, opening up enhanced employment opportunities. Second, because of a fairly high turnover rate, women are able to move up the ladder in a shorter amount of time. Third, wages are low for both women and men. Finally, women tend to have longer tenure due to their greater commitment to the mission of the agency, thereby increasing their advancement opportunities. Yet, each of these four attributes demonstrated evidence of male bias and exemplified the institutional roadblocks faced by women on their journey into management. Three steps forward and two steps backward is how Guy (1993) proclaimed that women's advances toward equality progresses.

Volunteers and Employees

It's been said that women are less selfish and more devoted to public issues than men (Themudo, 2009). Specifically, they are acknowledged as altruistic (Eckel and Grossman, 1997) more likely to assume the helper role (Eagly and Crowley, 1986), and demonstrate more commitment to justice and equality (Andreoni and Vesterlund, 2001), which is portrayed in their high level of volunteer work (DiMaggio and Louch, 1997). Additionally, when women volunteer, they are likely to lend their financial support to the cause to which they devote their time (DiMaggio and Louch, 1997; Minter, 2009). As a result of these characteristics, it stands to reason that women are more likely than men to be employed in the nonprofit sector.

Since women volunteer at higher rates than their male counterparts, one would expect that there would be a correlation between the number of women volunteers and their role as leaders. However, board membership and ED positions do not support this expectation. As Minter (2009) questioned, "If women's giving is catalyzed by their involvement, and they like to volunteer, why are they underrepresented in the volunteer leadership ranks?" (p. 3). She suggests four actions that boards should initiate to capitalize on women's strengths as charitable and volunteer leaders: (1) Stipulate financial contributions as an aspect of leadership, (2) mandate diversity in board membership, (3) instigate a myriad of volunteer options for opportunities and assignments, and (4) extinguish patronizing behavior.

Women in leadership positions are role models and mentors for those women who report to them, inspiring their female staff to take on responsibilities that may help in staff advancement. However, women's organizations and women in all nonprofits must examine how standards of power are validated; challenge the status quo to increase diversity, and examine power differentials not just between women and men, but also between women (Lott, 1994).

Executive Directors

The journey to the top rung of the management ladder in the public interest organization requires a unique blend of characteristics (Herman and Heimovics, 1991); specifically, it requires a "special mix of political entrepreneurialism and management ability" (Shaiko, 1996, p. 305). Leadership in the NPS requires a combination of skills and knowledge that is often attributed to the for-profit sector, such as marketing, fundraising, political savviness, technical expertise, and emotional intelligence (Young, 1987). Additionally, the search for an executive director (ED) involves candidates outside the organization (Shaiko, 1996). Individuals who have been employed in high-level federal government positions and in an area that is well versed in the policy concerns of the public interest group's mission are sought out to undertake the ED role (Shaiko, 1989). The limited number of women in high-level government positions means there is not an adequate pool of women from this source. Not surprisingly, then, it is men who are most likely selected. Shaiko (1996) found that 20 percent of public interest groups were directed by women, 75 percent of whom had come from the nonprofit sector. Conversely, the male EDs brought significant government experience; only half had any training in NPS advocacy.

Women make up 50 percent of the EDs in small (less than $1 million in expenditures) nonprofit organizations, 34 percent in medium-sized (between $1 million and $50 million) nonprofits, and only 14 percent in large (expenditures of over $50 million) nonprofits (Gibelman, 2000; Guidestar, 2007). Women's higher level of volunteering and philanthropy is positively associated with their empowerment in the NPS (Themudo, 2009).

The mission of the NPS agency may dictate the percentage of women EDs within each agency (Shaiko, 1996). Of the 20 percent female EDs, those organizations whose mission is related to, for example, business and/or economics, international affairs, public interest law firms, universities, and mental/physical rehabilitation institutions, tend to be less amenable to women EDs; whereas women account for half of the EDs of consumer/health organizations. Shaiko identified four indicators of the gender variant—the size, age, and location of the organization, and the number of female board members. Women hold management positions in the less-dynamic agencies, while their male peers govern the more prestigious organizations (McPherson and Smith-Lovin, 1982, 1986).

Shaiko (1996) found that older agencies and those with budgets exceeding $1 million are more likely to be led by male EDs. Likewise, if an organization's headquarters is located in Washington, D.C., which is increasingly true, male directors are more likely to be at the helm. Those public interest groups whose boards are largely made up of women and have mostly women as members are more likely to have a woman director. Women celebrities (such as Ellen Burstyn, Marsha Mason, Anne Bancroft, and Julie Child) and women who serve in political public service organizations (such as Elizabeth Dole, Diane Feinstein, and Susan Estrich) are frequently board members.

Pynes's (2000) hefty study of the greater St. Louis metropolitan area nonprofit sector found 78 percent of employees were female and 22 percent were male. Organizations surveyed came from sectors such as arts and culture; education; health; human services/social welfare; international organizations; religious; and "other," such as youth, neighborhood, volunteer, and housing services, to name a few. Despite the much larger female sector, there were 50 male and 53 female CEOs. Six males had budget responsibilities of $10,000,000, compared to only three women. Despite the fact that only 22 percent of employees were male, the majority of board members (56%) were male, as were board presidents (77 male presidents compared to 25 female presidents). The number of male and female vice presidents was similar, with 49 men and 42 women. Twice as many men as women were treasurers and secretaries. Across the entire sector of organizations surveyed, men were the gender most represented as well as holding positions of power on the boards.

Mixer (1994), however, posited that because women now outnumber men in fund-raising associations, the glass ceiling is weakening. He argued that the 1990s fund-raising efforts brought a change from men as the dominate development director (fund-raiser) to agencies selecting women. Unfortunately, African American, Latina, and Asian American women are grossly underrepresented.

Women EDs were found to prefer working with colleagues who share their commitment to the goals of the organization rather than working with colleagues with whom they have a kindred, personable relationship (Beale, Thompson, Kaufmann, Hollenshead, and Gibbs, 2008). The authors found that an ED's job satisfaction is enhanced when she is working with those who are geared toward a common goal, because it is a catalyst to execute organizational objectives. This is in contrast to other studies that emphasized the personal/emotional aspects of collegial relationships as an impetus to job satisfaction (Buelens and Broeck, 2007; Handy and Eliakim, 1998). The researchers also found that female executives' job satisfaction was not as extrinsically motivated by salary and recognition as it was by intrinsic rewards, such as position challenge and skill development.

Pay

The pay gap between male and female nonprofit executives has narrowed within the last several years; however, females continue to earn less than their male peers, with men making almost 26 percent more in salary in 2005 (Lipman, 2006). That's good news, considering the pay gap in 2000 was nearly 46 percent. One of the reasons attributed to the narrowing disparity in pay is that women account for 57 percent of executives in those nonprofits making $1 million or less compared to 36 percent of larger organizations. Those executives at the helm of larger organizations garner substantial pay raises, a median pay of a little less than 7 percent in comparison to the smaller organizations' executives increase at just under 4 percent. Female executives' salaries grew faster than their male counterparts in almost every size organization. For example, women who managed budgets of $50 million or more experienced an 8.5 percent jump in pay compared to their male peers, whose pay rose a little less than 7 percent. Women with budgets of less than $250,000 saw their compensation increase by 3 percent compared to an increase for men of 2 percent. Despite the fact that women comprised 44 percent of the top executive positions, they received only 33 percent of the total compensation. One of the difficulties with pay for women is that they often expect less and therefore ask for less money than do men during salary discussions at the time of hire.

It wasn't only female executives that received less pay, but women in all levels of organizations of every size (Lipman, 2006). There was gender compensation inequality in the financial, educational, development, and program positions: women were paid less. This was even apparent in those charities with budgets less than $250,000 in which female workers were the dominant employee. The smaller charities were more likely to employ a woman as the financial administrator, with her pay a mere 75 percent of a man's pay in the same position.

Steinberg and Jacobs (1994) asserted that maintaining the invisibility of the low value of women's work is essential to preserve their continued low pay. In general, women executives working in health care and in medical and scientific research were paid more than those working in human services, religious organizations, and the arts.

Gibelman (2000) found that the gender of the worker was the third-strongest indicator of salary, preceded by age and education. Men's minority status was not an indicator of salary; however, women of color earned less than white women. Taking into consideration education, age, and type of degree, women were likely to earn about $5,000 less than their male peers. Women were not only unlikely to hold management positions but also earned a lower salary than men no matter what their position within the organizational structure.

Boards of Directors

Similar skills are required whether one is on a corporate or nonprofit board (Shaiko, 1996), including specific knowledge and talent. Board membership generally seeks a balance of the following attributes: status as a celebrity, ability to contribute financially, management expertise, and representation of the constituency of members and those clients whom the agency serves (Drucker, 1990; Stone, 1991). Interestingly, Odendahl and Youmans (1994) discovered that the roles of men and women who serve on nonprofit boards vary, and vary based on the type of board on which they serve. Some boards are gender segregated; for example, women hold positions in which they plan a celebratory charity event while the men make decisions. Health and human services boards are more likely to include an equal number of men and women; this is an exception to most boards that lack gender parity.

There are few statistics about women of color on boards (Odendahl and Youmans (1994). Less than 25 percent of women and only 6 percent of Asian, African, and Latino women were represented on boards (Gittell, 1990, cited in Shaiko, 1996).

A board of directors is pivotal in the selection of an executive director for their nonprofit agency (Shaiko, 1996). In Shaiko's study, one-fifth of the agencies studied had female board members, and all were governed by a male executive. The agencies with a large number of female members were more likely to have female board members. Boards and managers tend to hire those who are like themselves. Considering that most boards are male, they tend to hire male EDs—a person they consider a peer—creating a challenging situation for women. However, men still tend to have the upper hand in being selected for the ED position, even when the board is open to job candidates of either gender (Joslyn, 2003). Boards of health care, universities, and other large organizations are predominantly male (Odendahl, 1994).

A question one can't help but ponder is why women are able to influence public interest agencies when they are underrepresented in managerial and board positions. Surprisingly, wealthy women are significant financial contributors to the agencies, and may serve on the boards not as decision makers or policy developers but merely to lend their name, clout, and wealth (Pynes, 2000). One example is Teresa Heinz, chairwoman of the Heinz Family Philanthropies, who focuses on the needs of the poor and elderly female population (Davidson, 2003). A second rationale for women's influence is whom they know in Washington, D.C., often as wives of politicians or because they held political or other influential office themselves (Pynes, 2000).

Research by Bradshaw, Murray, and Wolpin (1996), discovered that organizations with a woman CEO were more likely to have more women on their board. The more women on an agency's board, the less prestige was granted the organization. Also, board members determine how much the ED will earn and are therefore largely responsible for the ongoing gap in salary between female and male directors (Joslyn, 2003).

When boards elect board members, there is a difference in the type of board: membership is often awarded to those who have been loyal to the agency for years and have worked their way up to the privilege and honor of servicing on the board.

Conclusion

There is a lack of research examining the role of women in nonprofit organizations, in particular women's role in the governance of NPS. The NPS is somewhat of a dichotomy in that women are more likely to be volunteers and staff members and have opportunities to garner management experience, yet men are primarily the leaders of the organizations and receive a higher wage. However, it appears that some change is occurring, with women assuming more fund-raising responsibility. Additional research may hopefully provide essential knowledge to help kindle a more equitable sector that recognizes the contributions of women and minorities.

Women's funds and community-based agencies offer "the potential to provide alternate legitimating institutions that are more representative of a diverse nation" (Lott, 1994, p. 178.). Women, whether as an NPS volunteer or staff member or within the governance structure, tend to be more inclusive and use social change as an avenue of growth for the nonprofit agency itself.

References

Andreoni, J., and Vesterlund, L. (2001). Which is the fair sex: Gender differences in altruism. *Quarterly Journal of Economics, 116*(1), 293–312. Retrieved from EBSCO database on March 5, 2010.

Beale, R. L., Thompson, H., Kaufmann, S., Hollenshead, C., and Gibbs, T. (2008). Job satisfaction in nonprofit female executive directors: The significance of shared goals vs. congenial colleagues. *Review of Business Research, 8*(5), 107–115.

Berry, J. M. (1977). *Lobbying for the people: The political behavior of public interest groups.* Princeton, NJ: Princeton University Press.

Bradshaw, P., Murray, V., and Wolpin, J. (1996). Women on boards of nonprofits: What difference do they make? *Nonprofit Management & Leadership, 6*(3), 241–254.

Buelens, M., and Van den Broeck, H. (2007). An analysis of differences in work motivation between public and private sector organizations.*Public Administration Review, 67*(1), 65–67. Retrieved from EBSCO database on May 3, 2010.

Burbridge, L. C. (1994). The occupational structure of nonprofit industries: Implications for Women. In T. Odendahl and M. O'Neill (Eds.), *Women and power in the nonprofit sector* (pp. 121–154). San Francisco: Jossey-Bass.

Davidson, E. M. (2003). Report on: Women's philanthropy in the United States: Trends and Developments. Retrieved from www.philanthropy.org/publications/online_publications/women_paper.pdf on September 21, 2010.

DiMaggio, P., and Louch, H. (1997). *Who volunteers? Dominant and relevant statuses.* Washington, DC: Aspen Institute; Nonprofit Sector Research Fund.

Drucker, P. F. (1990). *Managing the nonprofit organization.* New York: HarperCollins.

Eagly, A. H., and Crowley, M. (1986). Gender and helping behavior: A meta-analytic review of the social psychological literature. *Psychological Bulletin, 100*(3), 283–308. Retrieved from psycARTICLES database on March 5, 2010.

Eckel, D. D., and Grossman, P. J. (1998). Are women less selfish than men? Evidence from dictator experiments. *Economic Journal, 108*(448), 726–735. Retrieved from EBSCO database on February 23, 2010.

Gibelman, M. (1995). Purchasing in social services. In R. L. Edwards (Ed.), *Encyclopedia of social work*, 19th ed. (pp. 1998–1007). Washington DC: National Association of Social Workers Press.

Gibelman, M. (2000). The nonprofit sector and gender discrimination: A preliminary investigation into the glass ceiling. *Nonprofit Management and Leadership, 10*(3), 251–269. Retrieved from EBSCO database on February 23, 2010.

Glass Ceiling Commission. (1995). *Good for business: Making full use of the nation's human capital.* Washington, DC: U. S. Department of Labor.

Grey, S., and Katz, H. (1996). Women still lag at the top. *The Chronicle of Philanthropy, 8*(10), 36–38.

Guidestar. (2007). *Nonprofit compensation report.* Williamsburg, VA: Author.

Guy, M. E. (1993). Three steps forward, two steps backward: The status of women's integration into public management. *Public Administration Review, 53*(4), 285–292. Retrieved from EBSCO database on February 23, 2010.

Handy, F., and Eliakim, K. (1998). The wage differential between non-profit institutions and corporations: Getting more by paying less. *Journal of Comparative Economics, 26*(2), 246–261. Retrieved from ScienceDirect database on May 3, 2010.

Hayes, A. (1999). The new presence of women leaders. *The Journal of Leadership Studies, 6*(1/2). 112–121. doi: 10.1177/107179199900 600108.

Herman, R. D., and Heimovics, R. D. (1991). *Executive leadership in nonprofit organizations,* San Francisco: Jossey-Bass.

Hernandez, A. (1994). A Latina's experience of the nonprofit sector. In T. Odendahl and M. O'Neill (Eds.), *Women and power in the nonprofit sector* (pp. 255–266). San Francisco: Jossey-Bass.

Hodgkinson, V. A., Weitzmann, M. S., Toppe, C. M., and Noga, S. (1992). *Nonprofit Almanac 1992–1993: Dimensions of the independent sector.* San Francisco: Jossey-Bass.

Hodgkinson, V. A., Weitzman, M. S., Abrahams, J. A., Crutchfield, E. A., and Stevenson, D. R. (1996). *Nonprofit almanac 1996–1997: Dimensions of the independent sector.* San Francisco: Jossey-Bass.

Joslyn, H. (2003). Board members play crucial role in closing the gender gap in pay. *The Chronicle of Philanthropy, 15*(11), 49-51. Retrieved from EBSCO database on February 24, 2010.

Kanter, R. M. (1977). *Men and women of the corporation.* New York: Basic Books.

Katz, M. B. (1986). *In the shadow of the poorhouse: A social history of welfare in America.* New York: Basic Books.

Lipman, H. (2006). Pay gap narrows for male and female nonprofit executives, study finds. *Chronicle of Philanthropy, 19*(1), 13. Retrieved from EBSCO database on February 24, 2010.

Lott, J. T. (1994). Women, changing demographics, and the redefinition of power. In T. Odendahl and M. O'Neill (Eds.), *Women and power in the nonprofit sector* (pp. 155–182). San Francisco: Jossey-Bass.

McCarthy, K. (1994). The history of women in the nonprofit sector: Changing interpretations. In T. Odendahl and M. O'Neill (Eds.), *Women and power in the nonprofit sector* (pp. 155–182). San Francisco: Jossey-Bass.

McPherson, J. M., and Smith-Lovin, L. (1982). Women and weak ties: Differences by sex in voluntary associations. *American Journal of Sociology, 87*(3), 883–904. Retrieved from JSTOR database on March 4, 2010.

McPherson, J. M., and Smith-Lovin, L. (1986). Sex segregation in voluntary associations. *American Sociological Review, 51*(1), 61–79. Retrieved from JSTOR database on March 4, 2010.

Minter, M. (2009, March 5). Seeking volunteer leaders: Tips for increasing women's giving. *On Philanthropy.* Retrieved from http://onphilanthropy .com/2009/seeking-volunteer-leaders-tips-for-increasing-womens-giving/ on March 9, 2010.

Muncy, R. (1991). *Creating a female domination in American reforms, 1890–1935.* New York: Oxford University Press.

Odendahl, T., and Youmans, S. (1994). Women on nonprofit boards, In T. Odendahl and M. O'Neill (Eds.), *Women and power in the nonprofit sector* (pp. 183–221). San Francisco: Jossey-Bass.

O'Neil, M (1994). The paradox of women and power in the nonprofit sector, In T. Odendahl and M. O'Neill (Eds.), *Women and power in the nonprofit sector* (pp.1–16). *San* Francisco: Jossey-Bass

Preston, A. E. (1990). Women in the white collar nonprofit sector: The best option or the only option. *Review of Economics and Statistics, 72*(4), 560–568. Retrieved from EBSCO database on March 8, 2010.

Preston, A. E. (1994). Women in the nonprofit labor market. In T. Odendahl and M. O'Neill (Eds.), *Women and power in the nonprofit sector* (pp. 39–77). San Francisco: Jossey-Bass.

Pynes, J. E. (2000). Are women underrepresented as leaders of nonprofit organizations? *Review of Public Personnel Administration, 20*(2), 35–49. doi: 10.1177/0734371x0002000204.

Roper, B. C. (1994). Women and volunteer activity: One practitioner's adventures in leadership. In T. Odendahl and M. O'Neill (Eds.), *Women and power in the nonprofit sector* (pp. 267–294). San Francisco: Jossey-Bass.

Salamon, L. (1999). *America's nonprofit sector, a primer*, 2nd ed. New York: The Foundation Center.

Shackett, J. P., and Trapani, J. M. (1987). Earnings differentials and market structure. *Journal of Human Resources, 22*(4), 518–531. Retrieved from EBSCO database on March 28, 2010.

Shaiko, R. G. (1989). *The public interest dilemma: Organizational maintenance and political representation in the public interest sector.* Unpublished doctoral dissertation, Maxwell School of Citizenship and Public Affairs, Syracuse University.

Shako, R. G. (1996). Female participation in the public interest nonprofit governance: Yet another glass ceiling? *Nonprofit and Voluntary Sector Quarterly, 25*(3), 302–320. doi:10.1177/0899764096253003.

Shimmel, D. (n.d.). Women's use of the nonprofit sector as an alternative power source. Retrieved from http://learningtogive.org/papers/paper70.html on March 6, 2010.

Steinberg, R. J., and J. A. Jacobs. (1994). Pay equity in nonprofit organizations; Making women's work visible. In T. Odendahl and M. O'Neill (Eds.), *Women and power in the nonprofit sector* (pp.79–120). San Francisco: Jossey-Bass.

Stone, M. M. (1991). The propensity of governing boards to plan. *Nonprofit Management and Leadership, 1*, 203–215.

Themudo, N. S. (2009). Gender and the nonprofit sector, *Nonprofit and Voluntary Sector Quarterly, 38*(4), 663–683. doi: 10.1177/0899764009333957.

U. S. Department of Labor. (1991). *A Report on the Glass Ceiling Initiative.* Washington, DC: U.S. Department of Labor.

Wellford, W. H., and Gallagher, J. G. (1988). *Unfair competition: The challenge to charitable exemption.* Washington, DC: National Assembly of National Voluntary Health and Social Welfare Organizations.

Young, D. R. (1987). Executive leadership in nonprofit organizations. In W. W. Powell (Ed.), *The nonprofit sector: A research handbook* (pp. 167–179). New Haven, CT: Yale University Press.

7

The Stained Glass Ceiling: Women Leaders in Religion[*]

J. Harold Ellens

Introduction

During most of the last 7,000 years, religious functions in society have been in the hands of male leadership in nearly every human culture. This should be more of a surprise to us than it seems to be. There are archaeological and philological indications that in prehistory, male dominance in things religious was not the case; indeed, that prior to 5000 BCE, matriarchal cultures were as customary, or more so, than patriarchy. Whatever the revolution was that shifted cultural and social preferences to male-dominated shamanism and priesthood at that time, we have no good clue to account for it. It is even more surprising that in the history of Christianity, women should have been reduced to second-rate roles or lacked any role at all during most of the history of that dominant Western religion.

In Jesus's own life time—if we can take the gospel narratives as indicators—women were as prominent in his support community and ministry as were the 12 specially chosen males. Moreover, in the Pauline mission churches, the dominance of women is remarkable, including the function of women as bishops,[1] pastors (Epp, 2005), priests, and leaders of those new worshipping and working communities of faith (Torgeson, 1993).

---

[*]Sections of this chapter were adapted from Ellens (2010).

Women persisted in the leadership of Christian communities well into the second century, and in some cases, such as the Montanist denomination, into the third and perhaps the fourth century. The definitive death knell of women's prominence in religious leadership in Christendom seems to have been sounded by Constantine in 325 CE. When he ordered the production of a unifying Christian Creed, a universally agreed-upon authoritative scripture, and a universally church polity in which the managers of the religious communities were also appointed as managers of the urban-centered regions of the empire, the jobs were filled exclusively with males.

That state of affairs persisted into the twentieth century. In the late 1930s, the Methodist Church in the United States began to ordain women into the ministry of the word and sacraments on an equal basis with men. The Presbyterian communion followed in the 1950s; the Episcopal Church achieved this milestone much more recently. However, despite this progress in the last century, the potential for women to achieve the senior offices of these churches remained very difficult and a precarious quest. The stained glass ceiling seemed to most women an impenetrable obstacle to the highest offices in religious leadership.

Exposition

The twentieth-century phenomenon that most extensively changed cultural values in the United States regarding women leadership in all societal structures was the social revolution that took place between 1965 and 1975. During this time, the corporate structures throughout the society felt intense pressure to open the doors of equal opportunity to all minorities in America, and particularly to women. Concomitantly, we began to hear much about the glass ceiling, which allowed women to advance to a certain corporate level but shut off the highest, most powerful, and choicest positions from access by talented women. Women in ministry seemed initially less concerned about the glass ceiling, but were winning their way to ordination in many or most Protestant denominations by superb service and wise leadership at the parish level.

Nonetheless, in the last two decades the woman's movement in many denominations has matured to the point of competition among women for the senior positions in the church hierarchy. The assignment of woman as bishops in the Episcopal Church in the United States has succeeded, but not without major controversy at nearly every step of the way. The stained glass ceiling has been penetrated, but it has not been removed everywhere. In most Protestant denominations, it remains true that the choice senior positions consistently go to men more often than to women, despite the fact that women are the majority gender in church membership.

Of course, it is a tragic fact that one hardly needs to mention the thoroughgoing intransigence of the Roman Catholic Communion in its opposition across the board, so to speak, to women in any ecclesiastical leadership roles whatsoever. Pope John XXIII clearly intended by the proceedings of Vatican II to move the church to greater openness toward the role of women and other disadvantaged groups. The present pope, Benedict XVI, has completely rolled back the advances of Vatican II, both during his tenure as chief of the Curia during the papacy of Pope John Paul II, and now during his own papacy. The stained glass ceiling not only remains solidly in place in the Roman Catholic Church but has been so enormously reinforced by the present pope that is impossible to see through it or discern any light "at the end of the tunnel."

However, as hinted in the introduction, the history of this matter is not only still a tragic shackling of the talents, energy, and imagination of woman, thus preventing from employment in Christian ministry some of the best and most redemptive energy and thought of which humans are capable, but this state of affairs, the impenetrability of the stained glass ceiling, prevails generally in all other religions much more severely than in Christendom. Islam, for example, is universally and incorrigibly patriarchal in principal and practice. This is not only true of its religious structures and behavior but of its entire body of social ethics and values and its legal theory and prescriptions. Shariah law and culture reflect those aspects of the Qur'an, Muhammad's teaching, and the Hadith, the commentary on the Qur'an that requires the suppression of women under male authority. Similarly, Judaism has retained its patriarchy since the formulation of the Hebrew Bible, so that woman may not be ordained except in the very liberal movements, such as Reformed Judaism. Even in Reformed and Humanistic Judaism, in practical fact, few women are ordained to the Rabbinate or to leadership of the Synagogues. This is also characteristic of Buddhism, Hinduism, The Saithya Sai Baba Movement, and Taoism in China and Japan.

The repression of women has been a burden on the hearts and minds of a great percentage of human beings, particularly Americans. Indeed, many of us have felt infuriated by the relentlessness of it in all aspects of world society, while feeling quite unsure about how to influence its repair. The feminist and womanist movements have achieved decided gains over the last three or four decades, again largely in North America. However, some of the phases of both of these movements have functioned counterproductively. The rage-driven first phase of the feminist movement may have been justified and necessary, but it produced more push back from society than forward movement for the cause. That resistance was reduced considerably when the second phase of the movement brought a reasoned imperative before the general society and dispassionately challenged it to a new set of values in which women were overtly valued and rewarded for the quality of the abilities, motivations, and contributions. This has led, I think, to a generally improved valuing of women as persons of equal or superior potential contribution to the well-being of humanity, compared with men. Some of us even believe that after 7,000 years of testosterone running this world so poorly, it is time for a shift to estrogen for a few millennia.

It is unclear whether the women in other cultures and religions lack the interest or motivation to definitively change their status, or whether they are so boxed in that it is not even possible for them to think of a more liberated and effective role in life. In any case, the movement to break through the stained glass ceiling by women in religious leadership has taken on the character of a crusade. This is particularly the case in Western culture, and more particularly in North America. Karen Torgeson, for example, accuses the Roman Catholic Church outright of intentionally subverting the truth when it denies that women were priests in the early church. She declares, "Giorgio Otranto, an Italian professor of church history, has shown through papal letters and inscriptions that women participated in the Catholic priesthood for the first thousand years of the church's history" (Torgeson, 1993, p. 2).

Surely it is obvious that Jesus treated women as equals without making an issue of it in principle or practice. He cared very much about those about whom others cared very little: women, children, the poor, outcasts, and the devalued stranger. He attacked all forms of social or ethical structure that were not authentic, useful, and productive of equality in relationships. He was close friends with the up-and-out as well as the down-and-out, but just as much with those of the establishment who would hear his challenging assault on superficial or trivial and trivializing values and practices. Jesus launched a broadside campaign against the patriarchal authority structure in the family and in the religiosocial rigidity of his time. He seemed to have a clear vision that the entire message of divine grace was at stake in his crusade. He endeavored to empower those whom that structure disempowered. When the religious authorities counterattacked, Jesus would not back down in these matters, so they killed him.

Torgeson (1993) gives us data. "When Jesus gathered disciples around him to carry his message to the world, women were prominent in the group. Mary Magdalene, Mary of Bethany, and Mary his mother are women whose names survived the retelling of the Christian story in the language and literary conventions of Roman patriarchal society. Paul's letters reflect an early Christian world in which women were well-known evangelists, apostles, leaders of congregations, and bearers of prophetic authority" (p. 4). Torgeson notes that Celsus, a second century critic of the Christianity, dismissed it as a women's movement, so prominent were they in its leadership (p. 81). Origen, the noted third-century Church Father, was sponsored by leading church wokers, in his rise to leadership in the church and headmaster of the Catechetical School of Alexandria. Nonetheless, he was very ambivalent about women's leadership in the church as he moved further toward the fourth century (Torgeson,1993, pp. 113–114).

For the first 250 years, Christianity was mainly local in private societies and house churches, in which the leadership of women was natural, as in the management of Greek and Roman households. When the Christian movement gained great numbers by the beginning of the third century, more formal structures were necessary and the local congregations acquired or built public buildings as churches and basilicas. Formal administrative organizations were developed and officials appointed to manage them efficiently. It was in this era leading up to the Constantine reorganization of the church that women seem to have been eased out of definitive leadership roles, though Torgeson argues that they were prominent in such roles for the first 1,000 years. "As Christianity entered the public sphere, male leaders began to demand the same subjugation of women in the churches as prevailed in Greco-Roman society at large. Their detractors reproached women leaders, often in strident rhetoric, for operating outside the domestic sphere and thus violating their nature and society's vital moral codes. How could they remain virtuous women, the critics demanded, while being active in public life?" (Torgeson, 1993, pp. 37–38).

Torgeson (1993) named the Constantinian revolution and its women-suppressive antecedents the scandal of their subordination. In elegant elegiac prose, she regales us with a story that fixes her thesis firmly in empirical historical data. She writes:

> Under a high arch in a Roman basilica dedicated to two women saints, Prudentiana and Praxedis, is a mosaic portraying four female figures: the two saints, Mary, and a fourth woman whose hair is veiled and whose head is surrounded by a square halo—an artistic technique indicating that the person was still living at the time the mosaic was made. The four faces gaze out serenely from a glistening gold background. The faces of Mary and the two saints are easily recognizable. But the identity of the fourth is less apparent. A carefully lettered inscription identifies the face on the far left as Theodora Episcopa, which means Bishop Theodora. The masculine form for bishop in Latin is *episcopus*; the feminine form is *episcopa*. The mosaic's visual evidence and the inscription's grammatical evidence point out unmistakably that Bishop Theodora was a woman. (pp. 9–10)

Similarly, on Santorini, the Greek Island of Thera, a grave site bears the epitaph of a woman named Epiktas, who was a priest sometime between 200 and 400 CE.

Theologians often think that this shift against women's leadership had biblical or theological justification, but they miss the point that women were prominent, if not dominant, for the first two to three centuries. If they had not been, there would have been no need for all the fulmination against them in the third and fourth centuries as the church shifted to the adoption of the value structures of the Greco-Roman secular world, at the expense of the unique set of values for which Jesus lived and died. Karen Gaca has explicated this important, life- and society-shaping movement as a result of the church leadership endeavoring to determine its own philosophy of sexual ethics (Gaca, 2003). Gaca points out that the struggle was about whether the church would adopt the communal sexual model of the early Stoics, Zeno and Chrysippus, and Plato, dependent as it was upon

Pythagorean philosophy; the liberal sexual ethics model of Epiphanes, on the opposite extreme; or the later Stoic familial model of moderation, monogamy, and heterosexuality.

Both Gaca and Torgeson suggest that the issue of women's leadership in the church ultimately was shaped by the church adopting the reigning cultural ethical values of its day, and the political ideals implied in them. That is, Greco-Roman notions of the uncoupling of women as sex objects from women as domestic managers and procreators resulted in the devaluation of women in Christian society to the domestic-maternal role or the erotic whore role. Both roles subjected women to Greco-Roman male sexual dominance. Gaca and Torgeson see the demise of the equality of women—as Jesus had apparently envisioned it, and hence women as priests and bishops in the church—as a casualty of the politics of Greco-Roman sexual dynamics as it shaped the gender models dominant in the church.

Those gender models have prevailed consistently in Christian religious practice ever since, with the rare exception of women leadership in the feminine religious orders. Unfortunately, those hardly count in the issue of equality of leadership, since they are gender-exclusive and do not speak of or to the general pattern in the church. Moreover, even these singularly able women and their orders achieved legitimate status mainly as adjunct to male orders. Another exception is that of such figures as Jean d'Arc, Theresa of Avila, Hildegard of Bingen, and Julian of Norwich. However, these are merely exceptions that prove the rule of general gender inequality and the suppression of the voice of women in the history of the Christian religion.

This denigration is not intrinsic to Christianity. Quite the opposite, it is alien to its essence. It is a product of the influence of Hellenistic culture, as I have argued, but it is also a carryover of the patriarchal model from that old Jewish story in the Hebrew Bible. All three of the Abrahamic religions are infested with that old Jewish story, with the same wretched consequences. Indeed, it is this old Jewish story from which the patriarchal model in the Qur'an derives, and thus that story is responsible for the suppression of women in Islam as well as in Judaism, and residually in Christianity. We must get rid of that old Jewish patriarchal story from the Hebrew Bible, the Old Testament.

The history of the liberation of women in religious ministries is an odyssey of fits, starts, and regressions; of spectacular successes and pitiful failures. This is true of all faith groups. The great variety of religions throughout history have been the matrix of a painful and precarious pilgrimage for women endeavoring to express their inherent desire and heroic struggle for certification in authentic religious leadership roles as priests and bishops.

There are at least five different Jewish "denominations" and that, undoubtedly, does not indicate the subdivisions within each. Buddhism, while it is constituted mainly by the distinctive schools of Mahayana, Vajrayana, Theravada, and Hinayana communities, is almost infinitely divided into more than 50 specialized subgroups within each of the four major "denominations." Recently the various forms of Islam—al Qaeda, Sufism, Shi'ite, and Sunni Muslims—have come to our attention. Every one of these religious systems has been an arena in which the issue of women in religious leadership has been a significant contest and noteworthy ferment.

As a father of four daughters of superior quality, ability, and heroism, and the husband of one gracious wife, I am personally grieved and enraged by the fact that in all facets of all societies the role of women has been repressed, suppressed, and oppressed. Whether consciously intentional or motivated by other drivers, the story is one of power brokering in which women have been most of the time disempowered. The most unfortunate aspect of this tragic narrative is the fact that religious institutions have, until recently, been the most powerful agents and agencies of this injustice. The misfortune is compounded by the fact that repressing the contribution of women has been a deprivation of those very societies and cultures that have perpetrated this unwisdom and injustice. I resent and reject, as ought all responsible humans, the difficulty we have created for women to penetrate the stained glass ceiling in church ministry.

In the struggle for women's ordination to the ministry of the word and sacraments, Independents and Pentecostals were far ahead of the established churches. However, these instances were fairly isolated cases of exceptional, independent, charismatic, self-appointed, and self-made prophets such as Aimee Semple McPherson and Mary Baker Eddy. Judaism was not so marked and Islam has never had a woman Imam. Consequently the regularization of the roles of women in religious leadership at the official level is very recent and sparsely distributed among the religious institutions of the Western world.

In 1999, Audrey Brosnan wrote an interesting study of women going through transition in ministry roles in the Roman Catholic Church. She focused on the perplexities and pain of women in religious leadership in the Roman Catholic faith community. She pointed out that the issue at stake is a woman's clear discernment of authentic vocation and the mode and method of ministry to which she is called. Every Catholic movement for women in religious leadership was resisted, criticized, and obstructed until they were organized into identifiable movements that could appeal to the ecclesiastical authorities for institutionalization in the form of religious orders of cloistered women. That hardly solves the problem.

Despite the fact that there are a hundred religious orders, each having numerous daughter organizations in various countries of the world (Wikipedia, 2009), none of the women in divine vocation can ever be ordained to the priesthood. Highly accomplished women in heroic and profound forms of ministry stand out in this historic tradition over the centuries. Women of today who have a vision and vocation of ministry as women in religious leadership strongly wish a place at the table where the decisions are made for the future of women in the church. In mainline Presbyterian and Methodist churches in the United States, in which ordination is now equally accessible to women as it is to men, many if not most of the major committees and commissions at the national organizational level of those denominations are led by women, and the percentage increases every year.

In denominations in which women still cannot be ordained, there is a sturdy undercurrent of desire for such certified roles of women religious leadership. As I write this, the Roman Catholic Curia under Pope Benedict XVI is carrying out a systematic assessment of all women religious orders with the purpose of weeding out those progressive-thinking women who militate in favor of women's ordination to the priesthood in the Roman Catholic Communion. This is a step further along a course instituted by Benedict XVI both before and during his papacy. A decade or more ago, he carried out a housecleaning in all Roman Catholic Seminaries in the United States. In that intervention ecumenical initiatives by the seminaries toward other denominations were curtailed, non-Catholic faculty members were removed from Catholic seminaries, non-Catholic students could no longer matriculate in or even attend the Masters of Divinity courses leading to ordination to the priesthood, and non-Roman Catholic students were systematically amortized from the master of arts program in religious studies at the seminaries. This will cause a significant distancing of the Roman Catholic communion from other communities of Christian faith, as well as from those in Catholic membership who feel that the restrictions of the church against women in religious leadership is neither biblical, nor wise, nor fair. The predicament of such women in Roman Catholic communities is paradigmatic of that of women in any denomination or walk of life in which gender is an obstruction to vocation, promotion, and achievement. The situation places women, with skills, talents, natures, and divine vocations for ordained religious leadership, in an impasse in which they are unable to be true to their own authentic selves. They are forced to decide whether they should simply continue alone in the pursuit of an interior personal spirituality or persist in pressing for such ordination, promotion, and leadership roles as permit them to exercise their sense of divine vocation. Are they to be satisfied with personal contemplation of the mystery of a meaningfully transcendent private spirituality or militate for the institutionalization of their rightful sense of vocation?

There have always been those women in regressive and oppressive religious communities who have sublimated their loss of certification and ordination by pouring their spiritual energies and sense of vocation into some kind of personal ministry. They are the ones who chose to move away from the struggle for ordination and immersed themselves in ministry to specific human needs, such as teaching or care of the needy and suffering. "They are the ones who bore the burden and the heat, while they could have been those who spiritually conquered and subdued the land." These women apparently prefer to stay in the community, adapt to its prescriptions, define themselves in terms of its rubrics, and enjoy that traditional *status quo*. Such women tend to move to the margins and work in peripheral ministries without pursuit of ordained leadership roles. Others enter the academy and invest their energies there instead of in the church, and still others simply abandon the cause of religious service and move into a kind of forced secularity. Other Catholic women see it as a matter of ethical integrity to stay and fight. It is these women that the present papal housecleaning of the female orders is endeavoring to eliminate from places of influence.

If this were only true of the Roman Catholic Church and the Muslim congregations and Mosques-centered communities, it might be possible for most of us to ignore them and leave them to their benighted and misbegotten selves. However, the trouble, as hinted above, lies in the fact that this ancient mode of repressing women in religious institutions tends to reinforce the long-standing pattern of those same regressive values and behaviors in the culture and society in general. When the biblical community of Israel became an empire under David's dynasty, prophets arose to remind them that this was not the intent of the covenant. Prophets challenged the *status quo*, claiming that God does not have a predestined system of order that is unfolding in history, no matter how humans behave. The prophets claimed that the world is not the way God intended it and humans are responsible to set it right.

Consequently women should not simply stay in repressive institutions and roles, acquiesce to the exploitation, and rationalize away the perfidy and immorality of such religious or societal structures! We are *all duty-bound* and under ethical imperative to rectify repressive institutions or get out of them and find or create an alternative structure that will function morally. It is an extension of the institutional oppression for any of us to leave women in the situation in which they must make their own personal decision regarding the tipping point of this ethical and personal dilemma. Wherever repression and oppression of any kind have prevailed in this world, it has often been up to women to initiate ministry and service to the marginalized, victimized, outcast, and disempowered. It was usually women that opened the doors and windows of new initiatives and experimental ministries for the needy, helpless, hopeless, and forlorn (Wink, 1984, 1986, 1992, 1998). How often throughout history the prophetic voices of women have given the sturdy and challenging leadership that delivered all kinds of persons from the denigration of their humanness, and so greatly relieved the human spirit of its travail! (Wink, 2002, 2003).

Surely this is the reason that Jesus's message and style had such inordinate appeal to women, and that they have always sought official and certified ministry in his name. Jesus stood against all forms of entrenched power and oppression throughout his ministry. That was certainly the main point of his very existence. That is also the reason why, from the outset of his ministry, his interventionary voice and his unconventional claims on the sources of power in his society were suppressed and ultimately exterminated. Jesus stood against the powers of this world and so was himself oppressed, suppressed, and cast out. He cared greatly for the outcast, suppressed, and oppressed.

Women understood immediately and intuitively the sounds, signs, and significance of such a mission as Jesus's, and its importance for the unempowered. They had been there, done that, and gotten the T-shirt, so to speak. So it should not surprise us that throughout history there have risen to the top of the tide of human endeavor women of great ability and redemptive presence who have called for a legitimation of all forms of women's religious leadership. They have long known the essential issues, have long sought deliverance, and they have militated appropriately for their opportunity to bind up the broken hearted and afford the ministry of deliverance and hope to all who are oppressed. Moreover, they saw that in the final analysis, for them to accomplish this without oppressive limitations they needed to smash the ecclesiastical stained glass ceiling.

The net outcome of this long historic struggle for the equality of women, for their freedom from sick dependencies and oppression, and for their ordination to and/or certification in religious leadership roles, turns out to be very interesting in many ways. This observation applies equally to women in the political arena, in social services agencies, in the academy, and in ordained religious roles—in those communities of faith of every religion and denomination that allows it.

The fact that is most interesting about this modern-day outcome is as follows. In the historically most highly regarded professions in the Western world, namely, religion, medicine, and university faculties, men are no longer the most prominent candidates or appointees. I came into the university scene in 1970 and had a lovely time for a decade. However, in the subsequent quarter of a century, key university posts tended to be given to women or black candidates. If you were a qualified black woman, your chances were even better for an appointment. If you were a black Puerto Rican woman of Spanish extraction whose mother tongue was Hebrew, it was a cinch.

The very specific reasons for this lie in two facts. First, is the wholesome advantages of equal opportunity legislation; second is the fact that during the last two generations, males with first-line brains, so to speak, have not sought out the ministry, medicine, and the academy as of primary interest to them. They have tended strongly, instead, to professions having to do with research, technology, and computer engineering, rather than the humanities and social sciences.

At the same time, equal opportunity legal provisions opened the doors for women with first-line brains to seek and find significant appointments in ordained ministry, medicine, and university faculties. In those communions of faith and those institutions of medicine and learning that were open to senior roles for women, this began to provide the opportunity for woman of superior ability and training to acquire the leading positions in these historically esteemed professions. Thus, in Christian churches that now ordain women to religious leadership positions, we are getting a preponderance of women with first-line brains entering our seminaries and our significant positions of religious leadership as ordained clergy. At the same time, a high percentage of the males who are going into ordained ministry, medicine, and university professorships have third- and fourth-line brains; that is, they are of far less ability, skill, motivation, and productivity than their women colleagues. This is not true of all males, but a high percentage of those becoming ordained ministers, doctors, and university professors. Conversely, excellence does not mark all women entering the historically prized professions, but only a high percentage of them. This sociological and psychological shift represents a major modification in our culture. The glass ceiling is disappearing from the churches.

I was, for the first half of my professional career, an ordained minister in a denomination that would not ordain women to the roles of either deacon or teaching and ruling elders (preachers and pastors). Many of us young men carried a brilliantly burning torch for the cause of women's ordination. We were fathers of brilliant and appropriately passionate daughters whose future in ordained ministry was quite obvious. We gained some ground in the late 1970s and succeeded in getting women ordained as deacons. When we overturned the denomination to ordain women as elders and ministers, an aggressive political counterforce both denied the overture for ordination of women as ministers and rescinded the previous decision of years before regarding ordination of women deacons.

After a decade of this struggle, constantly failing in our objective, I left that denomination on the grounds of its failure to measure up to the biblical and ethical imperatives for the equality of women and their opportunities as women religious leaders. I tried hard to smash the stained glass ceiling. This struggle continues in many religious communities. The Roman Catholic Church, for example, is rushing rapidly into the Middle Ages. All prospects of any gains in ordained women in religious leadership in that most influential of all Christian communions is being set back at least a century.

So the picture and prospects for women as religious leaders in the Americas, and throughout the Western world, are quite ambiguous. In the Christian denominations and non-Christian communities of faith that invite women as religious leaders, women are generally doing brilliant work and providing exceedingly effective service to those institutions and their constituencies, as the effectiveness of males in comparable roles is in decline. The stained glass ceiling is largely melted away.

On the other hand, in those religious groups who resist women as religious leaders, the antifeminine prejudice is hardening and becoming more and more regressive, to the great detriment of those institutions and their constituencies, especially of the women in their communions. The stained glass ceiling is thickening and becoming ossified. There seems to be more and more likelihood that women will increase in prominence and effectiveness in religious leadership where they are certified to do so; and less and less likelihood that women will ever have that opportunity in such regressive communions as the Roman Catholic Church—at least under the present Medieval papacy.

I have addressed in this chapter mainly the ethical issues of an impenetrable stained glass ceiling. Implied in this discussions has been the detrimental psychological impact upon women specifically and the society in general. Along the way, I have hinted at the unacceptable distortion of society and its deprivation of the ingenuity of more than half of its creative constituents. What I have not addressed as extensively is the loss of productivity that any culture experiences when it fails to allow women to participate and contribute in the roles for which they are best prepared by nature and motivation; and to which they sense the urgent imperative of a divine vocation (Ellens and Paludi, in press). I watched my daughters, particularly my eldest, struggle with this, and the suffering and repression were, from my point of view, infinitely unacceptable. She is the brightest, most able person I know, and in a culture like ours has been for the last 50 years, too much of her energy had to be poured into the quest to get her footing. She deserved a smooth and inviting pathway to the richness of her singular role, achievement, and contribution in life and history.

Note

1. Ellens, J. H. (2010). Women as religious leaders: Advances and stalemates. In M. Paludi (Ed.), *Feminism and women's rights worldwide*. Vol.1: Heritage, roles and issues (pp. 85–95). Westport, CT: Praeger.

References

Brosnan, A. (1999). *Discerning ministerial transition.* Unpublished dissertation at Catholic Theological Union, Chicago, IL.

Ellens, J. H. (2010). Women as religious leaders: Advances and stalemates. In M. Paludi (Ed.), *Feminism and women's rights worldwide* (pp. 85–95). Westport, CT: Praeger.

Ellens, J. H., Paludi, M., and Paludi, C. (in press). Religious discrimination. In M. Paludi, C. Paludi, and E. DeSouza (Eds.), *Praeger handbook on understanding and preventing workplace discrimination.* Westport, CT: Praeger.

Epp, E. (2005). *Junia: The first woman apostle.* Minneapolis, MN: Fortress.

Gaca, K. (2003). *The making of fornication, eros, ethics and political reform in Greek philosophy and early Christianity.* Berkeley, CA: University of California Press.

Torgeson, K. (1993). *When women were priests: Women's leadership in the early church and the scandal of their subordination in the rise of Christianity.* San Francisco, CA: HarperCollins.

Wikipedia. (2009). *Denominations.* Retrieved from http://www.wikipedia.org/ on August 22, 2010.

Wink, W. (1984). *Naming the powers: The language of power in the new testament.* Philadelphia, PA: Fortress.

Wink, W. (1986). *Unmasking the powers: The invisible forces that determine human existence.* Philadelphia, PA: Fortress.

Wink, W. (1992). *Engaging the powers: Discernment and resistance in a world of domination.* Minneapolis, MN: Fortress Augsburg.

Wink, W. (1998). *When the powers fall.* Minneapolis, MN: Fortress Augsburg.

Wink, W. (2002). *The human being: The enigma of the son of the man.* Minneapolis, MN: Fortress Augsburg.

Wink, W. (2003). *Jesus and nonviolence.* Minneapolis, MN: Fortress Augsburg.

8

Latinas and Leadership in a Changing Cultural Context

Silvia L. Mazzula

Introduction

The face of the United States changed dramatically in the 1960s, following President Kennedy's campaign to erase legally sanctioned immigration quotas based on national origin. The termination of these quotas allowed legal entry and residency in the United States to racially and culturally diverse immigrant groups (i.e., Asians and Hispanics[1]), who until then had been denied entry. Since then, the changing demographic composition of the United States has resulted in increased racial and ethnic diversity not only in society at large but also in the workforce (Bass and Bass, 2008). As a result of additional key historical events, such as the civil rights and feminist movements, there has been increasing participation of women in the workforce in general (U.S. Department of Labor, Bureau of Labor Statistics; USDL, 2009, September) and in leadership positions in particular (Carli and Eagly, 2001). Over the past several decades, we have also seen an increase in full-time working women and mothers (USDL). In addition to notable gender diversity, we have also witnessed increasing representation of Hispanics, whose population growth rate is higher than all other racial ethnic groups in the United States. Their growth is projected to continue over several decades and will become a pronounced voice in the workforce and in the leadership of the United States.

Currently, Latinas make up almost half (47.3%) of the Hispanic workforce (USDL, 2009C). In 2009, Latinas represented 6.8 percent of the total noninstitutionalized U.S. workforce although they constituted 12.6 percent[2] of all American women in the workforce. However, 59.2 percent of Latinas participated in the workforce, compared to 60.4 percent of white women and 63.4 percent of black/African American women (USDL, 2010A, 2010B). However, according to the National Council of La Raza (Elliott, 2005), Latinas make a significant contribution to the American economy and their family's economic well-being. For example, according to current data, 24 percent of Latinas were financially responsible for maintaining their family (with no spouse present), compared to 44 percent of black, 15 percent of white, and 12 percent of Asian women in 2008 (USDL, November 2009). Furthermore, almost half of Latinas are married, and data show that the median income for married Hispanic families increases significantly when Latinas work (Elliott).

Their participation in the workforce, however, has not necessarily translated into professional advancement. The gender inequity in leadership positions has been well documented, with women occupying significantly fewer leadership roles compared to their male counterparts. Although we have seen an increase of women working in management, professional, and related occupations, Latinas are disproportionally represented compared to women of other racial groups. In 2009, only 23.3 percent of Latinas held management, professional, or related occupations compared to Asian (47.6%), white (41.5%), and black (33.5%) women (USDL, 2010A). On the contrary, Latinas were more likely to hold service occupations compared to women of other racial groups (Latinas, 33.8%; blacks, 27.7%; Asians 20.2%; and whites 19.5%; USDL, 2010B).

Despite their overrepresentation in service occupations, Latinas' employment in management, professional, and related occupations has increased in the past decade (Escamilla, 2009). We have seen recent historical undertakings by Latinas in leadership positions. Examples that come to mind are Justice Sonia M. Sotomayor, the first Hispanic and third woman Supreme Court justice; and Dr. Melba Vazquez, the first Latina and woman of color to serve as president of the American Psychological Association, out of 120 presidencies. Public television figures include Judge Cristina Perez, J.D., who hosts *La Corte de Familia*; and Cristina Saralegui, a veteran journalist and influential role model for today's Latinas who is the host of *El*

Show de Cristina. Notable activists include poet Julia de Burgos, who is an advocate for Puerto Rico's independence as well as an activist for women and African American Caribbean writers; and Gloria Anzaldúa, a scholar on social and cultural marginalization, particularly among Chicanas. In addition to these notable Latinas, Latinas in general have a long history of political activism, of organizing their communities and participating in labor rights movements throughout U.S. history (e.g., Prindeville, 2003; Segura, 2003).

The lower workforce participation of Latinas and their underrepresentation in professional occupations coupled with the notable achievement of many Latinas currently and throughout the history of America highlight the importance of understanding how Latina leaders have "made it." Two specific questions are warranted: What are the structural, cultural, and racial barriers that Latinas encounter in leadership, and how have they navigated their identity successfully within a cultural context? This chapter seeks to understand Latina leadership and their leadership role within a racial, cultural, and gender context. It also explores how Latinas may navigate their multiple identifies (e.g., role of family member, mother, wife, etc.) and reviews those factors that may explain workforce and occupational disparities, highlighting issues that may hinder or serve as positive influences in obtaining and remaining in leadership positions.

Theoretical Background

While incorporating sociopolitical factors, I make certain assumptions throughout this chapter: First, leadership is not determined solely on individual characteristics or attributes but is also shaped and informed by its context. Second, leadership among Latinas, who are members of marginalized communities based on gender, race, or cultural heritage, cannot be understood without an understanding of racial and cultural factors. The chapter is grounded in systems theory of understanding groups in general. Systems theory provides a useful way to understand " . . . the context in which a behavior occurs and the sociopolitical factors that may influence an individual's behavior" (McRae and Short, 2010, pp. 2). Although a detailed review of the complexities of systems theory and the integration of racial and cultural dynamics in organizational life is beyond the scope of this chapter, readers are encouraged to see McRea and Short (2010).

I also make several assumptions from a systems perspective: First, individuals are part of multiple systems (e.g., organizations, culture, family, ethnicity, racial group, etc.) and are multidimensional beings. Second, as members of these various systems, we endorse values, ideas, assumptions, and beliefs about ourselves and others on both a conscious and unconscious level. Lastly, our worldview plays a role in organizational life, drives our interactions (or lack thereof) with members of the organization, and shapes our experience in the workforce. Throughout the chapter, I use the term "group" broadly to identify the professional organization, the racial or cultural group of Latinas, and the culture of those that Latinas will lead in their professional roles.

This chapter is divided into three sections. The first provides an overview of the demographic characteristics of Hispanics in the U.S. The second section provides the profile of Hispanics in the workforce and their standing with respect to correlates of professional advancement (e.g., employment status, education level, generation status, etc.). The last section discusses leadership within a multicultural context and the racial and cultural factors that are important in understanding Latina leadership.

The Hispanic Profile

Currently, Hispanics are the fastest-growing and largest ethnic minority group in the United States, with a population of approximately 45 million (15% of the total U.S. population), excluding another 3.9 million residents of Puerto Rico (U.S. Bureau of the Census, 2008). Population projections estimate that by 2050, Hispanics will represent 20 percent of the U.S. population. Despite the use of global categorical descriptors (i.e., Hispanic or Latino/a), Hispanics are a heterogeneous community and their diversity continues with the increasing influx of immigrants from nontraditional Hispanic groups. Historically, the largest groups of Hispanics in the United States were immigrants from Mexico, Puerto Rico, and Cuba (Logan, 2003). However, recent statistics show an increase in people from the Dominican Republic, as well as South America, such as Colombians, Ecuadorians, and Salvadorians (Logan; Schwartz and Zamboanga, 2008).

In addition to their diversity with respect to nationality or ethnicity, Hispanics are racially heterogeneous representing people from all racial backgrounds. The racial identification of Hispanics is a complex issue and thus they tend to be globally identified as Hispanic or Latino/a or by their national heritage (Nicholson, Pantoja, and Segura, 2005). For example, although Puerto Ricans can be racially white, black, or mestizo (racially mixed), they are most often identified as Puerto Rican. However, Hispanics can be of any race, regardless of their ethnic or cultural self-identification. There are many other within-group differences, such as immigration status, acculturation, cultural values, ethnic/racial identity, etc., which have all been shown to shape the worldview of Hispanics (e.g., Mazzula, 2009). In addition to the aforementioned differences that need to be considered when understanding Latina leaders, it is important to highlight the reality of Latinos in general and Latinas in particular on issues related to the workforce and professional attainment.

Reality and Correlates of Professional Advancement

Although women in general continue to be underrepresented and experience glass ceilings, Latinas encounter several other barriers that warrant discussion, particularly as they relate to Hispanics' economic standing and educational attainment, which have been correlated with professional advancement for the general population. Although an in-depth discussion on any of these factors is beyond the scope of this chapter, they highlight the social and political reality that Latinas must navigate in their professional advancement.

Hispanics in the Workplace

Hispanics in general constituted 14.5 percent[3] of the American workforce in 2009. This was proportionally representative of the total Hispanic U.S. population, as the overall workforce participation for all Americans was 65.2 percent.[4] Hispanics continue a previously noted pattern of having the highest workforce participation of all racial ethnic groups (USDL, 2010B). For example, in 2009, 68 percent participated in the labor force (USDL, 2009B), compared to 66 percent of Asians, 65.8 percent whites, and 62.4 percent of blacks/African Americans (USDL, 2010B; USDL, 2009A). Hispanics born outside of the United States are also more likely to seek employment or be employed compared to U.S.-born Hispanics; almost 70 percent were active in the workforce in 2006 (NLPA, 2007).

Although Hispanics have the highest representation in the American workforce, their representation varies by occupation. For example, in 2010 only 18.7 percent of Hispanics held management, professional, and related occupations compared to Asians (48.1%), whites (38%), and blacks (29.8%); however, they were overrepresented (27.3%), in service occupations compared to other racial groups such as blacks (24.7%), Asians (17.7%), and whites (16.5%). Hispanics are also overrepresented in office and administrative support occupations, and over half of Hispanic men were employed in natural resources, construction, maintenance-related occupations, transportation, and material moving occupations in 2008 (USDL, November 2009)

Employment Status
The American labor market has experienced considerable challenges since the recession of 2007. Although all Americans were affected by this recession, Hispanics in 2008 had the second-highest unemployment rate, 7.6 percent, preceded by 10.1 percent of blacks/African Americans and compared to 5.2 percent of Asians and 4 percent of non-Hispanic Whites (USDL, November 2009). Despite these unemployment rates, in 2008 Hispanics were more likely to be employed (63.3%) compared to whites (62.8%) and blacks (57.3%). Furthermore, although Hispanic men had the highest employment–population ratio, Hispanic women (20 years or older) had the lowest employment rates (54.6%) compared to their Asian (59.3%), black (59.1%), and white (57.5%) female counterparts (USDL) and were almost twice as likely to be unemployed than white women. For example, in 2009, 7.7 percent of Hispanic women were unemployed compared to 4.9 percent of white women (USDL, September 2009).

According to the USDL (November 2009), the problems associated with higher unemployment rates for Hispanics and African Americans are related to many factors, such as level of education, employment in occupations with limited security, limited job opportunities as a result of working in urban areas, and possible discrimination. Further indicating that not all of these factors are measurable; although I would argue that many are when explored within a racial and cultural context. I will interpret these statistics throughout this chapter within a multicultural and systemic context, specifically addressing Hispanic cultural values that may interact with Hispanic socioeconomic standing and in part explain these discrepancies.

Occupational Representation

Similar to Hispanics in general, Latinas are disproportionally represented in leadership roles. Although women accounted for 51 percent of those employed in management, professional, and related occupations in 2008 (USDL, September 2009), only 23.3 percent of Latinas held those occupations compared to Asian (47.6%), white (41.5%), and black (33.5%) women in 2009, (USDL, 2010B). On the contrary, Latinas (33.8%) were more likely to hold service occupations compared to women of other racial groups (blacks, 27.7%; Asians, 20.2%; whites, 19.5%; USDL, 2010B). However, Latinas' employment in management, professional, and related occupations has increased in the past decade (Escamilla, 2009). In an analysis of government-wide occupations from 2007 to 2008, Hispanics in professional occupations also increased, albeit the figure still remains significantly low, accounting for only 3.8 percent of professionals employed (U.S. Office of Personnel Management, April 2010). However, it's unclear how many of professional government occupations are held by Latinas.

An increase in self-employed status among Latinas and Latina-owned businesses has also been noted. Over three million Latinas were self-employed in 2004 (Elliott, 2005). Almost a third (31.5%) were self-employed in education and health services and 18 percent in professional and business services. In 2002, Latina-owned businesses had almost doubled since 1997 and represented 2.4 percent of all U.S. firms. Latina-owned businesses also contributed over $36 million to the American economy (Elliott). Furthermore, among Hispanic workers, recent population data show that 40.5 percent of Latinas were employed in management, professional, and related occupations compared to 34.5 percent for their male counterparts; 21.3 percent worked in service occupations compared to 14.3 percent of Hispanic males. Interestingly, a close examination of these data reveals Latinas who identified racially white were more likely (41.4%) to be employed in management, professional, and related occupations and less likely (20.1%) to be employed in service occupations compared to black Latinas, 21.3 percent and 28.5 percent respectively (USDL, 2009C). The data show racial disparities within Hispanics as well, yet relatively little attention is given to racial differences among Hispanics in general (Mazzula, 2009) and there are no empirical studies that have addressed this issue as it relates to Latina leadership.

Educational Attainment

In general, 68 percent of Hispanics in the workforce had completed high school compared to 90 percent of Asians, blacks, and whites in 2008 (USDL, November 2009). Only 16 percent of Hispanics had a college degree compared to Asians (54%), whites (34%), and blacks (24%), although the proportion of college graduates has increased over time among all racial groups (USDL). Hispanic women in particular tend to achieve significantly lower levels of educational attainment. Although women's educational attainment has increased and the proportion of women who obtain college degrees has almost tripled since 1970 (USDL, September 2009), this has not been the case among Latinas. For example, 41.8 percent of Latinas did not finish high school, compared to black (22.7%), white (17.1%), and Asian women (15.6%) in 2004. Of Latinas who graduated high school, 54 percent pursued higher education compared to black (58.2%), white (65.6%), and Asian woman (76.4%) (Elliott, 2005).

Some researchers have found women with higher educational attainment are more likely to be employed and that education explains the racial and ethnic disparities in employment in the United States (England, Garcia-Bea, and Ross, 2004; Reid, 2002). However, irrespective of educational level, Hispanics are more likely to be employed than whites or Asians (USDL, September 2009). In 2006, Hispanics had the highest employment rate of those who had less than a high school diploma, and 59 percent of those without a high school degree were employed. Similarly, those with some college experience were more likely to be employed compared to other racial groups and native-born Hispanics with a college degree or higher more than whites or blacks to be employed (NCLR, 2007). While educational attainment is not necessarily related to employment for Hispanics, it remains unclear if that is the case with respect to management, professional, or related occupations. Furthermore, cultural values associated with collectivism above individual achievement may in part explain these statistical data, as well as other institutional and structural barriers such as discrimination, lack of role models, and lack of support.

Generation Status

Generation status has been used as a proxy of acculturation[5] among Hispanics and has been related to the endorsement of American values, mobility, and access to resources in general, as well as to educational attainment and professional advancement. Current statistical data show that foreign-born women in general are less likely to be in the labor force and more likely to be unemployed compared to native-born women, although the opposite is true among foreign-born men (USDL, September 2009). Although attention has been given to gender and immigration issues (e.g., Pedraza, 1991) and the experience of immigrant women who are employed (Hondagneu-Sotelo, 1997; Romero, 2002), relatively little is known about Latinas. However, some within-group differences have been noted in empirical studies (see England et al., 2004, for review). For example, Cooney and Ortiz (1983) found that Puerto Rican women born on the mainland were more likely to be employed than Puerto Rican, Cuban, and Mexican immigrants and that English proficiency assisted Mexican and Puerto Rican women's employment.

In a study of 2001 population data examining the impact of immigration status among Latinas (i.e., Mexican, Puerto Rican, and Cuban descent), non-Hispanic blacks, and non-Hispanic whites, England et al. (2004) found immigrant women across all racial groups—except non-Hispanic blacks—were less likely to be employed. The authors also found immigrants with longer residency (i.e., 11 years) were more likely to be employed compared to recent immigrants (i.e., less than four years) and that immigrants who had been in the United States for more than 11 years were not significantly different from those who were U.S. born. The authors concluded that lack of social network, limited English proficiency, and experience working within the U.S. culture make it difficult for more recent immigrants to be employed. The authors also noted that over 50 percent of Latinas were immigrants, compared to whites (5%) and blacks (9%), and that this may explain some of the lower employment rates of Latinas compared to white women. It is also possible that in addition to the factors noted by the authors, legal status, racial and ethnic discrimination, and perceived acceptance by white-dominated employment settings may contribute to Latinas' underrepresentation. In general, although these studies highlight the relationship between generation status and employment, albeit limited compared to the proportion of Hispanics in the U.S., its relationship to leadership or professional advancement is unclear.

Family and Motherhood

In general, Latinas tend to have lower rates of participation in the workforce. In 2009, 59.2 percent participated in the workforce, compared to 60.4 percent of white women and 63.4 percent of black/African American women (USDL, 2010A, 2010B). Almost half of Latina women are married, and data show that the median income for married Hispanic families increases significantly when Hispanic women work (Elliott, 2005). Yet, married Latinas are less likely to participate in the workforce compared to other Latina women, or black, white, or Asian married women (Elliott). However, with no spouse present, 24 percent of Latinas were responsible for maintaining their family compared to 44 percent of black, 15 percent of white, and 12 percent of Asian women in 2008 (USDL, November 2009). Among mothers, 71 percent participated in the labor force, yet when racial ethnic differences were considered, only 61.4 percent Latinas participated compared to 68.8 percent of Asian, 76.7 percent of black, and 70.8 percent of white mothers (USDL).

It has been long documented that children often prevent women of all racial groups from employment and that mothers tend to be the primary caretakers (e.g., England et al., 2004). The lower representation of women in the workforce has often been attributed to gender roles dictating that men should provide the income and women should attend to their children and housework. However, recent scholarship notes a change in this pattern. While having young children tends to be related to lower workforce participation, the role of the husband's income may no longer apply (Cohen and Bianchi, 1999). However, some researchers found that marriage deterred employment for Latinas—but not for white or black women—and that although there was no relationship between Latinas' employment and their husband's income, there was an inverse relationship among white married women (see England et al., 2004, for review). Recently, in a study exploring population data, England et al. found no statistically significant differences in employment between married and never married women across a racially diverse sample. They did find that husband's income level was related to fewer married women being employed across all racial groups, except blacks. However, they noted the findings to be insignificant and concluded that marital status and husband's income may no longer be related to women's participation in the workforce.

The findings indicate that whereas husband's income may not be related to women working, at least among women of color, marriage itself was a determent for Latinas. Some studies have found that Latinas are more likely to report home or family reasons for not working. In 2003, almost a third of Latinas (64.3%) did not work for family or home-related issues compared to 57.3 percent of Asian women, 47.8 percent of white women, and 29.8 percent of black women (USDL, 2003). There are many likely explanations for these findings. First, considering the cost of child care and that Latinas tend to have less educational attainment and higher employment in lower-income occupations, it appears plausible that Latinas may find themselves struggling to outweigh the cost of paid work vs. nonpaid work in their home and community. Second, Hispanic workers are less likely to receive health coverage from work (NCLR, 2007) (despite a survey by the Business and Professional Women's Foundation (*Working Mother*, June 2005) that found that Latinas rated child care and family-related benefits more important than did their white and black women peers). Third, underrepresentation in the workforce may not hold the negative connotation perceived from white American culture. Hispanic cultural values and gender roles revere mothers and their role in the home and family. Latina women themselves may choose to remain in the home for their family and feel positive about doing so. Thus, it appears highly important to understand how Latinas navigate their multiple identities (e.g., role of family member, mother, wife, etc.) in general as they relate to their employment status, but in particular with regards to their professional attainment and leadership roles.

Summary of Hispanic Profile

In summary, statistical data show that Latinas have the lowest workforce participation, have the lowest educational attainment, and are underrepresented in professional and related occupations while overrepresented in service occupations. Although we can assume that some of these statistics have been impacted by the recent recession, it has been well documented that this has been a reality for Hispanics in the United States for decades. A discussion on the effects of the recession on all Americans is beyond the scope of this chapter, as are the systemic issues associated with the poor socioeconomic status of Hispanics in general and Latinas in particular. However, the profile in this chapter highlights some of the structural and systemic barriers that Latinas encounter, setting the context in which Latina leadership can be understood. It also highlights the resilience and determination of those Latinas who have "made it" and underscores the importance of incorporating these issues when understanding Latina leadership. Furthermore, while these statistics are alarming and have significant implications on Latinas' employment status, the data also show the importance of familial values among Latinas. Therefore, understanding Latina leadership warrants an exploration within a racial and cultural context. The racial and cultural dynamics in organizational life in general, and in Latina leadership are rarely addressed (McRae and Short, 2010); however, the intersection of leadership with race, ethnicity, gender roles, and national origin must be examined.

Latina Leadership in Context

Latina Leadership Research

Relatively few studies have been conducted on women's leadership (Eagly and Johannesen-Schmidt, 2001) and most have focused on the experiences of white women. Despite the growing diversity in the workforce and the increasing scholarship on gender issues, an understanding of racial and cultural factors in organizational life remains limited (McRea and Short, 2010). Therefore, relatively little is known about women of color leaders in general, and Latinas in particular (Hite, 2007; Prindeville, 2003). This is interesting, considering that Latina women have worked as political activists throughout the history of the United States (Garcia, 2005). The limited studies that have examined ethnic or racial differences tend to examine minority leaders within the context of white cultural values (Eagly and Johnson, 1990). Those studies that have explored Latina leadership without using white cultural norms have found that Latinas in leadership tend to struggle with issues of acculturation, belonging, discrimination, and family–work balance (Hite, 2007; Segura, 2003).

Although there is little research evidence to support this claim, the history of Latina's contributions as movers and shakers in their communities appears to align with more recent approaches to leadership. Although previous research on leadership focused on task-oriented leadership styles, current approaches have begun to focus on leaders' ability to inspire, encourage, and empower others. According to Okasi, Smith, Clark, and Sherman (2009), ethnic minority leaders tend to lead by connecting with others in meaningful ways and by being more nurturing and engaging; their approach appears more congruent with the transformational leadership model (Ardichvili, Mitchell, and Jondle, 2009). Ethnic minority leadership style also seems congruent with collectivist values; thus suggesting that cultural background is directly related to the leadership styles of ethnic minorities (Hetty van Emmerik, Euwema, and Wendt, 2008).

While ethnic minority leadership appears consistent with current approaches to leadership, this approach has not penetrated organizational life. Therefore, ethnic minority leaders who may lead in this way may encounter conflicts with dominant Western cultural values in general—and dominant leadership styles in particular—that continue to be more task-orientated, rigid, and driven by individualism (Okasi et al., 2009). This may in part explain the lack of research in ethnic minority leadership. However, research that has examined Latina leadership specifically within a social cultural framework have found Latinas' leadership style to be consistent with the style of transformational leaders, who inspire and are interpersonally concerned about their groups' advancement. For example, in a study examining Chicana faculty, Segura (2003) noted the following reasons why her participants entered academia:

> ... to challenge hegemonic discourse in their respective disciplines, articulate the needs of their diverse communities mindful of the danger of false representation, serve as role models for members of historically disenfranchised groups, and to contest racially gendered limitations imposed on their communities. (p. 47)

In essence, these women served as agents of change and were personally and interpersonally invested in the advancement of their people (Segura). This leadership style, although rarely documented in scholarship, is characteristic of the many Latina community organizers and indigenous healers who have been pivotal to Latino communities throughout the history of Latinos in the United States (Prindeville, 2003; Segura, 2003).

Although the number of Latinas leaders in recognized leadership positions is increasing, the dearth of scholarship on Latina leadership style highlights the limited representation of Latinas in leadership positions (Catalyst, 1999; USDL, November, 2009) and the lack of role models for future Latina leaders. It also highlights the potential value judgment on whom and what type of leadership style is worth scholarly attention. For example, while Latinas have served as leaders in their communities, these women are rarely discussed. It also highlights the diversity among Latinas (e.g., race, social class, generation status, etc.), which at times may make it difficult for researchers and scholars to truly capture racial and cultural factors that may be related to their experience as leaders. Lastly, it highlights the importance of understanding the factors that hinder or serve to facilitate Latina leadership and how they have navigated their changing cultural labyrinth.

Individualistic and Collectivist Values

Although the United States is mainly characterized as an individualistic culture (Stewart and Bennett, 1991), many Americans identify with collectivist[6] values (Constantine, Robinson, Wilton, and Caldwell, 2002). Hispanics, African Americans, and Asian Americans are typically considered collectivist cultures, while Western or Euro-Americans are typically considered individualist cultures. Considering that some Hispanic ethnic groups have been found to endorse a collectivist worldview, an understanding of how these values interact within a dominant individualistic workforce is important. In collectivist cultures, individual members tend to evaluate their sense of worth, well-being, and satisfaction with life based on the evaluation of external sources such as social norms, family expectations, relationships, and interactions with members of their group. Families tend to include the nuclear unit, as well as extended family members and members of the community (Santiago-Rivera, 2003). In contrast, individualistic cultures are characterized by a worldview that values independence and individual attributions (e.g., autonomy, self-reliance, and uniqueness), and families that are composed of the nuclear unit (Stewart and Bennett, 1991).

Traditionally, research and notions of leadership in the United States emphasized individualistic cultural values, such as the leader's ability to demonstrate self-initiative and self-determination, and to be the authority on how things should be accomplished. Leaders from more collectivist cultures, such as the Hispanic and African American cultures, tend to endorse transformational leadership styles as previously noted (Ardichvili et al., 2009). However, among Latinas, retention of collectivist values and or endorsement of more individualist values are dependent on their level of acculturation. Level of acculturation may impact the worldview of Latina leaders and their leadership style. Acculturation considers how members of different cultural groups interact, how they adapt, and the changes that occur for members of each group (Kohatsu, 2006; Sam and Oppedal, 2002). These include individual changes in identity, values, attitudes, and behaviors (Berry, 2005, 2006a). Until the 1960s, immigrants were expected to assimilate, or adopt "middle-class cultural patterns of largely white Protestant, Anglo-Saxon origins" (Gordon, 1964). However, in the last 40 years, notions of assimilation have been increasingly challenged. The shift away from the expectation and requirement of assimilation is reflected in the many organizational diversity initiatives to foster inclusion.

However, very little is known about its relationship to leadership and the workforce. What can be helpful in understanding Latina leadership is that acculturation is related to both well-being and distress among Hispanics and other ethnic minority groups. Distress can result from multiple factors, such as language and family cohesion (Miranda and Matheny, 2000) and differences in cultural values and gender roles (Ramos, 2005). It has been documented that as Hispanics' residency in the United States increases, their traditional values tend to decrease, although family has been shown to continue to be a central aspect of Hispanics' self-identity throughout generations. Due to the limited representation of Latina leader role models, some Latinas may observe the mainstream culture and imitate behaviors driven by dominant individualist values as a way to prevent being an outcast or in order to fit in (Hite, 2007). This has implications for Latinas' well-being in general. Fitting in would require a Latina to abandon certain aspects of their Hispanic culture (or, acculturating in American culture). Although being bicultural has been shown to be optimal, some scholars suggest that distancing completely from one's culture of origin results in negative psychological consequences. Moreover, it is possible that Latinas who immerse themselves in white American culture as a means of professional advancement may experience familial conflicts and or isolation from their community.

A Latina leader who endorses more collectivist values may seek support from her community and family as a means of buffering negative work experiences. For example, she may be overtly or covertly informed about the discomfort that her subordinates may experience as result of her "new" leadership style. She is also likely to experience barriers and discrimination based on her gender, race, and ethnicity, especially if she is less assimilated. Although minority, and Latina, leadership style appears to encompass notions of transformational leadership (Ardichvili et al., 2009), it seems particularly important for Latina leaders to be aware of the way in which their cultural values have shaped their leadership style and the way in which they problem solve and engage others, as well as their expectations of subordinates. Considering the low representation of Latina leaders in the workforce and the racial disparities in advanced professional organizations, it is safe to assume that both their subordinates and superiors will be of different racial and cultural groups, and will most likely find themselves in predominantly white working environments. Therefore, Latina leaders who are aware that they endorse collectivist values must also be aware of how their approach might be perceived by others. For example, it is possible that Latina leaders who focus on collaborative problem solving may be incorrectly perceived by dominant racial groups as having less initiative or knowledge about the task at hand.

There are multiple ways in which acculturation interacts with cultural values and in turn influences leadership style, but relatively little has been done to understand these interactions. However, as the population growth rate of Latinas continues in the United States and the discussion of the importance of being bicultural continues, it is safe to assume that some Latinos/as will continue to retain values from their culture of origin. Therefore, further research in this area will make a significant contribution to understanding Latinas in general and Latina leadership in particular.

Authority and Leadership

The literature on racial and cultural dynamics in organizational life suggests that the race and culture of individuals will impact how they perceive their ability to lead and their leadership style. Specifically, "racial and cultural identities affect the ways in which individuals are authorized in the role and the power available to them to fully take up leadership" (McRae and Short, 2010, p. 93). Oftentimes, although these perceptions and assumptions impact our behavior and those we interact with in organizations, they are outside of our immediate awareness. The power of Latinas to make decisions or the authority they have in that role will be impacted by specific racial and cultural values.

Collectivist values and Hispanic gender roles may interact with the authority of Latinas and their power to lead. The Hispanic cultural values of *respeto, sympatía*, and *personalismo* may all play a role in the leadership style and decision-making approach of Latinas, albeit often out of their conscious awareness. For some Hispanic ethnic groups, Latinas are "expected" to be subordinate, therefore rendering them powerless and helpless in decision making. Assertiveness and independence are highly discouraged. While holding leadership positions imply the existence of hierarchy (e.g., Bartunek, Walsh, and Lacey, 2000), this notion is in direct conflict with these collectivist values. These values revere friendliness, respect of others when interacting, and likeability. Yet, individualist cultural values engrained in organizations may create dissonance in the subordinates of Latinas, questioning their ability to lead and their power to make decisions effectively. In other words, Latinas may be found to lack the necessary "this is how you do it" attitude. Some have noted these values to reflect sexist notions and to counter feminism movement (Zavala-Martinez, 1987). While I do not disagree, I also believe that this is a strength for Latina leaders: they may be able to connect with those they lead in a more meaningful way and use these values to serve as transformational leaders in their organizations.

Cultural values of *familismo,* which reveres family unity, honor, and loyalty above individual needs and goals (Sue and Sue, 2008), may also impact the leadership of Latinas, and negotiating these identities may be critical for Latinas in leadership positions. This is not to say that white women do not value family, but the sanctioning of group identity vs. individual identity may be more salient among Latina leaders. Similarly, although scholarship on the relationship between balancing family and work is fairly new in organizational literature (Hite, 2007), the centrality of *familismo* values have been salient for decades in the Hispanic community. Although relatively little has been researched as family relates to *familismo* and leadership, one study of Latinas in managerial and professional occupations (Hite) noted that family was a central aspect of their identity and navigating work, and that family was significant in their leadership. Hite also noted a difference in family values by generation status, such that first-generation women noted more concrete ways in which they are connected to their family (e.g., working to support their family) vs. later generation leaders. This is an area for further research, considering that the role of family and children in deterring women from professional advancement has been well documented.

Lastly, gender roles have also been found particularly salient among some Hispanic ethnic groups and may consciously or unconsciously be related to the perceived power of Latinas to lead. The gender role of *marianismo*, which is now receiving scholarship attention, characterizes the Hispanic woman as self-sacrificing and "living in the shadows" of her husband, family, and children (Gil and Vasquez, 1997). Traditional Western-based leadership style was characterized by more masculine behaviors, yet some of these may now be considered gender neutral (Escamilla, 2009). However, this shift remains to be examined among Latinas in general and Latina leaders specifically. However, we can assume that Latinas who endorse *marianismo* values may have to determine how to assert their leadership and power in ways that remain congruent with their self-identity. Latinas must find ways to reconcile being a wife, mother, and family member with her leadership role, which has been noted to be a salient struggle and challenge among minority leaders, which are often tokenized within organizations (Hite, 2007; Pettigrew and Martin, 1987).

Although racial and cultural dynamics in organizational life remains a fairly marginalized area of scholarship, the brief discussion mentioned above reflects the structural, cultural, and systemic issues that must be addressed and explored in order to understand Latinas' authority and power in their leadership role. Latinas who have "made it" appear to have learned how to navigate conflicting cultural values and how to rely on their culture as a source of strength in their leadership. However, this is subject to further empirical investigations.

Structural Barriers

The last important factors to consider are structural barriers related to racism and discrimination. The United States society has been marked by notions of inferior and superior peoples based on the social construction of race. Therefore, there must be a discussion of power differentials between minority and majority groups in order to understand the experience of Latina leaders. For example, England et al. (2004) noted that women who are privileged (i.e., belong to the perceived dominant group) based on their race, national origin, and immigration status are more likely to have employment. While all women continue to experience barriers related to gender, Latinas as women and as members of marginalized ethnic and racial groups face additional obstacles in the workplace and in their leadership roles.

According to Elliott (2005), discrimination charges filed with the EEOC in 2003 by Latinas had increased significantly since 1992. For example, there was a 68 percent increase in sexual discrimination charges, a 120 percent increase sexual harassment charges, and a 183 percent increase in racial or ethnic discrimination charges. The increase suggests the persistence of discrimination that Latinas continue to experience in the workforce and also highlights the importance of attending to racial and ethnic discrimination when discussing Latinas in leadership positions. It also highlights the importance of understanding racial and cultural dynamics in organizational life.

Theories of racial identity have implications for some of these statistics. Helms (1995) suggested that racial identity might operate at a psychological level as a worldview to understand oneself as a racial being, which in turn may affect perceptions of discrimination. However, understanding the meaning of race and racial identity among Hispanics is complicated by several issues, such as 1) the lack of uniformed understanding of what it means to be a race among Hispanics, 2) the fact that they are racially diverse, and 3) the many ways in which race is interpreted by Hispanics depending on their national origin or ethnic heritage (Mazzula, 2009). Currently, there is a dearth of literature on the racial dynamics at play in Latina leadership. Although a discussion of racial identity and racial discrimination is beyond the scope of this chapter, it is important to note that we have little understanding of racial dynamics in the workforce in general, or how they are related to Latinas in leadership in particular. Racial and ethnic identity scholarship, however, suggests that identifying positively with members of one's racial/cultural group serves to buffer against stressors, such as prejudice and discrimination (Phinney, 1996). Yet personal struggles may arise when minorities internalize negative attitudes about their perceived minority racial group membership. Internalizing inferior notions and negative stereotypes about their racial group may result in Latinas' perceived incompetence to lead effectively, irrespective of their ability or capability. On the contrary, Latinas who have positive racial and ethnic identity may not internalize discriminatory or stereotypical messages that they may receive in the workforce and may be more able to navigate racial and cultural dynamics without them interfering with their authority and leadership or their experience in general.

In addition to racial and ethnic discrimination, Latinas face additional obstacles related to their immigration status. As noted previously, more than half of Latinas in the workforce are immigrants. Furthermore, acceptance of different cultures is a relative new phenomena. Traditionally U.S. society held the expectation that individuals had to abandon their ethnic cultural behaviors in order to become American and gain access to American opportunities—anything that connected them to their culture of origin (i.e., native language or ethnic enclaves) was seen as negatively affecting assimilation (Berry, 2006). Despite diversity initiatives in the workforce, the notion of the "other' (i.e., those who are not representative of dominant white American culture) remains a central aspect of American society and organizational life. Therefore, Latinas in leadership may find themselves having to "prove" that they are capable of effectively leading those who may not perceive them as a member of their group or who perceive that they lack the ability to lead. Oftentimes, Latinas experience these types of discriminatory experiences as microaggressions (i.e., subtle, often unconscious forms of racism) related to their racial or cultural background, leaving them feeling puzzled by those interactions (Hite, 2007). Latinas also often find themselves as "tokens" in organizational life, which implies their otherness (Hite), and may find themselves learning to navigate these experiences regularly in their leadership roles.

Although I in no way condone this, Latinas' experiences with racism and discrimination may serve to strengthen their leadership role. For example, experiences of oppression may be related to Latina leaders' long history of political activism; their efforts in grassroots organizing reflects their personal and interpersonal investment in serving as agents of change for the advancement of people (Segura, 2003). Furthermore, racial and ethnic stereotypes that question the competence of minorities to lead has helped some minority leaders assist in and validate the experience of their subordinates (Trevino and Nelson, 2004). Similarly, in her study of Latinas in professional occupations, Hite (2007) found that some Latinas' persistence is driven by their need to challenge some of these racial and ethnic stereotypes.

Conclusion

In conclusion, the statistical data and structural and systemic barriers that Latinas encounter in society at large and in leadership in particular highlight the resilience and persistence of the many Latina leaders who have "made it." Although women in general continue to experience glass ceilings in leadership, the challenges of leadership is even greater for Latinas who are members of marginalized groups based on gender, race, ethnicity, and culture. It appears that Latina leaders who have "made it" today and throughout the history of America have found ways in which to navigate oppression, racism, and cultural values that at times are in direct opposition to the dominant white American cultural values embedded in American organizational life. Latina leaders also appear knowledgeable about themselves as racial and cultural beings, are able to navigate these barriers while remaining grounded in their identity, and make a connection with their subordinates in a personally and interpersonally meaningful way. As Latinas take on more leadership roles, they will continue to serve as agents of change in various aspects of American life and serve as a significant proportion of transformational leaders in the United States.

Notes

1. The terms *Hispanics* and *Latinos* are used interchangeably throughout this chapter to identify people from Mexico, Cuba, Puerto Rico, Central America, and South America. The term *Latina* refers to a Hispanic woman; *Latino* refers to a Hispanic man. Hispanics can be of any racial group.

2. These percentages were calculated for the purpose of this chapter from the 2009 U.S. Department of Labor, Bureau of Labor Statistics, Current Population Survey, Table 3 and Table 4.

3. Ibid.

4. Unless otherwise noted, the statistical data represents noninstitutionalized individuals who are 16 years or older.

5. Acculturation is a multidimensional construct capturing behavioral, affective, and cognitive domains and bidirectional. Traditionally, acculturation was understood as a unidirectional construct with movement away from one's culture of origin toward endorsement of the dominant group's culture. Currently, some acculturation researchers suggest that membership in each cultural group should be considered independently to understand the experience of bicultural people. Thus, new terms have been introduced and the construct of acculturation has been expanded. Acculturation is now considered by some scholars as the continuum that captures the socialization or adjustment into the mainstream culture (e.g., dominant culture continuum or Anglo-American culture) and enculturation as the continuum that captures the retention of the individual's culture of origin (e.g., nondominant or home culture continuum). The complexity of acculturation and enculturation is not discussed in this chapter for the sake of simplicity. However, when using the term acculturation, I assume its multidimensionality and bidirectionality.

6. Throughout this chapter, I make reference to Hispanics' endorsement of collectivist values. Collectivism is characterized by several distinct values and not all Hispanics may endorse all these values equally. Similarly, most of the research conducted with Hispanics on collectivism has been conducted with specific Hispanic ethnic groups (e.g., Mexican Americans). The extent to which this is generalizable to other Hispanic ethnic groups remains an area of further investigation. Therefore, while I compare collectivist and individualistic cultural values throughout the chapter, readers are warranted not to overgeneralize these discussions. Similarly, collectivism and individualism are at the extreme poles of a spectrum and significant within-group differences are found between both of these worldviews.

References

Ardichvili, A., Mitchell, J. A., and Jondle, D. (2009). Characteristics of ethical business cultures. *Journal of Business Ethics, 85*(4), 445–451.

Author. (June 2005). Diversity at work: Women of color crave family benefits. *Working Mother.*

Bartunek, J. M., Walsh, K., and Lacey, C. A. (2000). Dynamics and dilemmas of women leading women. *Organizational Science, 11*(6), 589–610.

Bass, B., and Bass, R. (2008). *The Bass handbook of leadership: Theory, research, and managerial applications*, 4th ed. New York, NY: Free Press.

Berry, J. W. (2005). Acculturation: Living successfully in two cultures. *International Journal of Intercultural Relations, 29*, 697–712.

Berry, J. W. (2006). Contexts of acculturation. In D. L. Sam and J. W. Berry (Eds.), *The Cambridge handbook of acculturation psychology* (pp. 27–42). Cambridge, NY: Cambridge University Press.

Carli, L., and Eagly, A. (2001). Gender, hierarchy, and leadership: An introduction. *Journal of Social Issues*, 57(4), 629–636.

Catalyst (1999). *Women of color in corporate management: Opportunities and barriers.* New York, NY: Author.

Cohen, P. N., and Bianchi, S. M. (1999). Marriage, children, and women's employment: What do we know? *Monthly Labor Review, 122* (December), 22–31.

Constantine, M., Robinson, J., Wilton, L., and Caldwell, L. (2002). Collective self-esteem and perceived social support as predictors of cultural congruity among Black and Latino college students. *Journal of College Student Development, 43*(3), 307–316.

Cooney, R. S., and Ortiz, V. (1983). Nativity, national origin, and Hispanic female participation in the labor force. *Social Sciences Quarterly 64,* 510–523.

Eagly, A. H., and Johnson, B. T. (1990). Gender and leadership style: A meta-analysis. *Psychological Bulletin, 108*(2), 233–256.

Eagly, A., and Johannesen-Schmidt, M. (2001). The leadership styles of women and men. *Journal of Social Issues*, 57(4), 781–797.

Eagly, A., Johannesen-Schmidt, M., and van Engen, M. (2003). Transformational, transactional, and laissez-faire leadership styles a meta-analysis comparing women and men. *Psychological Bulletin, 129*, 569–591.

Elliott, M., (2005). Hispanic women at work, Statistical Brief No. 6. Retrieved from National Council of La Raza Web site, http://www.nclr.org/content/publications/detail/32940/, on June 15, 2010.

England, P., Garcia-Bea, C., and Ross, M. (2004). Women's employment among Blacks, Whites, and three groups of Latinas: Do more privileged women have higher employment? *Gender and Society, 18*(4), 494–509.

Escamilla, O. M. (August 2009). How women lead: A look at leadership, values, and leadership behavior in Hispanic women. In *Communiqué: Ethnic Minority Leadership*. Retrieved from American Psychological Association, Office of Ethnic Minority Affairs Web site, http://www.apa.org/pi/oema/resources/communique/2009/08/august-special.pdf, on [date].

Garcia, E. (2005). *The Ohtli encuentro: Women of color share pathways to leadership*. Boerne, TX: Sor Juana Press.

Gil, R. M., and Vasquez, C.I. (1997). *The Maria paradox: How Latinas can merge old world traditions with new world self-esteem*. New York: G. P. Putman's Sons.

Gordon, M. M. (1964). *Assimilation in American life: The role of race, religion, and national origins*. New York: Oxford University Press.

Helms, J. E. (1995). An update of Helm's White and people of Color racial identity models. In J. G. Ponterotto, J. M. Casas, L. A. Suziki, and C. M. Alexander, (Eds.), *Handbook of multicultural counseling* (pp. 181–198). Thousand Oaks, CA: Sage Publications.

Hetty van Emmerik, I., Euwema, M. C., and Wendt, H. (2008). Leadership behaviors around the world, the relative importance of gender versus cultural background. *International Journal of Cross-Cultural Management, 8*(3), 297–315.

Hite, L. (2007). Hispanic women managers and professionals: Reflections on life and work. *Gender, Work, and Organization, 14*(1), 20–36.

Hondagneu-Sotelo, P. (1997). Working "without papers" in the United States: Toward the integration of legal status in frameworks of race, class, and gender. In E. Higginbotham and M. Romero (Eds.), *Women and work: Race, class and ethnicity* (pp. 101–125). Thousand Oaks, CA: Sage.

Kohatsu, E. L. (2006). Acculturation: Current and future directions. In R. T. Carter (Vol. Ed.), *Handbook of racial-cultural psychology and counseling: Theory and research*, Vol. 1 (pp. 207–231). New York: Wiley.

Logan, J. R. (2003). *The new Latinos: Who they are, where they are*. Retrieved from Lewis Mumford Center for Comparative Urban and Regional Research, University at Albany Web site, http://www.shccnj.org/ new_latinos.htm, on January 12, 2009.

Mazzula, S. L. (2009). *Bicultural competence: The role of acculturation, collective self-esteem and racial identity.* Doctoral dissertation. Available from ProQuest Dissertations database. UMI No. 3388463.

McRae, M. B., and Short, E. L. (2010). *Racial and cultural dynamics in group and organizational life: Crossing boundaries.* Thousand Oaks, CA: Sage Publications, Inc.

Miranda, A. O., and Matheny, K. B. (2000). Socio-psychological predictors of acculturative stress among Latino adults. *Journal of Mental Health Counseling, 22(4),* 306–317.

National Council of La Raza (2007). The status of Latinos in the labor force: Fact sheet. Retrieved from http://www.nclr.org/content/publications/download/50719 on.

Nicholson, S. P., Pantoja, A. D., and Segura, G. S. (2005). *Race matters: Latino racial identities and political beliefs.* Paper WP2005-47. Retrieved from http://repositories.cdlib.org/igs/WP2005-47 on June 18, 2010.

Pedraza, S. (1991). Women and migration: The social consequences of gender. *Annual Review of Sociology, 17,* 303–325.

Pettigrew, T. F., and Martin, J. (1987). Shaping the organizational context for Black American inclusion. *Journal of Social Justice Issues, 43,* 41–78.

Phinney, J. S. (1996). When we talk about American ethnic groups, what do we mean? *American Psychologist, 51,* 918–927.

Prindeville, D. M. (2003). Identity and the politics of American Indian and Hispanic women leaders. *Gender and Society, 17*(4), 591–608.

Ramos, B. M. (2005). Acculturation and depression among Puerto Ricans in the Mainland. *Social Work Research, 29*(2), 95–106.

Reid, L. (2002). Occupational segregation, human capital, and motherhood: Black women's higher exit rates from full-time employment. *Gender and Society 16,* 728–747.

Romero, M. (2002). *Maid in the U.S.A.,* 2nd ed. London: Routledge.

Sam, D. L., and Oppedal, B. (2002). Acculturation as a developmental pathway. In W. J. Lonner, D. L. Dinnel, S. A. Hayes, and D. N. Sattler (Eds.), *Online readings in psychology and culture* (Unit 8, Chapter 6). Retrieved from Center for Cross-Cultural Research, Western Washington University Web site, http://www.wwu.edu/~culture, on June 23, 2010.

Santiago-Rivera, A. (2003). Latinos values and family transitions: Practical considerations for counseling. Counseling and Human Development. Retrieved from Commonwealth of Virginia Department of Mental Health, Mental Retardation and Substance Abuse Services Web site, http://www. dmhmrsas.virginia.gov/2008CLC/OHRDM -CLC-Diff-Communities.htm on June 23, 2010.

Schwartz, S. J., and Zamboanga, B. L. (2008). Testing Berry's model of acculturations: A confirmatory latent class approach. *Cultural Diversity and Ethnic Minority Psychology, 14*(4), 275–285.

Segura, D. (2003). Navigating between two worlds: The labyrinth of Chicana intellectual production in the academy. *Journal of Black Studies, 34*(1), 28–51.

Stewart, E. C., and Bennett, M. J. (1991). *American cultural patters: A cross-cultural perspective,* 2nd ed. Yarmouth, ME: Intercultural Press, Inc.

Sue, D. W., and Sue, D. (2008). *Counseling the culturally diverse: Theory and practice,* 5th ed. New York, NY: Wiley.

Trevino, L., and Nelson, K. (2004). *Managing business ethics: Straight talk about how to do it right.* New York, NY: Wiley.

U.S. Bureau of the Census (2008). U.S. Hispanic population surpasses 45 million now 15 percent of total. Retrieved from http://www.census.gov/Press-Release/www/release/archives/population/011910.html on July 27, 2010.

U.S. Department of Labor, Bureau of Labor Statistics (July 2008). *Highlights of women's earnings in 2008.* Report No. 1017. Retrieved from http://www.bls.gov/cps/cpswom2008.pdf on July 27, 2010.

U.S. Department of Labor, Bureau of Labor Statistics. (2003). Current population survey, Table 8. Employment status of persons by presence and age of own children, sex, race, Hispanic or Latino ethnicity, and marital status, annual average 2003.

U.S. Department of Labor, Bureau of Labor Statistics. (2009A). Current population survey, Table 3. Employment status of the civilian noninstitutional population by age, sex, and race. Retrieved from http://www.bls.gov/cps/cpsaat3.pdf on July 28, 2010.

U.S. Department of Labor, Bureau of Labor Statistics. (2009B). Current population survey, Table 4. Employment status of the civilian noninstitutional population by age, sex, and race, and Hispanic or Latino ethnicity. Retrieved from http://www.bls.gov/cps/cpsaat4.pdf on July 27, 2010.

U.S. Department of Labor, Bureau of Labor Statistics. (2009C). Current population survey, Table 10. Employed persons by occupation, race, Hispanic or Latino ethnicity, and sex. Retrieved from http://www.bls.gov/cps/cpsaat10.pdf on July 30, 2010.

U.S. Department of Labor, Bureau of Labor Statistics (September 2009). *Women in the labor force: A databook*. Report No. 1018. Retrieved from http://www.bls.gov/cps/wlf-intro-2009.pdf on July 30, 2010.

U.S. Department of Labor, Bureau of Labor Statistics. (November 2009). *Labor force characteristics by race and ethnicity, 2008*. Report 1020. Retrieved from http://www.bls.gov/cps/cpsrace2008.pdf on July 27, 2010.

U.S. Department of Labor, Bureau of Labor Statistics. (2010A). Current population survey, Table A-20. Employed persons by occupation, race, Hispanic or Latino ethnicity, and sex. Retrieved from http://www .bls.gov/web/empsit/cpseea20.pdf on July 30, 2010.

U.S. Department of Labor, Bureau of Labor Statistics. (2010B). Labor force statistics from current population survey: Databases, tables and calculators by subject. Retrieved from http://www.bls.gov/data on July 28, 2010.

U.S. Office of Personnel Management. (April 2010). *Ninth annual report to the president on Hispanic employment in the federal government*. Retrieved from http://www.opm.gov/Diversity/Hispanic/annual/ reports/April2010/HispanicEmployment-2010.pdf on July 30, 2010.

Zavala-Martinez, I. (1987). En la lucha: The economic and socioemotional struggles of Puerto Rican women. *Women and Therapy, 6(4)*, 3–24.

9

Living the Questions

Karen Dill Bowerman

As the years pass, I realize that there are more authentic questions about women's lives as leaders than there are authoritative answers. Women's leadership in business and organizational life is both a macro- and individual phenomenon of our culture. We grapple with the personal issues and find our way. Those macro questions—particularly when prescriptive in nature—may remain elusive for a long while.

As our professional lives evolve, we work through personal questions that we have for that moment in time. For example, to a young woman and future leader, there will come an individual question that should be a conscious question. The answer should not be given simply by her biological clock, but by her mind and heart. How will you answer the young woman who asks you for guidance? Should she choose to marry and become a parent? If so, when? We know that still today, marriage and parenting are linked with higher salaries for men; however, the opposite is true for women. Is salary the driving force for the individual? Should it be the driving force? Each young woman should answer these kinds of questions thoughtfully for herself. If she chooses to become a parent, should she drop out of the workforce? Studies have shown that women workers with children, even when they have an MBA, worked fewer hours per week and therefore interrupted career progression more frequently than men, which led to divergence of salaries. Again, what is the driving force for the individual? Each mother should answer these kinds of questions pensively for herself. These individual questions are critical, and we tend to work—or muddle—through them for that moment in time. For example, we end up with a partner who cherishes an equal, or we don't. We change careers, or we don't, and the individual's personal question is answered.

The global cultural questions about women's lives as leaders remain vibrant and sometimes vexing. *Live the questions now*, as Rainer Maria Rilke advised in *Letters to a Young Poet* in 1903:

> . . . I would like to beg you dear Sir, as well as I can, to have patience with everything unresolved in your heart and to try to love the questions themselves as if they were locked rooms or books written in a very foreign language. Don't search for the answers, which could not be given to you now, because you would not be able to live them. And the point is to live everything. Live the questions now. Perhaps then, someday far in the future, you will gradually, without even noticing it, live your way into the answer.

Perhaps you have also worked in a "man's world." I shall never forget the reality of looking around the conference table after being on a new job for many days and realizing that there were no other women there. How shocking not to have noticed! As a woman who was even then conscious of data and research about the low numbers of women in top management, how amazing it was not to have seen! Living the moment, rather than living the questions, closes our eyes and minds to the full experience of life as a woman and a leader.

Leadership is a process of social influence to move others toward a desired goal. Managers who are not capable of influencing others in their organizations and for their organizations are not leaders. You may have read the cry of even high-ranking women who feel invisible in certain organizational settings. Consider the following experience, which is not uncommon to women: A woman contributes significant and unique insights at a meeting that are later credited to a garrulous male in the group. I wonder if that woman is even capable of social influence in her organization, given what transpires, or if her leadership is actually achieved (even though the male is given credit) because her unique insight is given credibility? I contend that the answer to this question, when it finally comes, does matter. It matters because if the woman whose contributions are impactful is herself invisible, her organization is likely to lose out on her higher-level contributions in the future (invisible people are promoted less frequently). For the organization to live only the moment, rather than living the questions, closes its eyes and minds to the full experience of its human resources.

There is not one leadership profile. Leaders can be charismatic or boring. They can be older or younger. They can be male or female. Advocates of the traits approach to the study of leadership from the past century gave up on its attempt to identify *the one complete list* of traits that all leaders must have. So, why is it that many still attribute leadership characteristics to the male stereotype—competitive, results-oriented, self-confident and competent, or taking charge (versus "taking care," as women are characterized in the corresponding female stereotype)? Such a perspective is not new, whether looking at the credit given to Aristotle for styling women as "unfinished men" or noting the title of a 1920 movie release, *The Inferior Sex*. But does this perspective even matter, given that thoughtful people *know* there is not one leadership profile, and that stereotypes are nothing more than generalizations that fail to apply to you or me as leaders? Do not search too hard right now for the answer, because there is no immediate correct answer. Instead, live the question. As Rilke said, we are not to search for the answers which cannot be given to us now, because we would then be unable to live them. And the point is to live everything.

We in Western society focus on what makes men and women different as leaders. Why do we do that? Over 2,500 years ago, Confucius said that all people are basically the same—just their habits differ. If one thinks about the commonalities of the human condition, indeed we all have more in common than that which is different. We need clean water, food, and sleep; we crave love; and we want a social existence with friendship (see the movie *March of the Penguins* if you think this phenomenon is limited to the human condition). We seek achievement and respect from others, we enjoy music, we want to understand why we exist on earth. To focus on both our commonalities and disparities is indeed healthy; however, to ignore one at the expense of the other is limiting in both sensitivity and in harnessing diversity.

In speaking about men and women as leaders, I often refer to remarks made by the cofounder of Honda Motor Company, Takeo Fujisawa. He said that Japanese and American managers are 95 percent the same, but differ in all important respects. Similarly, I contend that men and women as leaders are 95 percent the same, but that the 5 percent difference can make diversity a tremendous asset, or lead to intolerance. Leaders play a key role in living the question in order to help ensure in the long run that diversity, including diversity of gender, is a source of strength rather than a weakness.

Some self-help/motivational books for women leaders are very good, or even useful. Some are well intentioned, but focus exclusively on how to improve *the woman*. How many times do we need to hear that leaders need to work hard and play hard, and become balanced? The fact is that if discrimination or harassment reigns in an organization, improving oneself may have little bearing on one's potential for becoming a leader and influencing others. If top management values only those employees who work 65 hour weeks, then striving for a work–life balance is nothing more than a dream anyway. Some change for women clearly comes from the advancement of individual women leaders, but lasting improvement comes from *organizational* development toward the advancement of women leaders in general. Why do some well-intentioned women (and men) in management concentrate on self-help books for women as opposed to helping the organization improve its practices? Are they, in fact, leaders? As we live such questions and gradually improve policies for organizational development, we will someday live our way into the answer.

Research shows that women who successfully lead transformational change often feel that they pay a personal price. Adversaries of change set the price and then try to force payment, whether successfully or not. It may come in the form of relentless opposition to future inconsequential matters, with the apparent intent of wearing down the leader, who may not have arranged for enough outspoken political advocates. All such feelings of having to pay a price for leading change are not gender-based; transformational change, by its nature, brings some managers out of their comfort zones. Responses to women leaders may often be idiosyncratic, however. For example, some studies have shown that when leadership requires a person who is both respected and liked, women may face a trade-off that men are unlikely to face. Thus the transformational change may take place out of respect, but the trade-off for the woman leader over the longer term is that she will be less liked. (Alternatively, the change may take place because she is liked, but after the transformation, she will be less respected.) Is the cost to bringing transformational change due to the leader's behavior, or due to the followers' reaction to a woman leader? Perhaps we will gradually live our way into the answer sometime in the distant future.

Like most teenage girls, I thought I had answers. I know now that I do not have them. But I've also lived for years with the questions (and others) that I've raised in this short chapter. By living these questions, I am living! I could not understand why there weren't more women at the conference table (mentioned above), much less why one would not have noticed their absence, even though there was progress in women's pay, in occupational clustering, and in hammering against what we now call the glass ceiling. Early in my career, I identified with the woman who felt invisible, and "hoped" that she had consummated her leadership when her perspective was adopted because I had been taught that it is our responsibility as women to make our world a better place. I carried unresolved the question of why many attribute leadership characteristics to the male stereotype, and fundamentally hoped that both men and women could happily and equally adopt those characteristics of the male stereotype in organizational life (until I realized mid-way in my career that I had chosen not to live stereotypical male organizational attributes!). I assumed initially that we focus on what makes men and women different as leaders only because it entertains us and even makes us laugh. However, later the question persisted because my assumption became suspect. I had never wanted to read self-help books for women, but did not realize why until I was mid-way in my doctoral program and the idea of focusing on *organizational* improvement became exciting. I questioned the price women leaders pay personally when they bring transformational change because I grew up revering women like Eleanor Roosevelt. Why should a price be waged?

As managers and leaders, we prepare ourselves for the constantly arriving and inherently dynamic future if we live the questions about women as leaders now.

Reference

Rilke, R. M. (1903). *Letters to a young poet.* Retrieved from http://www .carrothers.com/rilke_main.htm, on August 7, 2010.

10

Social Psychological Perspectives on Discrimination against Women Leaders

Nicole L. Cundiff and Margaret S. Stockdale

About a decade ago, one could count the number of female CEOs of *Fortune* 500 companies on one hand. By 2010, it took two hands and a foot (*Fortune*, 2010). Despite this modest growth in women in top business leadership positions, women have made meaningful advancements in other leadership positions. The percent of managerial posts in the United States occupied by women has grown from less than 14 percent in the 1950s to almost 51 percent by the year 2007 (Catalyst, 2008). Over 40 percent of the global workforce are women, and in more developed countries (Europe, North America, Australia/New Zealand, and Japan), women make up 46 percent of the workforce (LABORSTA, 2009).

Although these statistics appear promising, there is disturbing evidence that women may not be catching up to men on important career outcomes as quickly as hoped. Blau and Kahn (2006) studied the change in the gender pay gap in the United States and noted that since the early 1990s, the gap was not closing as rapidly as it had been in the 1970s and 1980s. Their careful analysis showed that human capital arguments could not adequately explain the slowdown because women have had higher educational attainment than men in the past couple of decades. Also, women have been moving into higher-paying sectors, leaving room for questions about the persistent inequality of women's wages compared to men's. This unexplained variance in the pay gap suggests that discrimination may be playing a significant role.

Evidence of discrimination can also be found in the upper echelons of organizations. *Catalyst*, a leading research and advocacy organization for women business leaders, recently reported that the percent of women on *Financial Post* 500 boards (representing 4,505 directors) increased only 1 percent from 2007 to 2009 (to 14%) and that 42 percent of these boards still had no female directors (Catalyst, 2010). In a separate study, *Catalyst* researchers tracked over 4,000 male and female MBA alumni who graduated from the top 25 business schools in Asia, Canada, Europe, and the United States between 1996 and 2007 and compared them on starting salary, entry position level, current salary, current position, and salary growth (Carter and Silva, 2010). The results were astonishing. Controlling for industry type and geographic region, women started at lower positions and earned significantly lower salaries than men—on average $4,600 less per year—and differences between men and women in both salary and position level only increased as they progressed through-out their careers (i.e., men's salaries increased faster than women's, and men were quicker to climb the career ladder). The results did not change when looking only at the subsample who aspired to CEO and senior exec-utive positions or the subsample who did not have children (Carter and Silva, 2010). Additionally, women MBAs who pursued nontraditional careers in public and not-for-profit sectors had slower salary and career growth than women who chose traditional career paths in private industry, but pursuing nontraditional paths did not adversely affect men's careers (Carter and Silva, 2010).

As more women advance in the workforce, it is imperative to have a better understanding of the current issues they face. For instance, many women entering the labor force are still in feminized occupations and industries, such as social work and education (Betz, 2005; Eagly and Carli, 2007; Garcia-Retamero and López-Zafra, 2006; Reskin, 1993); according to *Catalyst*, these types of occupations tend to hinder salary and advancement for women. Therefore, gaining insights on the barriers that women encounter during their careers can help educate current and future leaders about the need for gender equity in leadership positions. This chapter will focus on identifying and addressing discrimination as it applies to female leaders.

Gender Discrimination against Female Managers and Leaders

Prejudice and discrimination exist and are reinforced within organizational systems; these systems require effort and resources to change the culturally embedded processes that keep them grounded in the status quo. Discrimination against women in leadership positions can be manifested in terms of access or treatment. Disproportionately selecting men for management positions or for other career paths that could lead to leadership and compensating men at disproportionately higher rates than women in similar occupations qualify as access discrimination. Judging the performance of female leaders (or women in occupations with a leadership career path) to be inferior to men's; regarding such women as being less likable; shutting these women out of important developmental, mentoring, and networking opportunities; and creating a hostile or chilly work environment are examples of treatment discrimination. Ample evidence has been amassed from experimental social psychology–based laboratory studies, as well as field research, to document these forms of discrimination in a variety of samples (Beilby and Baron, 1986; Blass, Brouer, Perrewe, and Ferris, 2007; Cuddy, Fiske, and Glick, 2004; Garcia-Retamero and López-Zafra, 2006; Green, 2009; Heilman, 2001).

For instance, Garcia-Retamero and López-Zafra (2006) found that promotion perceptions for women were highest in feminized industries (i.e., clothing manufacturing), but in masculine (i.e., auto manufacturing) and gender-neutral industries (i.e., marketing), men were perceived as more promotable. Further, promotion perceptions of men in feminized industries were similar to the women in these industries. Therefore, women, though not disadvantaged, did not enjoy an advantage over men even in feminized industries. Men, on the other hand, were advantaged in both masculine and gender-neutral industries.

Through the popular press and personal experiences, working women are familiar with the concept of the glass ceiling—the point at which women's career advancement becomes stifled. However, obstacles in women's careers do not necessarily occur directly before reaching the upper echelons of organizations. Women encounter discrimination from early childhood and throughout their lives, which interferes and dissuades them from entering into desired professions. For instance, women and girls are faced with disproportionate displays of heroes, historical figures, and role models of the opposing sex throughout their educational and professional advancement (Betz, 2005). This sends a message that women are not as important as men, potentially affecting young women's self-efficacy and self-esteem (Bandura, 2001; Lent, Brown, and Hackett, 1994).

Other barriers that women face in their ascension to leader positions include a lack of social support and mentors, sexual harassment and sexism, and the need to maintain multiple roles (family and work) (Betz, 2005; Eagly and Carli, 2007). Despite these disadvantages, women are starting to reach the upper echelons of organizations by breaking through some of the barriers that have detained them throughout the last few decades.

Alice Eagly and Linda Carli (2007) developed the metaphor of a labyrinth to illustrate the experiences and barriers facing women who aspire to leadership positions. They reported that women face a situation that can best be described as moving through a labyrinth when it comes to their careers; they must learn to negotiate through this labyrinth in order to obtain top leadership positions, as opposed to straighter paths typically established for men. The theoretical labyrinth is full of dead-ends and obstacles; however, it is perceivably surmountable where "paths to the top exist, and some women find them" (Eagly and Carli, p. 6).

The women who eventually progress through the glass ceiling or the labyrinth and achieve a leadership position must maintain many social expectations. First, women in some positions may be tokens and may have restricted power and expectations to go along with customized ways of doing work (Eagly and Carli, 2007). Second, they may take on or display leader-appropriate behaviors and characteristics, therefore going against expectations that women display more communal behaviors (Eagly and Karau, 2002). Incongruities between displayed roles and expectations may hinder evaluations of female leaders. For example, Heilman (2001) suggested that prescriptive stereotyping of women in organizational settings (expecting women to display stereotypical characteristics and admonishing those who do not) could limit their access into upper-echelon positions.

Networking or making connections with influential members of an organization or occupation is important in order to have a successful career. Female leaders encounter issues in networking due to culturally engrained practices within organizations, such as their intentional and unintentional exclusion from formal and informal communication channels. Women also tend to encounter tokenism when they are promoted into leadership roles in which they are not given as much authority or are not viewed as valuable as their male counterparts (Lyness and Thompson, 1997). Therefore, female leaders are less likely than male leaders to be included in their organization's social networks.

Finding suitable mentors can also be a problem for women because women in organizational leadership positions are scarce. Mentors, however, are necessary in order to create networks of relationships that will be sustained once the mentor leaves the organization and to create links to informal social networks (Thomas, 2001). For instance, Blass et al. (2007) argued that mentoring helps increase the political skill necessary to become a successful leader in an organization. Unfortunately, when examining the amount of organizational politics mentees gained from their mentoring, they found that political understanding and networking occurred for men but not for women. In other words, women did not benefit from mentoring in terms of building influential social networks as did men. Therefore, finding suitable mentors for female leaders can be difficult and may potentially result in unsuccessful networking opportunities.

Gender role beliefs and stereotypes are other important factors that have strong impacts on discrimination and that can wreak havoc on women's leadership trajectories at various career stages. For instance, stereotypes can impact women at the beginning of their career, while they are applying for a leadership position; during the interview process; or when they are interacting with followers once they hold a management role. The following is a review of social psychological forces that impact women's interest and ability to occupy and succeed in top management positions.

Social Psychological Forces Shaping Gender Disparities in Leadership

Women may be less likely than men to obtain leadership positions because of conflicts with other roles, self doubts about their fitness for such roles, or others' beliefs that they are not appropriate for such roles. Well-entrenched patriarchic social structures that stress women's reproductive and caregiving capacities over economic and achievement-centered aspirations shape women's expectations about their own place in society as well as others' beliefs about appropriate roles for women. Although attitudes toward women and gender roles have become more progressive and egalitarian over the last several decades, as described below, these deeply-rooted social systems still manifest insidious effects on the ability of women to obtain and succeed in leadership positions.

Gender Role Socialization

Differences in the social and economic roles that women and men hold in society are a major source of sex differences in social behavior, including one's own and others' expectations about family and career roles (Eagly, 1987; 1997). "The expectancies associated with gender roles act as normative pressures that foster behaviors consistent with these sex-typical work roles" (Eagly, 1997, p. 1381). For example, the gender role for women arises from the compassionate and nurturing activities that they perform in the family and in many female-dominated occupations, such as teacher, nurse, and social worker. To the extent that expectations about gender roles become internalized, endorsement of gender roles may become part of individuals' self-concepts. But internalization is not necessary to produce gender differences. People can behave in gender-expected manners through self-fulfilling prophecies also known as behavioral confirmation (Zanna and Pack, 1975): "People communicate gender-stereotypic expectations in social interactions and can directly induce the targets of these expectations to engage in behavior that confirms these expectations" (Eagly, 1997, p. 1381). Over time, women and men learn to specialize in the skills sets and attend to beliefs and values associated with those roles.

Gender role beliefs have evolved, and both women and men espouse more egalitarian attitudes toward gender roles than in the past. Nonetheless, differences in such beliefs still exist, and those who endorse traditional gender role beliefs tend to follow career patterns that reinforce traditional disparities. For instance, Judge and Livingston (2008) examined the role of gender role attitudes in explaining the gender pay gap using data from the National Longitudinal Survey of Youth (NLSY), which has been repeatedly administered to a national probability sample who were between the ages of 14–22 when first surveyed in 1979. The researchers found that over time, possessing traditional attitudes toward gender roles (e.g., that a woman's place is in the home, not the office or shop) was associated with men pursuing high-paying male-dominated occupations and women pursuing low-paying female-dominated occupations.

The influences of gender inequity affect women beyond the office, as women have historically been responsible for the majority of domestic work and continue in this role. According to *Catalyst* (2009), 68 percent of women in their twenties and thirties cited a commitment to personal and family responsibilities as a barrier to women's advancement. Additionally, Galinsky, Aumann, and Bond (2008) in a national probability sample found that 41 percent of workers believe that men should make the money and that women should take care of the home and family; only 67 percent of male workers believe that a working woman could be a good mother, whereas 80 percent of working women believe that working women are good mothers; men and women spend almost similar amounts of time with children on weekdays, although the roles they are playing during this interaction are not reported (3 hours for men and 3.8 hours for women); 67 percent of working women claim that they take the most responsibility in child care; and 70 percent of working women report doing most of the cooking in the household. Although Galinsky et al. claim that attitudes toward women in the workforce and home are changing, it can be inferred that there is still a major gap between male and female domestic work. Further, it is encouraging to see increases in the amount of time that men spend with their offspring. However, other areas of domestic work are inequitable and restrict the amount of time women can spend on their careers; this potentially creates family–work conflict.

To assess the impact of family–work conflict, Hoobler, Wayne, and Lemmon (2009) asked male and female workers about the amount of family–work conflict they were experiencing. Interestingly, even though women report being more responsible for the family than men, they reported less family–work conflict than men. However, perceptions of potential family–work conflict may still have an impact on women's careers. For instance, Hoobler et al. (2009) examined the perceptions of superiors regarding family–work conflict of female workers. They determined that women's bosses expected to the women to be the caregivers of a household, which was found to interfere with perceptions of performance, person–job fit, and nominations for promotions. More specifically:

Women were rated lower on job and organizational fit and performance . . . [by] their managers' perceptions of their family–work conflict. In keeping with research on stereotypical attributes ascribed to women, it seems that women are less likely than men to be perceived as good "fits" and high performers because they are viewed as responsible for family, which may be seen as incompatible with holding leadership/managerial positions. It may be that managers feel that higher levels of family–work conflict make women less focused on their jobs and careers; consequently, managers presume that they are less committed. (Hoobler et al., p. 951)

Therefore, as women attempt to navigate their careers, expectations of their home life may still interfere with their success.

Based on this research, it can be concluded that gender role socialization strongly shapes women's and men's role behavior and occupational decisions. It also shapes expectations and beliefs about women and men in the workforce. In the next section, we discuss the role of stereotyping and bias and their basis for discrimination against female leaders.

Stereotypes

One of the most prevalent problems that women in organizations encounter is stereotyping. A stereotype is an automatic cognitive categorization of particular traits in connection with group membership; this categorization can lead to negative beliefs and reactions (Devine, 1989). For example, labeling women as warm and caring is a stereotype that stems from traditional sociogender roles (Eagly and Karau, 2002). Further, negative emotion directed toward women is considered prejudice, whereas the actual treatment of a woman differently than a man based on their gender is discrimination.

Stereotyping can be both descriptive and prescriptive. Descriptive stereotyping is the process of attributing traits or characteristics to members of social categories. Prescriptive stereotyping describes attitudes toward individuals who enact characteristics believed to be appropriate for their social category, and by contrast, attitudes toward members who enact characteristics counter to those expected for their category—a process sometimes referred to as proscriptive stereotyping (Rudman and Glick, 2001).

Descriptive stereotyping often means that women are simply not perceived as leaders. For instance, in a study of male and female African American leaders, Peters, Kinsey, and Malloy (2004) found students were less likely to differentiate between female targets on leadership attributes than they were among male targets. That is, participants accurately perceived differences among male targets in whether they possessed leadership characteristics, but they uniformly perceived female targets as not possessing leadership characteristics. Therefore, women were less likely to emerge as leaders within workgroups (Peters et al.).

Perceivers tend to implicitly label women as nonleaders, whereas they differentiate men on leadership status and abilities. In another study, conducted by Fiske, Xu, Cuddy, and Glick (1999), lower-status people individuated (i.e., perceived individual differences and characteristics among a group of people) higher-status people, but high-status people did not individuate those of lower status. To put this another way, stereotypes are less likely applied to evaluations of higher-status individuals than to evaluations of lower-status individuals. Therefore, working women may be implicitly stereotyped and thus less likely to be categorized as leaders because of the widely held belief that the female gender role does not accord the same economic and social status as the male gender role.

Furthermore, those responsible for evaluating female employees may not distinguish among those who do and those who do not possess leadership qualities. Therefore, even women who manage to emerge as leaders (usually as tokens) may suffer nondifferential evaluations and be categorized as belonging to the group of "nonleader-like women" from which they emerged. Descriptive stereotypic processes such as these could continue to damage women's progression through various leadership roles.

Prescriptive stereotypes are estimations for how women in organizations *should* behave. Prescriptive stereotyping has the potential to affect evaluations of female leaders, depending on the alignment between prescripted leadership roles and salient demographic roles. For instance, women are commonly believed to express communal characteristics (i.e., being nurturing and calm) based on stereotypical prescriptions for appropriate female behaviors, whereas prescriptions for men are to express agentic qualities (i.e., being dominant and independent; Eagly and Karau, 2002).

Because many aspects of business leadership subsume agentic qualities, aspiring female leaders are caught in a double bind. As women, they may not be perceived as having the requisite characteristics needed for leadership; however, if they demonstrate their leadership capacity by enacting agentic traits, they are summarily disliked (Eagly and Karau, 2002; Heilman, 2001; Schein, 2001). For example, self-promotion, which is commonly expected among leaders to verify their qualifications, is viewed much more negatively when enacted by women than by men (Moss-Racusin and Rudman, 2010). Similarly, female managerial candidates who negotiate (an agentic behavior) are perceived more negatively than negotiating male managerial candidates (Bowles, Babcock, and Lai, 2007).

The quintessentially communal quality of warmth and the agentic quality of competence further reveal the paradox of descriptive and prescriptive stereotyping. Albeit both positive in nature, different combinations of warmth and competence evoke very different reactions, and people in various roles tend to be automatically linked with one of these combinations. Around the world, high-status individuals, such as white men, Christians, and fathers tend to be viewed as high in warmth and competence and, as such, are well liked and highly rewarded. Low-status, out-group members, such as the poor and homeless, tend to be viewed as lacking in warmth and competence and tend to be disliked (Cuddy, Fiske, Kwan et al., 2009; Fiske, Cuddy, Glick, and Xu, 2002). Of most interest are those who appear to be high in one dimension but low in the other. For example, male and female working professionals who are or are not also parents.

Fiske et al. (2002) created such scenarios and asked Princeton college students to rate each individual's perceived warmth and competence and the Princeton students' willingness to hire, train, and promote them. Regardless of whether a male professional was also a parent, he was viewed as warm and competent and received high marks for hiring, training, and promoting. However, among professional women, those described as being new mothers were perceived as warmer but less competent than professional women who were not mothers. Professional women were perceived as more competent but less warm than their maternal counterparts. Furthermore, the maternal professionals received lower marks for hiring, training, and promotion than nonparental professional women or professional men, regardless of their parental status.

Researchers have also shown that regardless of parental status, individuals suspected to be low in warmth but high in competence are likely to evoke cooperation from most employees, as it is in their best interest to do so (Fiske et al., 2002). However, historically such individuals tend to be treated in an active-hostile manner, such as being targets of physical aggression or sexual harassment (Berdahl, 2007). In contrast, groups perceived to be high in warmth and low in competence (i.e., working mothers) may receive help from fellow workers but be patronized in other ways. For instance, they may suffer from passive stereotyping, such as being labeled incompetent. Therefore, women are particularly susceptible to different forms of prejudice throughout their careers: they are perceived as warm and likable when they assume traditional female roles (motherhood) but are viewed as incompetent for other roles; when they prove their competence in nontraditional roles (e.g., leadership) they are perceived as cold and unlikeable.

How women are perceived will influence whether they are selected for a leadership position and how they are sized up once in those positions. Inherently, people have different qualities or characteristics. Nonetheless, the same characteristic presented by a man or woman can be interpreted differently, thus affecting evaluations of the target individual (Eagly and Carli, 2007). This creates twofold issues for female leaders. If women conform to traditional female stereotypes, they are not perceived to have characteristics of a competent leader. If they steer away from traditional stereotypes and enact agentic traits, then they are perceived to be competent, but unlikable.

Women's Leadership Advantage

Despite prescriptive and descriptive stereotyping that impedes the perception and evaluation of women as leaders, women may have a slight advantage with regard to the contemporarily popular notion of transformational leadership. Transformational leadership occurs when leaders are able to motivate followers toward organizational goals and increase followers' sense of group identity over self (Seltzer and Bass, 1990). Transformational leadership includes a variety of substyles, such as individualized consideration, intellectual stimulation, and inspirational motivation (also known as charisma) and is perceived to be a highly effective leadership style (Avolio, Bass, and Jung, 1999; Bass, 1990). For instance, transformational leaders should be successful at obtaining motivation and commitment from followers due to more personalized interactions stemming from the individualized consideration subdimension.

Eagly and Johannesen-Schmidt (2001) found women to be slightly more transformational than men, whereas men more often than women took on a laissez-faire or unengaged leadership style. Additionally, Eagly and Johnson (1990) conducted a meta-analysis examining leadership styles between women and men. They found that women have a more interpersonal style of leadership and that men more task-oriented. Additionally, Nye and Forsyth (1991) found that female leaders with the highest leadership effectiveness ratings were the ones that demonstrated more role-congruent socioemotional or gender role–appropriate leadership orientations. However, for the most part, gender differences in leadership style have been small, and Eagly and Johnson's work shows that both women and men tend to exhibit effective leadership styles.

In more recent studies, perceptions of female leaders seem to be changing. For example, Powell, Butterfield, and Parent (2002) empirically examined stereotypical managerial characteristics and found that "feminized leadership" was more accepted than what had been found in past studies. However, managerial characteristics were still more masculine than feminine. Additionally, Eagly and Carli (2003) reviewed the literature and reported that female leadership styles are more effective in today's organizations, and that male and female managers rated successful female managers as having similar characteristics as successful middle managers (Duehr and Bono, 2006). More specifically, Duehr and Bono (2006) looked at how different categories of people are associated with various leadership characteristics, such as agentic, communal, task-oriented, relationship-oriented, and transformational leadership. Male and female managers as well as female students were as likely to associate women with successful middle-management characteristics as they were men. Only male business students held that men but not women were similar to traits ascribed to successful managers. In general, Duehr and Bono found both male and female managers are now being rated similarly on leadership characteristics by most groups of people.

Many studies have examined personality characteristics and leadership styles of male and female leaders. Based on these findings, we can conclude that there are only relatively small differences between men and women on these dimensions. Logically, no differences should be evident between women and men in selection for executive positions. However, objective measures depicting the raw numbers of men and women in top positions present a different story, most likely stemming from discriminatory practices toward women based on stereotypical perceptual bias.

Followers' Perceptions of Leaders

Once a woman becomes a leader, barriers shift from those associated with access into leadership positions to those associated with gaining the trust of followers (a form of treatment discrimination). Well-known leadership researchers Vroom and Jago (2007) suggested that leadership is a two-way process: the leader influencing followers' behaviors and followers influencing the leader's behavior. According to role congruity theory, the juxtaposition of prototypically female roles with leadership roles creates perceptions of role incongruity, and thus women are not perceived to be appropriate for leadership. For instance, Heilman, Block, Martell, and Simon (1989) found that men are perceived as leaders, but women, though viewed as similar to managers, were not categorized as leaders. Consequently, negative and automatic evaluations have the potential to influence female leaders' effectiveness in motivating and inspiring their followers.

If followers do not perceive deserving women as leaders, then female leaders are not likely to be viewed as charismatic (a subdimension of transformational leadership style), given that a characteristic of charisma is to stand out in the crowd or easily grasp the attention of the group. In global industries, having charisma is an important element to becoming a successful organizational leader, seeing how charismatic leaders are able to motivate subordinates to go beyond the call of duty in their obligations toward the organization (Bass, 1985, 2000). Additionally, women may have a harder time achieving the loyalty of followers if differentiation from one another is not present (Collinson, 2006).

As more women gain access to leadership positions, the perceptions and reactions of followers to these new leaders are highly important. In accordance, Lord and Maher defined leadership as "the process of being *perceived* by others as a leader" (emphasis added; 1993, p. 11). Therefore, the way that employees perceptually categorize a manager or executive is critical to whether they are perceived as having leadership characteristics. Theoretically, this perceptual process is influenced by schemas that followers hold for what constitutes a successful leader.

A schema represents knowledge and assumptions about abstract categories that is in an organized form. Leadership schemas are made up of prototypes and "they are stored in memory and are activated when followers interact with a person in a leadership position" (Epitropaki and Martin, 2004, p. 293). Understanding schemas in leadership perceptions is crucial, as much information processing occurs in leadership judgment and reaction. The perception of leadership takes on a top-down process, which is guided by the perceivers' schemas of appropriate leadership behavior and prototypical leadership characteristics (Lord and Emrich, 2001). Top-down processing is abstract processing based on information that has been stored in memory, whereas bottom-up processing is based on experiential data (Lord and Maher, 1993). For instance, assumptions and stereotypes about women are based on top-down processing. Lord and Emrich (2001) proposed that followers' schemas regarding leadership mediate leadership perceptions, such that followers' past experiences and general knowledge about leadership affect future perceptions of leaders.

Followers engage in both bottom-up and top-down processing in forming perceptions of leaders. A leader's outward characteristics, such as gender, along with contextual information from the organization (bottom-up processing) are used in conjunction with a follower's ideal representations of what constitutes a good leader (top-down processing) in order to categorize that person as a leader. Extending this thought, Hogg and Terry (2000) stated, "an intragroup prototypicality gradient exists—some people are or are perceived to be more prototypical than others" (p. 126). Therefore, some group members better match the expected prototype and are more likely to emerge as a leaders (Hogg, 2001). Leadership prototypes have the potential to benefit prototypical homogeneous group members and could act against members of minority groups, such as women, leaving room for majority group members to emerge as leaders (i.e., men). However, as we may be seeing in the current workforce, prototypical traits have the potential to shift over time and contexts (Hofstede, 1999; Hogg, 2001; Lord, Brown, and Freiberg, 1999).

Initial bias against women may dissipate quickly after followers get to know the female leader better; however, if there is enough information beforehand, then the bias may be moderated (Hogue and Lord, 2007). In other words, if there is enough information given to followers about a female leader before they enter into a new position then reduction in bias toward the leader can be expected (Landy, 2008). Some researchers, however, contend that additional information is not enough to create acceptance of female leaders. For instance, Heilman and Eagly (2008) stated that "the conditions that deter stereotyping are often absent in work settings ... Thus, stereotype-based perceptions of lack of fit are likely to take hold despite the availability of additional information" (p. 397).

Leadership prototypes may also change with environmental fluctuation in social expectations (Hogg, 2001; Hogue and Lord, 2007; Lord et al., 1999; Lord, Brown, Harvey, and Hall, 2001) relating to potentially shifting social/ leadership roles when it comes to women (Eagly and Carli, 2007; Schein, 2001). For instance, features of the social environment, such as organizational hierarchies, exemplars, and social networks, serve as input that shapes perceivers' connections between social categories, such as male with leader. As the social environment shifts, the connections between characteristics that represent a prototypical leader fluctuate. However, the adjustments occur slowly through a feedback process as the perceiver matches his or her prototypical representations with leaders' behaviors. Thus, although there are more women in management positions, it is going to take some time before followers' perceptions of female leaders at executive levels change.

Special Issues for Minority Female Leaders

While representation of women in management is low, representation of minority women in leadership positions is even lower, demonstrating the importance of understanding additional career barriers for people categorized into multiple nonprivileged groups (Hite, 2004). The theory of compounding oppression allocates that there are different categories of prejudice that can adversely affect people who have multiple disadvantaged social identities, such as being a women and an ethnic minority. For instance, although both white women and women of color are gaining access into organizations, the "glass ceiling" tends to be more prevalent for ethnic minority women than for white women (Eagly and Carli, 2007). This shows evidence that discrimination can have compounding effects on individuals depending on their unique characteristics. In accordance, Stanley (2009) reported that, "in predominantly White organizations, power dynamics may cause disempowering experiences for African American women that can occur in the form of challenging, resisting, resenting, undermining, or even ignoring a person's authority" (p. 552). Further, when it comes to wages, women fare remarkably poorly in comparison to men; women of color have even lower wages, with Hispanic women receiving the lowest rate (Eagly and Carli, 2007).

The leadership labyrinth, consisting of career-path obstacles and dead-ends, could be extended to nonmajority female groups to help explain the arduous path that they must take in order to obtain leadership positions within organizations. Eagly and Carli (2007) may be correct in their assertion that women no longer necessarily experience the "glass ceiling," and that this career ceiling may be deteriorating for minority groups in the United States, as well. The struggles that minority women experience and must maneuver through tend to be even more strenuous than for white women due to additional stereotyping related to multiple visible identities.

As previously discussed, leaders need to be accepted by their followers in order to be effective; however, many female minorities may have a harder time being accepted as a leader. Stereotyping based on minority status presents additional barriers for such women as they attempt to navigate and shape their careers. If minority women have a harder time influencing followers' behaviors, then they would unfairly have to spend extra effort in order to gain the trust and loyalty of their followers (House, Javidan, and Dorfman, 2001). Organizations need to be aware of the influences that multiple identities, such as gender and ethnicity, may have on their leaders, and extra steps need to be taken in order to ensure that the leaders will be supported during their crucial first weeks in office.

Recommendations

Many obstacles, some strenuous, seem to hinder women's advancement into leadership positions; unfortunately, the barriers to success do not stop once they get there. For instance, female leaders, once they start, have a harder time than their male counterparts at retaining tenure (Eagly and Carli, 2007). Many popular press publications on women in leadership instruct aspiring females to change their behaviors in a multitude of fashions. However, asking women to once again change in order to fit some prescribed standard is not only unfair but reinforces the standard instead of advocating for social change. If women are going to be perceived as equals to men, then social processes within organizations and society must change.

Employees and employers alike are going to have to challenge themselves to understand personal biases and automatic perceptual processes, as recognition is the first step to stopping stereotypical effects.

Organizations should strive to create change within their culture, emphasizing the inclusivity of female leaders. One cultural change that organizations could make to help shift perceptions of female leaders is to encompass values similar to feminine gender roles. For instance, Cundiff and Stockdale (2010) found that female leaders are perceived as more effective when they are embedded within collectivistic organizational cultures. Collectivistic cultures embrace team processes and group work and reward team-based rather than individual efforts (Hofstede and Hofstede, 2005). These types of activities tend to be more congruent with traditional female gender roles, such as being nurturing and community-oriented.

Organizations can also assist their female leaders by providing leadership development interventions that have been found to be equally successful for men and women. Leadership developmental programs, for instance, defined as "the development of the participant's knowledge, skills, ability, motivation, and/or perceived self-concept so as to enable him or her to exercise positive leadership influence" (Avolio, Mhatre, Norman, and Lester, 2009, p. 331), have had encouraging results for male and female aspiring leaders. Therefore, an equal opportunity-based leadership development program may help decrease the differences found between male and female leaders.

Conclusion

Members of many groups that have traditionally suffered discrimination are able to progress through organizations despite the barriers they encounter. Perhaps they have learned to ignore obstacles and been able to concentrate on negotiating the "labyrinth" of the workforce. However, career resilience or motivation to obtain one's career goals is a necessary element for women to persevere and overcome the barriers in their way; female leaders may need to have the "ability to adapt to changing circumstances, even when they are discouraging or disruptive" (London, 1998, p. 75). As reductions in inequalities and prescriptions toward gender roles in employment continue to become more egalitarian, more women will be found running the next generation of organizations.

References

Avolio, B. J., Bass, B. M., and Jung, D. I. (1999). Re-examining the components of transformational and transactional leadership using the multifactor leadership questionnaire. *Journal of Occupational and Organizational Psychology, 72,* 441–462.

Avolio, B. J., Mhatre, K., Norman, S. M., and Lester, P. (2009). The moderating effect of gender of leadership intervention impact: An exploratory review. *Journal of Leadership and Organizational Studies, 15,* 325–341.

Bandura, A. (2001). Social cognitive theory: An agentic perspective. *Annual Review of Psychology, 52,* 1–26.

Bass, B. M. (1985). Leadership: Good, better, best. *Organizational Dynamics, 13,* 26–40.

Bass, B. M. (1990). From transactional to transformational leadership: Learning to share the vision. *Organizational Dynamics. 18,* 19–31.

Bass, B. M. (2000). The future of leadership in learning organizations. *Journal of Leadership and Organizational Studies, 7,* 18–40.

Beilby, W. T., and Baron, J. N. (1986). Men and women at work: Sex segregation and statistical discrimination. *American Journal of Sociology, 91,* 759–799.

Berdahl, J. L. (2007). Harassment based on sex: Protecting social status in the context of gender hierarchy. *Academy of Management Review, 32,* 641–658.

Betz, N. E. (2005). Women's career development. In Brown, S.D., and Robert W. Lent (Eds.), *Career development and counseling: Putting theory and research to work* (pp. 253–277). Hoboken, NJ: John Wiley and Sons, Inc.

Blass, F. R., Brouer, R. L., Perrewe, P. L., and Ferris, G. R. (2007). Politics understanding and networking ability as a function of mentoring: The roles of gender and race.*Journal of Leadership and Organizational Studies, 14,* 93–105.

Blau, F. D., and Kahn, L. M. (2006). The U.S. gender pay gap in the 1990s: Slowing convergence. *Industrial and Labor Relations Review, 60(1),* 45–66.

Bowles, H. R., Babcock, L., and Lai, L. (2007). Social incentives for gender differences in the propensity to initiate negotiations: Sometimes it does hurt to ask. *Organizational Behavior and Human Decision Processes, 103,* 84–103.

Carter, N. M., and Silva, C. (2010). Pipeline's broken promise. New York: Catalyst. Retrieved from www.catalyst.org on May 26, 2010.

Catalyst. (2010). 2009 Catalyst Census: *Financial Post* 500 Women Board Directors. Retrieved from http://www.catalyst.org/file/369/2009_fp500 _core_report_final_021910.pdf on May 26, 2010.

Catalyst. (March 2009). Women in Their 20s and 30s, Quick Takes. http:// www.catalyst.org/publication/237/women-in-their-20s-30s.

Catalyst. (2008). *Women in U.S. management.* Retrieved from http://www .catalyst.org/file/193/qt_women_in_us_mgmt_1950-present.pdf on June 19, 2008.

Collinson, D. (2006). Rethinking followership: A post-structuralist analysis of follower identities. *The Leadership Quarterly, 17,* 179–189.

Cuddy, A. J. C., Fiske, S. T., and Glick, P. (2004). When professionals become mothers, warmth doesn't cut the ice. *Journal of Social Issues, 60,* 701–718.

Cuddy, A. J. C., Fiske, S. T., Kwan, V. S., Glick, P. S., Demoulin, S., Leyens, J-Ph., et al. (2004). Stereotype content model across cultures: Towards universal similarities and some differences. *British Journal of Social Psychology, 48,* 1–33.

Cundiff, N. L., and Stockdale, M. (August, 2010). *Past cares in research show results today: Perceptions of female executive's effectiveness.* Roundtable discussion for Academy of Management, Montreal, Canada.

Devine, P. G. (1989). Stereotypes and prejudice: Their automatic and controlled components. *Journal of Personality and Social Psychology, 56,* 5–18.

Duehr, E. E., and Bono, J. E. (2006). Men, women, and managers: Are stereotypes finally changing? *Personnel Psychology, 59,* 815–846.

Eagly, A. H. (1987). *Sex differences in social behavior: A social-role interpretation.* Hillsdale, NJ: Lawrence Erlbaum Associates.

Eagly, A. H. (1997). Sex differences in social behavior: Comparing social role theory and evolutionary psychology, *American Psychologist, 52,* 1380–1383.

Eagly, A. H., and Carli, L. L. (2003). The female leadership advantage: An evaluation of the evidence. *Leadership Quarterly, 14,* 807–834.

Eagly, A. H., and Carli, L. L. (2007). *Through the labyrinth: The truth about how women become leaders.* Boston, MA: Harvard Business School Press.

Eagly, A. H., and Johannesen-Schmidt, M. C. (2001). The leadership styles of women and men. *Journal of Social Issues, 57,* 781–797.

Eagly, A. H., and Johnson, B. T. (1990). Gender and leadership style: A meta-analysis. *Psychological Bulletin, 108,* 233–256.

Eagly, A. H., and Karau, S. J. (2002). Role congruity theory of prejudice toward female leaders. *Psychological Review, 109,* 573–598.

Epitropaki, O., and Martin, R. (2004). Implicit leadership theories in applied settings: Factor structure, generalizability, and stability over time. *Journal of Applied Psychology, 89,* 293–310.

Fiske, S. T., Cuddy, A. J. C., Glick, P., and Xu, J. (2002). A model of (often mixed) stereotype content: Competence and warmth respectively follow from perceived status and competition. *Journal of Personality and Social Psychology, 82,* 878–902.

Fiske, S. T., Xu, J., Cuddy, A. J. C., and Glick, P. (1999). (Dis)respecting versus (dis)liking: Status and interdependence predict ambivalent stereotypes of competence and warmth. *Journal of Social Issues, 55,* 473–489.

Fortune (2010). Women CEOs. Retrieved from http://money.cnn.com/magazines/fortune/fortune500/2010/womenceos/ on May 26, 2010.

Galinsky, E., Aumann, K., and Bond, J. T. (2008). Times are changing: Gender and generation at work and at home. *Families and Work Institute, National Study of the Changing Workforce.* www.familiesandwork.org.

Garcia-Retamero, R., and López-Zafra, E. (2006). Prejudice against women in male-congenial environments: Perceptions of gender role congruity in leadership. *Sex Roles, 55,* 51–61.

Green, F. (2009). Sex discrimination in job-related training. *British Journal of Industrial Relations, 29,* 295–304.

Heilman, M. E. (2001). Description and prescription: How gender stereotypes prevent women's ascent up the organizational ladder. *Journal of Social Issues, 57,* 657–674.

Heilman, M. E., Block, C. J., Martell, R. F., and Simon, M. C. (1989). Has anything changed? Current characterizations of men, women, and managers. *Journal of Applied Psychology, 74,* 935–942.

Heilman, M. E., and Eagly, A. H. (2008). Commentaries: Gender stereotypes are alive, well, and busy producing workplace discrimination. *Industrial and Organizational Psychology, 1,* 393–398.

Hite, L. M. (2004). Black and White women managers: Access to opportunity. *Human Resource Development Quarterly, 15,* 131–146.

Hofstede, G. (1999). Problems remain, but theories will change: The universal and the specific in 21st-century global management. *Organizational Dynamics, 28,* 34–44.

Hofstede, G., and Hofstede, G. J. (2005). *Cultures and organizations: Software of the mind,* 2nd ed. New York, NY: McGraw-Hill.

Hogg, M. A. (2001). A social identity theory of leadership. *Personality and Social Psychology Review, 5,* 184–200.

Hogg, M. A., and Terry, D. J. (2000). Social identity and self-categorization processes in organizational contexts. *Academy of Management Review, 25,* 121–140.

Hogue, M., and Lord, R. G. (2007). A multilevel, complexity theory approach to understanding gender bias in leadership. *Leadership Quarterly, 18,* 370–390.

Hoobler, J. M., Wayne, S. J., and Lemmon, G. (2009). Bosses' perceptions of family-work conflict and women's promotability: Glass ceiling effects. *Academy of Management Journal, 52,* 939–957.

House, R., Javidan, M., and Dorfman, P. (2001). Project GLOBE: An introduction. *Applied Psychology an International Review, 50,* 489–505.

Judge, T. A., and Livingston, B. A. (2008). Is the gap more than gender? A longitudinal analysis of gender, gender role orientation, and earnings. *Journal of Applied Psychology, 93,* 994–1012.

LABORSTA. (2009). Economically active population estimates and projections: 1980–2020. International Labor Office Bureau of Statistics. Retrieved from http://laborsta.ilo.org/STP/guest on May 29, 2010.

Landy, F. J. (2008). Stereotypes, bias, and personnel decisions: Strange and stranger. *Industrial and Organizational Psychology: Perspectives on Science and Practice, 1,* 379–392.

Lent, R. W., Brown, S. D., and Hackett, G. (1994). Monograph: Toward a unifying social cognitive theory of career and academic interest, choice, and performance.*Journal of Vocational Behavior, 45,* 79–122.

London, M. (1998). *Career barriers: How people experience, overcome, and avoid failure.* Mahwah, NJ: Lawrence Erlbaum Associates.

Lord, R. G., Brown, D. J., and Freiberg, S. J. (1999). Understanding the dynamics of leadership: The role of follower self-concepts in the leader/follower relationship. *Organizational Behavior and Human Decision Processes, 78,* 167–203.

Lord, R. G., Brown, D. J., Harvey, J. L., and Hall, R. J. (2001). Contextual constraints on prototype generation and their multilevel consequences for leadership perceptions.*Leadership Quarterly, 12,* 311–338.

Lord, R. G., and Emrich, C. G. (2001). Thinking outside the box by looking inside the box: Extending the cognitive revolution in leadership research. *Leadership Quarterly, 11,* 551–579.

Lord, R. G., and Maher, K. J. (1993). *Leadership and information processing: Linking perceptions and performance.* New York, NY: Routledge.

Lyness, K. S., and Thompson, D. E. (1997). Above the glass ceiling? A comparison of matched samples of female and male executives. *Journal of Applied Psychology, 82,* 359–375.

Moss-Racusin, C. A., and Rudman, L. A. (2010). Disruptions in women's self-promotion: The backlash avoidance model. *Psychology of Women Quarterly, 34,* 186–202.

Nye, J. L., and Forsyth, D. R. (1991). The effects of prototype-based biases on leadership appraisals. *Small Group Research, 22,* 360–379.

Peters, S., Kinsey, P., and Malloy, T. E. (2004). Gender and leadership perceptions among African Americans. *Basic and Applied Social Psychology, 26,* 93–101.

Powell, G. N., Butterfield, D. A., and Parent, J. D. (2002). Gender and managerial stereotypes: Have the times changed? *Journal of Management, 28,* 177–193.

Reskin, B. (1993). Sex segregation in the workplace. *Annual Review of Sociology, 19,* 241–270.

Rudman, L. A., and Glick, P. (2001). Prescriptive gender stereotypes and backlash toward agentic women. *Journal of Social Issues, 57,* 743–762.

Schein, V. E. (2001). A global look at psychological barriers to women's progress in management. *Journal of Social Issues, 57,* 675–688.

Seltzer, J., and Bass. B.M. (1990). Transformational leadership: Beyond initiation and consideration. *Journal of Management, 16,* 693–703.

Stanley, C. A. (2009). Giving voice from the perspectives of African American women leaders. *Advances in Developing Human Resources, 11,* 551–561.

Thomas, D. A. (April, 2001). The truth about mentoring minorities: Race matters. *Harvard Business Review,* 99–107.

Vroom, V. H., and Jago, A. G. (2007). The role of the situation in leadership. *American Psychologist, 62,* 17–24.

Zanna, M. P., and Pack, S. J. (1975). On the self fulfilling nature of apparent sex differences in behavior. *Journal of Experimental Social Psychology, 11,* 583–591.

11

"Wisdom Has Built Her House": From the Army to Motherhood to Management

Ayelet Giladi

Being invited to write a chapter on leadership posed a great challenge to me. It led me to access unconscious insights about my current work and my "journey" over the years, which I have attempted to put into words in this paper.

According to King Solomon, "Wisdom has built her house" (Proverbs 14:1, American King James Translation of the Bible). We live in an age of changes and opportunities. Active empowerment is one of the most important and central goals of those heading the managerial pyramid. Women bring their special brand of feminine innovativeness and insight to this role.

Today, I have a team of 17—14 women and three men—to assist me in writing these words. They are also involved in the important and never-ending task of promoting awareness to sexual harassment (SH) among young children. The common denominator is that all of us come from the fields of education, psychology, sociology, and social work, and we all understand the importance of empowerment and the hands-on approach in enabling young children to identify and deal with the realities in the world in which they live.

Four prevention programs have been or are being developed for young children:

1. *"Getting Along Together* – Preventing Sexual Harassment in Young Children" (for children aged four to seven—from kindergarten up to second grade).

2. *"Getting Along Together 10* – Preventing Sexual Harassment in Young Children" (for children aged eight to ten).

3. *"Getting Along Together Big Time* – Preventing Sexual Harassment in Young Children" (for children aged 11 to 13).

4. A program for seventh to ninth graders is now being developed.

These SH prevention programs, based on sociological perspectives, deal with important values, such as respect, dignity, and equality.

Looking at my role as the chief executive officer of the Voice of the Child Association through the lens of leadership, I am the guide who finds and shows the way. My leadership role was not exactly built in a clear and organized fashion. It grew out of being a pioneer in taking preventive measures against SH among young children. I brought to it my philosophy of life, theoretical knowledge in various areas accumulated over many years, and the skills acquired as a commander in the army and as a worker and manager of small- to medium-sized systems, in which I always stressed humanity. In addition, my skills as a mother undoubtedly helped forge my worldview as a manager and leader.

My success in leadership can be put down to various abilities. Describing these requires step-by-step reconstruction from the moment I first decided to promote SH awareness and prevention programs. Pioneering this field in Israel, I developed SH prevention programs, which were adopted by the Israeli Ministry of Education, and taught them in primary schools across the country. Every step was extremely difficult, requiring a great deal of hard work.

Eventually, I reached the most significant part of my life's work, requiring leadership abilities of a different kind: selecting and training others to work with me. The training process is long and meaningful, simulations and field work featuring significantly. As the leader and trainer in interaction with the trainees, several points are important.

The Ability to Present a Clear and Tangible Vision

Developing a vision suitable for adoption by society, which would lead to change, took time. It was the culmination of several years of study of relevant material in local and international settings, as well as theoretical analysis. I developed both a real, practical message for the short term, and a long-term vision. I then began looking for staff to join me in the fieldwork. In my view, presenting a consolidated vision with a pioneering spirit was crucial for attracting a suitable team.

Delegating Authority to Others without Reducing Their Responsibility

After suitable staff were selected, they were put through a long training program, including many simulations dealing with SH and prevention programs, to make them feel confident in their mission. In addition, staff attended a seminar in which both sides (trainer and trainee) examined whether they were suited to the work, and if they had mutual trust and a shared ideology necessary to serve as "SH ambassadors" in Israeli society. At the end of the seminar, those selected to continue felt a sense of mission to become initiators of social change beginning in early childhood.

The Ability to Imbue Others with Enthusiasm and Emotional Involvement

I will tell the story of one of the instructor-guides on my team to illustrate this point. She came to work with me after burnout in a highly paid job with a high-tech company. As she put it, she was looking for something "for the soul." I had already completed recruitment for the training group, but she convinced me in the interview that she was right for my project. The seminar, eight sessions lasting an average of 30 hours, not only presents the overall rationale, but also the programs. In the "Getting Along" prevention program, animal puppets are used to present to children the values of respect, honesty, and equality. After one of these sessions, this instructor told me what her husband had told her after a weekend visit from his parents: "You know, you didn't behave with respect, honesty, and equality toward my mother." Her story excited me because in the session before, I had taught these basic values, pointing out that they should be applied

204 Women as Transformational Leaders

not only to the children with whom the trainees work, but also in day-to-day life situations. Her husband understood that his words would explain what he was feeling inside, without starting an argument. This brought home to me how emotionally involved she was with her work, and made me realize what a good "ambassador" she would be for the program. Indeed, she is now one of our most requested instructors-guides.

Imbuing Others with a Sense of Confidence in Me as a Leader and in My Moral Infrastructure

In the seminar, transparency is the best way of creating a sense of trust in me and in my moral infrastructure. This means putting all my cards on the table, effectively making the following statement: "This is who I am and this is what I have to offer." Potential instructors realizing this transparency accept my values system. Most significantly, although they may not be aware of it at the time, this later enables them to pass on transparency to children in prevention programs in the classroom. I have coined the term "work at the eye level" to describe this process, which works in at least two ways, greatly enhancing the message of the SH prevention program and passing on a sense of mutual commitment and loyalty to the trainees.

Relating to the Staff as Equals, Taking into Account Their Feelings and Allowing Them to Express Their Doubts and Criticism

This certainly applies at all stages but particularly to the previous one, and in the work with both very young and more mature children.They are allowed to ask questions, criticize, and suggest new ways of "marketing" and transmitting the material in a rational fashion. In this process, the team leader clearly has the last word.

Serving as a Personal Example of the Values I Expect from my Staff

The personal example of the leader, expressed in constant preoccupation with the issue, even outside conventional work hours, gives moral and principled validity to work requirements from instructors and others.

It should be noted that the training process requires a considerable investment of time by the leader, sometimes at the expense of other things. However, developing a team to work in the field is significant and worthwhile in the long term. Instructors who are satisfied with their work, in the esteem they earn, and in the changes in behavior they see among the children in schools become "ambassadors" for the program. They are interested in continuing their work and, as a result, school principals request future participation in the program and even market it to other schools principals.

I hope writing about my work will help many other women make their personal "journeys." Women offer a different style of management and worldview. The women instructors working with me understood that their empathy and desire to change their immediate surroundings affects day-to-day discourse by bringing a different set of values not only to their work hours but also to their private lives. In this way, they become leaders who set the tone for future generations.

12

Global Leadership to Eliminate Violence against Women

Jeanine M. Galusha, Paula K. Lundberg-Love, Desiree L. Glaze, and Megan A. Brewer

Introduction

Violence against women does not discriminate. It spans all socioeconomic classes and ages and occurs worldwide. Oftentimes, women are too afraid or too ashamed to report the violence and instead are forced to suffer in silence. Even when the violence is reported, they often fear reprisal and at times are treated as criminals, instead of the victims that they are. Violence against women can and often does, have a lifelong impact. Interpersonal relationships may be destroyed, families torn apart, and incomes devastated by a complicated and frequently sluggish legal system. These women are often left with not only physical scars but psychological ones as well. Sometimes years of therapy may be required for full remission of their symptoms. Fortunately, not only has the United States recognized this growing problem and the lasting impact it can have, but so have many other countries. Even the United Nations has become involved in addressing this issue. Many studies have been conducted that examine not only the prevalence and impact of violence against women, but also review what our respective leaders are doing to combat it. A review of recent research and the actions that have been taken by various countries and other government organizations will be discussed within this chapter.

History of Violence against Women

Violence against women can take many forms. The United Nations Declaration on the Elimination of Violence against Women defines violence against women as " . . . any act of gender-based violence that results in, or is likely to result in physical, sexual, or psychological harm or suffering to women, including threats of such acts, coercion or arbitrary deprivation of liberty, whether occurring in public or in private life" (UN, 1993). Certain types of violence affect primarily young girls and adolescents. Child abuse and neglect occur in all countries of the world and include physical, sexual, and psychological abuse. There is also gender-based abuse of infants and female children. According to Krantz and Garcia-Moreno (2005), in some countries such as China, Taiwan, South Korea, India, Pakistan, and some sub-Saharan African countries, there is a longstanding cultural tradition favoring males. This social preference for boys leads to the neglect of girls. Finally, female genital mutilation (FGM) is an important issue. FGM is defined by the World Health Organization (1997) as the partial or total removal of the external genitalia or other injury to the female genital organs for cultural, religious, or other nontherapeutic reasons. WHO estimates that between 100 million to 140 million girls and women have undergone some type of FGM.

Other types of violence affect women of reproductive age and beyond. Intimate partner violence (IPV) and rape are two examples. IPV is abuse by an intimate partner or former partner. Rape is defined as forcing a woman to have sex against her will. Heise, Moore, and Toubia (1995) define sexual coercion as "the act of forcing (or attempting to force) another individual through violence, threats, verbal insistence, deception, cultural expectations, or economic circumstances to engage in sexual behavior against her/ his will." Because rape is often not reported to the police, existing statistics greatly underestimate the magnitude of the problem (Krantz and Garcia-Moreno, 2005). Another type of violence against women is dowry related. A dowry is the payment the bride's family makes to the groom's family so that the groom will marry their daughter. Dowry-related violence takes many forms in various cultures (Krantz and Garcia-Moreno, 2005). However, the size of the dowry is a common cause of disputes between families, which can lead to harassment of brides and also dowry-related deaths, particularly in parts of India and other countries in Southern Asia

(Krantz and Garcia-Moreno, 2005). Acid throwing, which involves the disfigurement of a woman by throwing acid and burning her, is another form of gender-based violence seen in some Asian countries such as India, Bangladesh, and Pakistan. An "honor" killing is the murder of a woman, usually by a brother, father, or other male family member, because she has allegedly brought shame to her family (Krantz and Garcia-Moreno, 2005). The basis for this phenomenon is the notion of male honor and female chastity that prevails in many countries in the Eastern Mediterranean region: a man's honor is linked to the perceived sexual purity of the women in the family (Krantz and Garcia-Moreno). If a woman engages in sex outside marriage or even if she is raped, she is thought to disgrace the family honor. In some societies, the only way to cleanse the family honor is to kill the woman/girl (Krantz and Garcia-Moreno, 2005).

The repeated depiction of women as victims, both directly and indirectly, implies that they are incapable of defending themselves or combating male violence on their own (Fong, 2007). This construct of women as passive victims of violent crimes can cultivate a sense of powerlessness in them, and thus trap them in the dynamic of a self-fulfilling prophecy (Fong, 2007). This portrayal of women also denies their sense of agency, which can discourage them from taking full control of their lives and thus force them to withdraw themselves from meaningful activities (Fong, 2007). A feminist political gender analysis has reframed the problem of violence against women as one of misuse of power by men who have been socialized to believe that they have the right to control the women in their lives, even through violent means (Walker 1989). While women do sometimes abuse other women, men, and children, feminist scholars maintain that men's socialized need for power is a component that underlies victimization against women. In the 1960s, it became apparent that there existed a need for a feminist analysis in psychology when those in the feminist movement began scrutinizing the contribution of gender-role socialization to the development of female and male behaviors previously considered innate and biologically determined (Maccoby and Jacklin, 1974). The integration of a feminist gender analysis into the psychological understanding of violence against women also resulted in the comprehension of the roles of powerlessness and oppression of women, as applied to individual situations. The roots of men's violence against women appeared to lie in the preservation of men's need for power and status (Walker 1989).

Research has shown that over time, violence between intimate partners tends to escalate, although there may be plateaus and even temporary reversals during periods of legal, extralegal, and psychological intervention (Walker, 1989). However, once the external scrutiny is removed and the stress reoccurs, the violence typically returns to its previous level and resumes its incremental nature (Walker, 1989). Cultural factors, including institutions that provide ineffective responses for the protection of women and children or those that promote traditional sociocultural norms that devalue women, can maintain the violence (Walker 1989).

Many battering relationships display a cycle of violence that appears to follow behavioral reinforcement theory (Walker 1989). The three-phase cycle of violence that Walker (1989) formulated as a framework for her investigation is based on a tension-reduction hypothesis. The first phase involves a buildup of tension during which the woman has minimum control over the situation. The second phase is the explosion, or acute battering incident. At this point, others may become involved, including the police. Although this is the shortest phase, it frequently causes the most physical harm. By the time the second phase is over, there is a physiological release of tension that acts a reinforcer (Walker 1989). Often there is a period of loving contrition that follows as the third phase, but in some relationships there is only a period of reduced tension that also serves as a reinforcer (Walker 1989). The battered woman may or may not be aware of this cycle and may blame herself for the violence.

Until the introduction of the method of feminist political gender analysis, battered women were often labeled as masochistic and blamed for their partner's dissatisfaction with them (Walker, 1989). Rape victims also were frequently blamed for the assaults. People did not recognize that rape occurred in the home or at the hands of an acquaintance or a dating partner, even though today we know that most sexual assaults are perpetrated by people known to the victims (Walker, 1989). Sexual access to a woman was seen as a man's right—his entitlement (Walker 1989).

According to Graffunder, Noonan, Cox, and Wheaton (2004), 20 years ago the words "violence" and "prevention" were rarely used in the same sentence. However, today, the idea that violence can be prevented is widely recognized. The Centers for Disease Control (CDC) is committed to violence prevention, including that which is obscured from public view. Violence against women is a hidden health hazard and a major public health problem that merits more attention. According to the National Violence Against Women Survey (Tjaden and Thoennes, 2000):

- Approximately 1.5 million women are raped and/or physically assaulted by an intimate partner each year
- Nearly 25 percent of women have been raped and/or physically assaulted by an intimate partner at some point in their lives, and more than 40 percent of the women who experience partner rapes and physical assault sustain a physical injury
- Nearly two-thirds of women who reported being raped, physically assaulted, or stalked since age 18 were victimized by a current or former husband, cohabiting partner, boyfriend, or date
- One of six U.S. women and 1 of 33 U.S. men have experienced an attempted or completed rape as a child and/or adult
- Of the women who reported an attempted or completed rape in their lifetimes, greater than 21 percent were younger than age 12 when they were first raped, and 32 percent were ages 12–17

These staggering statistics provide further evidence that significant attention is required on local, state, national, and international levels to reduce the prevalence of violence against women.

Violence against Women Act

Legislation proposing a federal response to the problem of violence against women was first introduced in 1990, although such violence was first identified as a serious problem in the 1970s (Laney, 2005). Congressional action to address gender-related violence resulted in the enactment of the Violence Against Women Act (VAWA), which is Title IV of the Violent Crime Control and Law Enforcement Act of 1994. Educational and social programs, as well as enforcement, were authorized under this bill, with local government programs being the focus of the funding. Sponsors of this bill believed that this was the most promising method to reduce crime and violence.

On October 28, 2000, President Clinton signed into law the Victims of Trafficking and Violence Protection Act of 2000 (P.L. 106-386). The Violence Against Women Act of 2000 (VAWA 2000) continued to support the original VAWA by reauthorizing existing programs and adding new initiatives, including grants to assist victims of dating violence, transitional housing for victims of violence, a pilot program aimed at protecting children during visits with a parent who has been accused of domestic violence, and protections from violence for elderly and disabled women (Laney, 2005). This bill also made technical amendments and required grant recipients to submit reports on the effectiveness of their respective programs. Furthermore, the bill provided protections for battered immigrant women so that they could leave their abusers without fear of deportation. Under the old law, these women could be deported if they left abusers who were their sponsors for residency and citizenship in the United States (Laney, 2005).

Another way the original VAWA sought to help combat violence against women was by rewriting several areas of federal criminal law. Penalties were created for interstate stalking or domestic abuse in cases where an abuser crossed a state line to injure or harass another, or forced a victim to cross a state line under duress and then physically harmed the victim during the course of a violent crime (Laney, 2005). VAWA called for pretrial detention in a federal sex offense or child pornography felonies and allowed evidence of prior sex offenses to be used in some subsequent trials regarding federal sex crimes (Laney, 2005). It also set new rules of evidence specifying that a victim's past sexual behavior generally was not admissible in federal, civil, or criminal cases regarding sexual misconduct (Laney, 2005). VAWA 2000 created new stalking offenses and penalties for a person who causes a spouse or intimate partner to travel in foreign or interstate commerce by force or coercion and during the course of such travel commits or attempts to commit an act of violence against that person (Laney, 2005). This bill added the intimate partners of the victims as people covered under the stalking statute and made it a crime to use the mail or any facility of interstate or foreign commerce to engage in conduct that would place a person in reasonable fear of harm to themselves or their immediate family or intimate partner (Laney, 2005). Moreover, VAWA 2000 created penalties for any person who travels in interstate or foreign commerce with the intent of violating a protection order or causes a person to travel in interstate or foreign commerce by force or coercion that violates a protection order (P.L. 106-386, Section 1107).

The original VAWA provided for many grant programs. These included (Laney, 2005):

- Law Enforcement and Prosecution (Special Training Officers and Prosecutors [STOP] Grants

  o The purpose of STOP grants, administered by the U.S. attorney general, was to help state governments, Indian tribal governments, and units of local government strengthen law enforcement, prosecution, and victims' services in cases involving violent crimes against women.

- State Domestic Violence and Sexual Assault Coalition Grants

  o These were distributed by the attorney general in order to enhance domestic violence or sexual assault intervention and prevention through information and training.

- Rape Prevention and Education Grants

  o These funds were added to the Preventive Health Service Block Grants monies already distributed to the states by the Department of Health and Human Services. These grants were to be used by states for rape prevention and education programs conducted by rape crisis centers or similar nongovernmental nonprofit entities.

- National Domestic Violence Hotline

  o These funds were authorized for the secretary of health and human services to make a grant to a private, nonprofit entity to provide for the operation of a national, toll-free telephone hotline to disseminate information and assistance to victims of domestic violence.

- Grants to Encourage Arrests Policies in Domestic Violence Cases

  o These grants were utilized to assist state governments, Indian tribal governments, and units of local government in treating domestic violence as a serious violation of criminal law.

- Grants for Battered Women's Shelters

  o These funds were distributed by the secretary of health and human services for battered women's shelters.

- Community Programs on Domestic Violence

  o Monies were provided by the secretary of health and human serv-
     ices to nonprofit private organizations for the purpose of estab-
     lishing projects in local communities to coordinate intervention
     and prevention efforts against domestic violence.

- National Stalker and Domestic Violence Reduction Grants

  o The attorney general was authorized to make grants to states and
     units of local government to improve data entry for cases of stalk-
     ing and domestic violence in local, state, and national crime infor-
     mation databases most notably the National Crime Information
     Center (NCIC).

- Rural Domestic Violence and Child Abuse Enforcement Grants

  o Funds were provided by the attorney general to states, Indian tribal
     governments, or local governments of rural states and to other
     public and private entities of rural states to further cooperative
     efforts and/or projects to investigate and prosecute acts of domestic
     violence, provide treatment and counseling to victims, and to work
     cooperatively to develop strategies at the community level.

- Victims of Child Abuse Grants

  o VAWA amended the Victims of Child Abuse Act of 1990 to pro-
     vide authorization for the following purposes: the court-
     appointed special advocate programs, child abuse training pro-
     grams for judicial personnel and practitioners, and grants for tele-
     vised testimony

- Federal Victims Counselors

  o Monies were allocated to the U.S. attorneys to appoint victims/
     witness counselors for prosecution of sex and domestic violence
     crimes where applicable.

- Grants to Reduce Sexual Abuse of Runaway, Homeless, and Street
  Youth

  o The secretary of health and human services was permitted to
     make grants to private, nonprofit agencies for the prevention of

sexual abuse and the exploitation of runaway, homeless, and street youth.

• Equal Justice for Women in the Courts

  ○ The State Justice Institute and the Federal Judicial Center were empowered to make grants to provide model programs involving training of judges and court personnel in state and federal courts on rape, sexual assault, domestic violence, and other gender-motivated crimes.

New grant programs in the Violence Against Women Act 2000 included the following: grants for legal assistance to victims, short-term transitional housing, funds to increase protection of older and disabled individuals, and the Safe Haven pilot program (Laney, 2005). Other initiatives included studies of insurance discrimination against victims of domestic violence, workplace effects of violence against women, unemployment compensation for women who are victims of violence, and parental kidnapping; the Battered Immigrant Women Protection Act of 2000; a definition of dating violence; and a task force on domestic violence (Laney, 2005).

United Nations' Efforts to Reduce Violence against Women

United Nations Secretary General Ban Ki-moon declared violence against women "an attack on all of us," and called on the world's men and women to stand together to end the intolerable violence "that destroys health, perpetuates poverty [and] strikes against equality and empowerment." On International Women's Day, 2009, Mr. Ban said "Violence against women cannot be tolerated in any form, in any context, under any circumstance, by any political leader or by any Government" (UN, 2009).

The United Nations comprises 192 countries, and although those countries have made some progress regarding violence against women, there is still much to be accomplished. In 2004, the UN passed a resolution concerning honor killings, which are still commonplace in several countries. Each March, the Commission on the Status of Women holds a meeting. Unfortunately, while the United Nations can make recommendations, it still faces many obstacles for their successful implementation. According to Dr. Janet Sigal (personal communication, January 11, 2010), the United Nations cannot interfere with the independence of a nation and thus lacks the ability to enforce resolutions that have been passed. The UN issues moral statements and judgments but there is no punishment and no enforcement if a country chooses not to comply (Sigal, January 11, 2010). One solution is for nongovernmental organizations (NGOs) to play a more prominent role in preventing violence against women. Another factor is that cultural change is required in countries that still condone such violence. But such a remedy requires a grassroots effort plus change at the government level in order to be effective. According to Dr. Sigal, for nations to achieve this goal, accurate data are needed and the nations need to be held accountable for developing a plan to collect such data.

Aja Isatou Njie Saidy, vice president of the Republic of The Gambia and minister of women's affairs, has stated that an existing web of protocols, conventions, and national frameworks that seek to end violence against women undoubtedly have laid a foundation for the work that must be done (UN, 2009). But while the responsibility to respond strongly and swiftly to end violence against women has fallen squarely on governments, only half the member states of the United Nations have enacted legislation to fight domestic violence or curb human trafficking (UN, 2009). Because the most prevalent form of aggression against women is domestic violence, it also needs to be targeted by the UN (UN, 2009).

Countries That Have Conducted Studies Concerning Violence against Women

World Health Organization Study

According to the results of a study by the World Health Organization (WHO), which involved a review of over 50 studies conducted in 35 countries utilizing samples representative of their respective populations before 1999, between 10 percent and 52 percent of women from around the world reported that they had been physically abused by an intimate partner at some point in their lives (Garcia-Moreno, Jansen, Ellsberg, Heise, and Watts, 2006). About 20 percent of those women also indicated that they had been sexually abused during childhood (Mercy, Krug, Dahlberg, and Zwi, 2002). In countries as diverse as Bangladesh, Cambodia, India,

Mexico, Nigeria, Pakistan, Papua New Guinea, Nicaragua, Tanzania, and Zimbabwe, studies find that violence is frequently viewed as a form of physical chastisement, that is, the husband's right to "correct" an erring wife. (Heise, Ellsberg, and Gottmoeller, 2002).

Generally, the prevalence of partner violence was much lower in industrialized settings than in other study sites (Garcia-Moreno et al., 2006). The estimates documented in the WHO study for Japan (Yokohama) and Serbia and Montenegro (Belgrade) were consistent with 12-month estimates of partner violence seen in other industrialized settings, including 1 to 5 percent in the United States, 4 percent in the UK, and 4 percent in Canada, which may suggest that women in these settings possibly have more options for leaving abusive relationships (Garcia-Moreno et al., 2006). This study confirms the pervasiveness and high prevalence of violence against women in a wide range of cultural and geographical contexts (Garcia-Moreno et al., 2006).

United States

After the United States passed VAWA, the Centers for Disease Control (CDC) sought to investigate a public health approach to preventing violence against women. In order to do that, Saltzman, Green, Marks, and Thacker (2000) described a four-step process that could be utilized to achieve this goal. The first step involved the definition and measurement of the types of victimization experienced by women. In step 2, researchers identified risk factors for such violence and factors that might protect women from violence. Interventions based on these factors were subsequently developed. Step 3 evaluated the public health interventions used in order to determine their impact, and step 4 consisted of the dissemination of promising strategies to ensure their widespread adoption by practitioners working to prevent violence against women.

In keeping with the CDC's emphasis on primary prevention, the Domestic Violence Prevention Enhancement and Leadership through Alliances (DELTA) program has been designed to build the capacity for and support the development of state-level leaders in the prevention of violence against women (Graffunder et al., 2004). This program focuses on building a primary prevention emphasis within a coordinated community response (CCR) (Graffunder et al., 2004). The focus of the CCRs is to coordinate the efforts of the criminal justice system with those of the social services agencies in cases of violence against women (Graffunder et al., 2004). The goal of the CCRs is to implement the appropriate protocols for responses to these cases by the various agencies involved. Additionally, they focus on community education efforts that increase awareness of the various issues related to violence against women. The CCRs seek safety for victims and accountability for perpetrators by recognizing the multifaceted dynamics of violence against women and respecting the sometimes divergent goals/mandates of the criminal justice system and social services agencies (Graffunder et al., 2004).

Another program that the CDC has designed to prevent violence against women is a social norms media campaign for sixth-, seventh-, and eighth-grade boys and girls (Graffunder et al., 2004). It builds on the effort to prevent teen dating violence by correcting the perceptions of a small subgroup of youth who believe that it is acceptable to physically or verbally abuse one's partner (Graffunder et al., 2004). This campaign strives to reinforce positive and healthy relationship values among the majority of teens because Graffunder et al. (2004) confirmed that the best way to effect social change is to begin teaching healthy attitudes and behaviors to young people.

Another effort launched by the CDC is the Rape Prevention and Education (RPE) program. This initiative works primarily through state health departments, state sexual assault coalitions, local rape crisis centers, and other state and local organizations to address the prevention of sexual assault (Graffunder et al., 2004). Authorized under VAWA (PL-106-386, October 28, 2000), this program funds the 50 states, the District of Columbia, and the U.S. territories to support efforts designed to increase the awareness of sexual violence (Graffunder et al., 2004). Thus, the CDC continues its goal of primary prevention in addressing the persistent problem of violence against women.

South Asia

In June 1980, the Women Lawyers Association of the Philippines organized a meeting in Manila. At the meeting, 13 South Asian countries presented reports in which they pointed out that there were no laws that were discriminatory toward women; rather, it was the common culture or traditions that were responsible for such attitudes toward them (Niaz, 2003). Perhaps one reason for these attitudes stemmed from the following events. Manu, the Hindu lawgiver, preached that girls should not be educated. He thought that women should restrict themselves to their homes and be prohibited from public life (Niaz, 2003). His dictum that a wife ought to respect her husband as God and serve him faithfully, even if he were vicious and void of any merit, was accepted as applicable to all women (Niaz, 2003). Under these laws, women become weak and subservient (Niaz, 2003). Buddhism further taught that women lure men away from the path of Nirwana or salvation (Niaz, 2003). Women were considered to be temptresses who hindered men's rise above the worldly status (Niaz, 2003).

Islam granted women the legal right to own property, marry, and divorce and elevated their status in the community to a level similar to men's, determined by their deeds (Niaz, 2003). However, with the passage of time and its basic teachings of tolerance and respect for other religions, Islam absorbed much from the local cultures in India and changed its view of women's status according to the culture of its host country (Niaz, 2003). Islam absorbed the Hindu cultural patriarchal values that supported female inferiority. These values were transmitted to the younger generations, resulting in tolerance of family violence as a male right to control those who are dependent (Niaz, 2003). Hence, in most countries of the world today, Islam is the male interpretation of uneducated or semieducated *Maulanas* (*Ulema*/priests), which has come to include many negative implications of other religions, such as the inequality and subjugation of women and the denial of women's rights of inheritance, divorce, and marriage (Niaz, 2003).

Cheshire, England

In the United Kingdom, it is clear that since the advent of the women's movement of the 1970s, activism—supported by research and service development—has transformed both the understandings of violence against women and the practice of many social care agencies (Hague and Bridge, 2008). In response to domestic violence in particular, Women's Aid has been the campaigning organization to lead the way, working with a variety of other women's groups, and now maintains a strong national presence (Hague and Bridge, 2008). As a result, policy change, research, and services have followed.

The Cheshire Domestic Abuse Project (CDAP) began in 2000 with Home Office funding for three years (see Hester and Westmarland, 2005; Hague and Bridge, 2008). It offered a complex and coordinated multifaceted response to domestic abuse across agencies and its work was evaluated as being extremely positively. It was able to foster strategy-building, and it was well regarded throughout the area (Hague and Bridge, 2008). The project's components included (Hague and Bridge, 2008):

- The Data-Collection/Monitoring Project provided a coherent data-monitoring system across the county and fed the results back into agency practice.

- The Police Project enhanced evidence gathering and provided "target hardening," personal safety videos, and improved training on domestic violence. In domestic violence police work, successful "target hardening" includes increasing the security of one's housing and the provision of personal alarms and mobile telephones for abuse survivors with the aim of reducing repeat incidents (Hester and Westmarland, 2005)

- The Outreach/Advocacy Project provided outreach support across the county to run women's support groups and to build networks with women's services.

- The Education Project developed domestic violence programs in schools to ensure that they were embedded within the curriculum.

The initiative also provided extensive domestic abuse training programs.

The coordinated community response developed in Cheshire has viewed domestic violence as a power issue in terms of gender. Its wide-ranging services support women victims and attempt to enable women experiencing abuse to escape the abuse, enter a network of support, and move toward violence-free lives (Hague and Bridge, 2008).

From the beginning, this initiative knew that in order to be successful, effective community services had to be developed. Both outreach/advocacy to empower survivors and help them learn from their experiences were viewed as essential components, without which success would be less likely (Hague and Bridge, 2008). The program was underwritten by data collection and monitoring so that the interventions were evidence-based and strategically unified (Hague and Bridge, 2008). Schools' initiatives provided a commitment to the next generation and the future. The unification of these various projects gave Cheshire a unique profile as a CCR within the UK (Hague and Bridge, 2008).

After evaluation, the Cheshire initiative was in most instances exceeding its target outputs and achieving projected outcomes in all areas (Hague and Bridge, 2008). The CDAP Data-Monitoring Project has produced assembled, systematic, and comprehensive data on domestic violence and converted these data into meaningful materials to inform service providers and impact wider strategic development (Hague and Bridge, 2008). The police have improved its domestic violence response as well by practicing positive policing that supports women and children. Additionally, police training and guidance with respect to comprehensive policy practices have improved the response of law enforcement (Hague and Bridge, 2008). Finally, "target hardening," a procedure that involves increasing the security of housing via the provision of personal alarms and mobile telephones for abuse survivors with the aim of reducing repeat incidents, has been effective (Hester and Westmarland, 2005). Other recommendations for the police had included the improvement of evidence collection in order to support successful prosecution. During this period, outreach/support was offered to over 1,000 women and over 1,600 children. The services were provided to a wide range of women from various cultures with different levels of employment and disability. The evaluation data sets, which rated the impact of the support received by the women, were very positive. A number of issues were assessed, including the provision of short- and long-term emotional support, advocacy, safety planning, needs assessment, treatment intervention, and court. The data indicated that the use of mobile phones and alarms enhanced the safety of the families, although the issue of rural isolation can be problematic in this respect. The women also reported that the process had improved their levels of self-esteem and confidence (Hague and Bridge, 2008). Finally, the Cheshire project developed a primary school educational project featuring a story performance to enable young children to begin to challenge attitudes to personal violence (Hague and Bridge, 2008). This project was presented to 7,500 children by more than 400 teachers in 80 schools (Hague and Bridge, 2008). The performances were followed up with children's workshops and special activities (Hague and Bridge, 2008). Several other programs were subsequently developed, and by the end of the evaluation period, domestic abuse education was significantly embedded in the curriculum and in all relevant strategic plans.

In summary, the Cheshire initiative resulted in large numbers of women and children (over 2,500) being effectively supported. The size and efficiency of the Data-Monitoring Project (over 14,000 cases) was impressive. Domestic violence education projects also were incorporated into a large number of school programs, such that over 24,000 children/young people in over 50 percent of schools received the information. Effective training interventions were provided for over 2,000 workers across the county by the Domestic Abuse Partnership's Training Programme. At the conclusion of the evaluation period (1998–2006) over 4,000 people had been trained (Hague and Bridge, 2008).

Pakistan

Seventy-five percent of Pakistan's female population live in rural areas, and the average Pakistani woman is burdened with the "crippling handicaps of illiteracy, constant motherhood and poor health" (Jalal, 1991). In 2003, The fundamental rights guaranteed in the 1973 Pakistan Constitution were suspended, including the right to be free of discrimination on the basis of sex (Niaz, 2003). In 1997, the new government, which assumed the office of prime minister adopted policies that appeared to block all opportunities for the advancement of women's rights. However, during 2003, under General Pervez Musharraf's government, women were encouraged to participate in national politics (Niaz, 2003). The discriminatory laws against women's rights are currently being examined for repeal of the previous ordinances.

Today, three federal ministers associated with the Departments of Education, Law, and Population are women, and women hold 33 percent of the seats in the National Assembly (Niaz, 2003). Women's awareness of their rights has increased, undoubtedly due to the relentless endeavors of Pakistani women's rights groups. Unfortunately, most women are still ignorant of their most basic rights because laws that discriminate against women remain on the books and are actively enforced. Discrimination in access to government resources and services continues unchecked and discriminatory practices go unpunished (Niaz, 2003). In Pakistan, as well as India, women are generally treated as second-class citizens and wives are battered for misconduct or minor mistakes. In India, nearly 25 percent of women suffer from physical abuse. In another study, 18 to 45 percent of married men in five districts of Uttar Pradesh acknowledged that they physically abused their wives (Niaz, 2003).

South Africa

According to a 1997 report by Human Rights Watch, "South Africa: Violence against Women and the Medico-Legal System," South Africa's criminal justice system exists in a sexist society that has historically disregarded or placed a low priority on the need to address discrimination and violence against women. Unfortunately, these women, who have been targets of rape or other assault, continue to face a system that is often hostile to their efforts to seek redress. The police are uninformed and unsympathetic. Prosecutors may often refuse to litigate domestic violence cases, and in rape cases often subscribe to the usual stereotypes, dropping cases where the women involved are not "good victims." This continues to occur despite South Africa's obligation under international law to ensure that women are guaranteed respect for their human rights and fundamental freedoms on the same basis as men. This obligation extends to the provision of an effective remedy if those rights are violated.

Guatemala

Feminicide is defined as the institutionalized killing of women. A review of the criminal investigation of the murder of Claudina Isabel Velásquez Paiz (one of 518 women murdered there in 2005) reveals the role of the state in Guatemala's feminicide and the omission of its responsibility to guarantee equal protection before the law to all of its citizens (Sanford, 2008).

The Genocide Convention was adopted by the United Nations General Assembly on December 9, 1948. Guatemala is a signatory to this convention, in which "genocide" means any of the following acts committed with intent to destroy, in whole or in part, a national, ethnic, racial, or religious group, such as (Sanford, 2008):

- Killing members of the group
- Causing serious bodily or mental harm to members of the group. Deliberately inflicting on the group conditions of life calculated to bring about its physical destruction in whole or in part
- Imposing measures intended to prevent births within the group
- Forcibly transferring children of the group to another group

In 1981, females (including adult women and girls) accounted for 14 percent of massacre victims in Rabinal. In June 1982, three months into Efrain Rios Montt's dictatorship, females made up 42 percent of massacre victims (Sanford, 2008). In mid-1982, the number of women and girls killed rose so sharply that the comparable percentage of male victims actually dropped. Many of these women had signs of torture and sexual abuse (Sanford, 2008).

The concept of feminicide builds on the term *femicide*, which refers to the murder of women in the criminology literature (Sanford, 2008). It also refers to a crime of hate against women in the emerging feminist literature that addresses the murder of women (Russell and Harmes 2001). Russell (2001) defines femicide not simply as the murder of females but as "the killing of females by males because they are females." Russell further categorizes femicide as "a form of terrorism that functions to define gender lines, enact and bolster male dominance and to render all women chronically and profoundly unsafe" (Russell, 2001, p. 177). According to Maldonado Guevara (as cited in Sanford, 2008), the concept of feminicide helps disarticulate belief systems that place violence based on gender inequality within the private sphere and reveals the very social character of the killing of women as a product of a relationship of power between men and women. This exists in Guatemala simply because of the absence of guarantees to protect the rights of women (Sanford, 2008).

The Inter-American Commission for Human Rights (IACHR) concluded that these assassinations are meant to signal to women to watch out and to return to the private sphere of home and their familial duties (Sanford, 2008). As women have taken on more public roles and are viewed as in competition with men, they are told to abandon the public arena and to give up on civic participation (Sanford, 2008). In fact, the report of the Commission for Historical Clarification (as cited in Sanford, 2008) confirms that the state of Guatemala trained its soldiers and other armed agents to rape and terrorize women. During the Guatemala war, army soldiers and other security officers were responsible for 99 percent of acts of sexual violence carried out against women (Sanford, 2008).

As Erturk (2005) concluded in her report on Guatemala, "Violence against women is met with impunity as authorities fail to investigate cases, prosecute and punish perpetrators. In this regard, the absence of rule of law fosters a continuum of violent acts against women, including murder, rape, domestic violence, sexual harassment and commercial sexual exploitation. Security and justice institutions have not responded adequately, most recently by failing to resolve a series of brutal murders of women."

Germany

"Domestic violence in immigrant communities is attributed to a backward, Muslim culture" (Weber, 2009). An invitation to consider and critique violence against women cannot ignore the activism of women who both affiliate themselves with a religious heritage or community and reject violence. An assumption that Islam is singular, unchanging, and immutable can only continue to reinforce dogmatic positions and cannot contribute to an effective integration of Germany's Turkish Germans (Weber, 2009).

The German Islam Conference (*Duetsche Islam-Konferenz*) discusses who can serve as the guardian of human rights, those of Muslims and, in particular of Muslim women. The first point is, rightfully so, equal rights for women. Since the so-called *Anwerbestopp* (end of labor recruitment) of 1973, dire warnings about the failed integration of immigrants in Germany have increasingly been linked to a discussion of the oppression of women in Islam and Muslim communities (Weber, 2009). These same immigrant women have taken active roles in challenging domestic violence from their positions within their communities—critiquing their community without rejecting it and linking domestic violence to violence in the larger society (Weber, 2009). The ironic result is that by asserting that immigrant and Muslim women have no voice within their own "culture," dominant groups deny those same women a voice in nationwide discussions (Weber, 2009).

Gayatri Spivak famously pointed out that Third World women had to choose between two narratives: one in which "white men are saving brown women from brown men" and one in which Third World women gain a strange sort of agency by acting on a desire to die by suttee, thus retaining or forging an anti-imperial claim to their "nation" (Weber, 2009). Within a colonial logic that legitimated Western colonization in the name of women's rights, women with feminist consciousness could only express that consciousness as a betrayal of their burgeoning national, anticolonial communities (Weber, 2009). If the consequences are less drastic, immigrant women, particularly Muslim women, are often forced to choose between two narratives, one in which German women are saving Muslim women from Muslim men by convincing them to reject affiliation with a religious or Turkish community, and the other, in which they consciously participate in or even desire their own oppression in order to retain a claim to their community (Weber, 2009).

Many scholars of Islam move from the assumption that Islamic law itself, properly interpreted, can promote women's rights, others point to the development of explicitly feminist movements in many Muslim countries, often by women who consider their Muslim identity to be primarily cultural rather than religious (Weber, 2009). Secularism, in this narrative, is a strategy for ending violence of religious conflict by managing the relationship between religion and the public sphere (particularly the State) (Weber, 2009). The law never seeks to eliminate violence because its object is always to regulate violence (Formations of the Secular 8) (Weber, 2009).

Challenges to the Western historicist narrative of secularism as modernity and as an appropriate strategy to ending violence also have been made from transnational feminist perspectives that include analysis of violence against women (Weber, 2009). Madhavi Sunder (2003, p. 1408) argues that within Enlightenment discourse, individuals are forced to choose between religious liberty in the private sphere and equality (outside of a normative community) in the public sphere.

Muslim women in Germany participate in immigrant activist groups that fight to recognize the specific position of Muslim women in Germany, but assume that structures of violence are changeable and that there are points of similarity with the lives of nonimmigrant women (Weber, 2009). Islam and women's rights in Germany continue to be largely shaped by two assumptions: Islam and women's rights to bodily integrity are mutually exclusive, and that Muslim women are unable to participate in activism for gender equality and women's rights particularly if they retain their religious affiliation (Weber, 2009).

Muslim women tell of violence at the hands of Muslim men, usually ending with an achievement of freedom from domestic violence by moving to Germany or by escaping their "Turkish" or "Muslim" community (Weber, 2009). Therefore, a crucial part of the women's survival is developing an independent, individual, "Western" identity that can combat the backwardness of communal identities (Weber, 2009). Groups such as *Ni Putes ni Soumises* (Neither Whores nor Submissives) have begun to think further about violence against women in Muslim communities in the context of a range of violence that exists, linked to forms of masculinities produced by complex intersections of "traditional" or "Muslim" cultures with the experiences of racism in French society (Weber, 2009). This organization was formed in response to an epidemic of gang rapes in the *banlieues,* drawn to public attention by the death of Sohanne Benziane, who was burned alive in October 2002 (Weber, 2009). The organization itself is deliberately inclusive of men, and though it expressly espouses a secularist agenda, it does so without rejecting Islam itself (Weber, 2009). The activism of the organization has constantly recognized racism, anti-Semitism, and misogyny as interlinked ideologies that lead to forms of physical violence that must be conceptualized and critiqued together (Weber, 2009). In the German context, violence due to "honor crimes" and one that specifically attributes violence against women in migrant communities to "Muslim culture" is a failure to "arrive" in German modernity (Weber, 2009).

There do exist organizations in Germany that refuse to choose between fighting for rights of immigrant communities and the rights of women. They simply do not find the public resonance of those in France. They wish to be against violence but find it difficult to do so on oversimplified, discursive grounds constructed by the women championed by dominant German society (Weber, 2009).

Indeed, given the feminist industry trading in stories of oppressed Turkish women, it may be more useful to think of an "indivisible" feminism relevant to all women, given that violence impacts everybody, as do employment inequalities (Weber, 2009). This sort of recognition of a more complex relationship between Islam, immigrant women, and feminism in the fight against gendered violence is also rarely represented in official conversations such as that taking place through the DIK (Weber, 2009). The discussion between Sezgin and Kiyak further suggests that exclusive attention to familial violence runs the danger of obscuring the economic and employment discrimination faced by women of immigrant heritage (Weber, 2009).

Mexico

The Mexican Institute for the Research of Family and Population (IMI-FAP) recognizes the progress made in the international sphere regarding violence against women and strives to reduce violence against women and girls through training programs that build skills and knowledge and by combating cultural norms and myths that generate, or at least condone, violence against women (Pick, Contreras, and Barker-Aguilar, 2006). IMIFAP's approach targets both the individual and community levels; it promotes new forms of coexistence and conflict resolution between men and women by enabling each to recognize the other's rights as individuals (Pick et al., 2006). The goal is to change attitudes, norms, and behaviors to achieve the common goals of improving the way men and women interact with each other (Pick et al., 2006).

In Latin America alone, more than one in every four women has been a victim of physical violence in the home (Saucedo et al., as cited in Pick et al., 2006). According to a 2003 survey conducted in Mexico by the National System of Statistics and Geographic Information (INEGI), 47 percent of Mexican women over the age of 15 who live with a partner suffer from some form of domestic violence (Pick et al., 2006). INEGI also reported that 96 out of 100 victims of violence in Mexico are women, while the remaining 96 are women (Pick et al., 2006). Data from the Secretary of Social Development indicates that 66 percent of women's deaths in urban areas occur due to violence in their own homes (Pick et al., 2006). Nationally, there are on average 14 deaths per day of women caused by violent acts (Pick et al., 2006). In the majority of domestic violence cases, the main aggressor is male; INEGI reports that 8 out of

10 women who fall victim to domestic violence suffer the most dangerous assaults from husbands or boyfriends (Pick et al., 2006). A diagnosis of the status of human rights in Mexico conducted by the Office of the United Nations High Commissioner for Human Rights indicates that there are 10 million women who suffer from violence in Mexico (Pick et al., 2006). Social inequality is compounded by economic inequality. According to the World Bank, women in the developed world earn 77 cents for each dollar that men earn in an equivalent job; in Mexico, women earn 68 cents for each dollar earned by men (Pick et al., 2006).

While the situation for women remains dismal, legal reforms in Mexico show that real change is occurring. In 1989, the Penal Code of Mexico City, which applies to most of Mexico City with its more than 18 million inhabitants, was reformed so that sexual crimes were recognized as "crimes against integrity and normal psycho-sexual development" and sexual violence was recognized as damaging one's physical and psychological integrity and sexual liberty (Pick et al., 2006). This same reform modified the concept of rape, once considered only vaginal, to include oral and anal penetration as well as to define sexual harassment and sexual abuse as a crime (Pick et al., 2006). The reform also eliminated the qualifying terms "honest and chaste" as a condition for lodging a claim (Pick et al., 2006). Before this, it was necessary to prove a woman's honesty and chastity prior to the crime in order to initiate an investigation into a sexual crime. In 1993, Article 20 of the national constitution was reformed to absolve minors of the obligation of confronting their aggressor in the case of rape or kidnapping, and to guarantee a victim's right to medical attention, judicial consultancy, the reparation of damages, and cooperation and collaboration with a public prosecutor (Pick et al., 2006). In 1997, the Mexican Congress approved reforms to the Civil and Penal Code regarding violence within the home; for the first time in Mexico, physical and psychological violence within the family was considered a crime (Pick et al., 2006). Other progress was made that resulted in the procurement and administration of justice, the agents of which are now obliged to take protective measures for the victims (Pick et al., 2006). As of September 2005, when the Supreme Court recognized the existence of marital rape, stated violence against one's wife is now considered a cause for divorce. In addition, when the violence is against minors, parent offenders can now lose guardianship of the children (Pick et al., 2006).

In 1999, the General Rule in Mexico (NOM-190-SSA 1-1999) was created to draw the attention of Mexican health services to domestic violence and to stimulate more thorough inquiries by medical personnel. These criteria and procedures are obligatory for all public and private health services in the national health system (Pick et al., 2006). In addition to these reforms, government agencies have initiated national such plans as the National Program for Equal Opportunity and Non-Discrimination against Women (President of the Republic, 2001), the National Program for a Life without Violence (INMUJERES, 2002a), and the Institutional Table (IN-MUJERES, 2002b) to coordinate preventive action and attention to domestic violence and violence toward women (Pick et al., 2006).

In Mexico, as in other countries, new legislation cannot and will not bring about all the change that is necessary. In a society where men feel entitled to make all decisions and women are reluctant to set boundaries within the relationship, change must occur on the individual level. IMIFAP's model is preventive. It is based on changing behaviors and sociocultural norms regarding coexistence and conflict resolution between men and women by recognizing each other's rights as individuals, in spite of what one may have learned from one's parents or from societal conceptions of gender inequality (Pick et al., 2006). The goals of IMIFAP's violence prevention programs are to develop skills in men and women to achieve common goals to improve the way they interact with each other (Pick et al., 2006). These skills include assertive communication, decision making, definition of priorities and future goals, self-knowledge, and active participation in one's health-related decisions as a means of preventing violence (Pick et al., 2006). Many women were surprised to learn that they had the power to communicate their needs to their husbands and had the rights to choose what they wanted. This type of assertive communication was indeed novel for these women, who had rarely voiced their wishes or set boundaries within their marriages (Pick et al., 2006). Another goal of IMIFAP was to promote masculine responsibility and equal relationships through comprehensive programs to achieve changes in gender roles (Pick et al., 2006). It is vital that men learn to control their anger and manage their anger effectively. Another important goal for IMIFAP was to educate and sensitize the health professionals who treat victims of domestic violence so that they develop skills, achieve more control over their lives, and enjoy improved well-being (Pick et al., 2006).

IMIFAP has developed numerous programs to address violence on a variety of levels. These include (Pick et al., 2006):

- I Want to, I Can . . . Prevent Violence (for adolescents)

  ○ The objective of this program is to prevent dating violence through information and education on how to detect the characteristics of potentially or openly violent relationships and to create alternative ways to build loving and more satisfying relationships.

- I Want to, I Can . . . Prevent Violence (for health personnel)

  ○ The goal of this program is to sensitize health personnel to their role regarding domestic violence and to teach them the skills necessary to detect, register, and focus attention on different causes of violence.

- I Want to, I Can . . . Prevent Violence (for females)

  ○ The objective of this program is to decrease the level of the incidence of domestic violence through the implementation of educational preventive programs that target women, men, adolescents, and representatives of the community.

- I Want to, I Can . . . Take Care of My Health and Rights (for females)

  ○ This program seeks to strengthen skills in rural women that are necessary to make decisions about health and family. These skills subsequently allow women to become the main health promoters in their respective communities,

- I Want to, I Can . . . Go into Business

  ○ Participants in this program wanted to complete their empowerment with full economic independence and asked for help to start their own small businesses. IMIFAP responded to their requests by piloting a micro-finance training program paired with small loans. This program has enabled poor and rural women to establish 500 sustainable businesses, of which a third have paid employees. The women who received training and loans repaid 100 percent of their loans.

- I Want to, I Can . . . Take Care of My Health and Rights (for males)

- ○ While this program is still in the process of development, its objective is to teach men how and where their concepts of masculinity have been formed, how this concept influences the manner in which they exercise their sexuality, reproduction, and health-related behaviors, and how this concept of masculinity affects their relationships with their families and their partners.

- I Want, I Love, I Can (for Children)

  - ○ The goal of this program is to teach children that they have rights, skills, and opportunities to express their emotions, to participate in tasks and games, to decide what they like, to live without violence, and to receive affection and all the basic elements for one's emotional and physical development.

The fight to end violence against women must involve more than just legislative reforms. According to Pick et al. (2006), only by targeting cultural norms through changes in behaviors and through sensitization, awareness training, and outreach can we change the sociocultural context. In order to do this, we must equip men and women with the proper skills to put their knowledge into practice and create lasting behavioral change.

Psychological and Medical Consequences of Violence

It is well documented that abused girls and women often suffer many sequelae associated with violence. These include adverse mental health conditions, such as depression, anxiety, and low self-esteem; poor physical health consequences, such as gynecological complications, chronic headaches, sleep disturbances, nausea, and a plethora of other poorly defined somatic complaints that often lack a clearly identified medical cause; and behavioral problems that further damage their health or put their lives at risk, such as substance abuse, alcoholism, and increased risk of suicide attempts (Graffunder et al., 2004). Domestic violence is frequently associated with injuries that do not match the explanation of how they occurred; a male partner who is overtly attentive, controlling, or unwilling to leave the woman's side; and physical injury during pregnancy. In addition, these women may also present with urinary tract infections and/or chronic pelvic pain.

Violence before and during pregnancy can have serious health consequences for women and their children. Pregnant women who have experienced violence are more likely to delay seeking prenatal care and to gain insufficient weight. They also are more likely to have a history of STIs, unwanted or mistimed pregnancies, vaginal and cervical infections, kidney infections, and bleeding during pregnancy. Violence has been linked with increased risk of miscarriages and abortions, premature labor, and fetal distress. Several studies also have focused on the relationship between violence in pregnancy and low birth weight, a leading contributor to infant deaths in the developing world (Heise et al., 2002).

A history of sexual abuse in childhood can indirectly lead to unwanted pregnancies and STDs by increasing sexual risk-taking in adolescence and adulthood (Heise et al., 2002). The studies also found a clear and consistent link between early sexual victimization and a variety of risk-taking behaviors, including early sexual debut, drug and alcohol use, more sexual partners, and less contraceptive use (Heise et al., 2002). Sexual and physical violence also appear to increase women's risk for many common gynecological disorders, such as chronic pelvic pain (CPP). Other gynecological disorders associated with sexual violence include irregular vaginal bleeding, vaginal discharge, painful menstruation, pelvic inflammatory disease, and sexual dysfunction. Sexual assault also increases the risk for premenstrual distress, a condition that affects 8 to 10 percent of menstruating women that causes physical, mood, and behavioral symptoms (Heise et al., 2002).

Conclusion

The data from Garcia-Moreno et al. (2006) add to the emerging body of research that confirms that violence by an intimate partner is a relatively common experience worldwide, and with the exception of one site in this particular study, women were more at risk of violence by an intimate partner than from any other perpetrator. In addition, these findings show that a large proportion of the violence is frequent and severe. Protections offered to battered women may still not be enough to protect them. According to Walker (1989), two-thirds of family violence deaths are women killed by their male partners, often when women attempt to leave their abusers. The fact that over half of all women homicide victims are killed by current or former partners further supports the gravity of this problem. Battered women accurately perceive their grave danger when they decide to leave their batterers, and have good reason to believe a man's threat to kill them if they leave the relationship.

As a result of decades of research on violence against women, many countries and entities—including the United States and the United Nations—have taken a more proactive approach regarding the prevention of violence against women. In the United States, passage of VAWA as well as the public health epidemiological approach of the Centers for Disease Control (CDC) have attempted to address this problem. The CDC's strategic approach toward violence against women has included a focus on primary prevention through a commitment to the advancement of the science of prevention, a focus on translating scientific advances into practical application through effective programs and policies, and the enhancement of the efforts of others by addressing existing gaps or needs (Graffunder et al., 2004). In England, the Cheshire Domestic Abuse Project reported significant success for a three-year study period. Pakistan has made strides to eliminate violence against women, although ignorance still remains a problem. South Africa, though obliged by international law to protect women's rights, still lags behind the efforts of other countries. Guatemala, unfortunately, continues to treat violence against women with apathy and, as of yet, has failed to provide women equal protection. Finally, in Mexico, while the outlook for women has been quite dismal, there is evidence that change is happening at last.

The purpose of this chapter has been to provide the reader with examples from various countries of the actions that have been instituted to eliminate violence against women. Violence against women can and often does cause a plethora of medical and psychological problems for the victims, young and old. It is only through effective leadership at the local, state, national, and global level that it can truly be eliminated.

References

Erturk, Y. (February 10, 2005). *Integration of the human rights of women and the gender perspective: Violence against women. Mission to Guatemala.* United Nations: Commission on Human Rights. Retrieved from http://daccess-dds-ny.un.org/doc/UNDOC/GEN/G05/108/17/ PDF/G0510817.pdf?OpenElement on June 1, 2010.

Fong, J. (2006). Psychodrama as a preventative measure: Teenage girls confronting violence. *Journal of Group Psychotherapy, Psychodrama & Sociometry, 59*(3), 99-108. doi: 10.3200/JGPP.59.3.99-108.

Garcia-Moreno, C., Jansen, H., Ellsberg, M., Heise, L., and Watts, C. (2006). Prevalence of intimate partner violence: Findings from the WHO multi-country study on women's health and domestic violence. *Lancet, 368*(9543), 1260–1269.

Graffunder, C., Noonan, R., Cox, P., and Wheaton, J. (2004). Through a public health lens. Preventing violence against women: An update from the U.S. Centers for Disease Control and Prevention. *Journal of Women's Health, 13*(1), 5–16. doi: 10.1089/154099904322836401.

Hague, G., and Bridge, S. (2008). Inching forward on domestic violence: The "co-ordinated community response" and putting it in practice in Cheshire. *Journal of Gender Studies, 17*(3), 185–199. doi: 10.1080/09589230802204134.

Heise, L., Ellsberg, M., and Gottmoeller, M. (2002). A global overview of gender-based violence. *International Journal of Gynaecology and Obstetrics: The Official Organ of the International Federation of Gynaecology and Obstetrics, 78 Suppl* 1S5–S14.

Heise, L., Moore, K., and Toubia, N. (1995). *Sexual coercion and women's reproductive health: A focus on research.* New York: Population Council.

Hester, M., and Westmarland, N. (2005). *Tackling domestic violence: Effective interventions and approaches.* Home Office Research Study 290. London: Home Office.

Jalal, A. (1991). The convenience of subservience: Women and the state in Pakistan. In Kandiyoti, D. (Ed.), *Women, Islam and the State* (pp. 77–114). Philadelphia, PA: Temple University Press.

Krantz, G., and Garcia-Moreno, C. (2005). Violence against women. *Journal of Epidemiology and Community Health, 59*(10), 818–821. doi: 10.1136/jech.2004.022756.

Laney, G. (2005). *Violence Against Women Act: History and federal funding.* CRS Report for Congress. Retrieved from http://opencrs.com/document/RL30871/ on January 13, 2010.

Maccoby, E. E., and Jacklin, C. N. (1974). *The psychology of sex differences.* Palo Alto, CA: Stanford Press.

Mercy, J., Krug, E., Dahlberg, L., and Zwi, A. (2003). Violence and health: The United States in a global perspective. *American Journal of Public Health, 93*(2), 256–261.

Niaz, U. (2003). Violence against women in South Asian countries. *Archives of Women's Mental Health, 6*(3), 173–184. doi: 10.1007/s00737-003-0171-9.

Observance of International Women's Day. (2009). *Meetings Coverage OBV/766.* Retrieved from United Nations Web site, http://www.un.org/News/Press/docs/2009/obv766.doc.htm, on June 15, 2010.

Pick, S., Contreras, C., and Barker-Aguilar, A. (2006). Violence against women in Mexico: Conceptualization and program application. *Violence and exploitation against women and girls* (pp. 261–278). Malden: Blackwell Publishing.

Russell, D. (2001). The politics of femicide. In D. Russell and R. Harmes (Eds.), *Femicide in global perspective* (pp. 177). New York: Teachers College Press.

Russell, D. and Harmes, R. (Eds.). (2001). *Femicide in global perspective.* New York: Teachers College Press.

Saltzman, L., Green, Y., Marks, J., and Thacker, S. (2000). Violence against women as a public health issue: Comments from the CDC. *American Journal of Preventive Medicine, 19*(4), 325–329.

Sanford, V. (2008). From genocide to feminicide: Impunity and human rights in twenty-first century Guatemala. *Journal of Human Rights, 7* (2), 104–122. doi: 10.1080/14754830802070192.

South Africa: Violence against women and the medico-legal system. New York: Human Rights Watch, 1997.

Sunder, M. (2003). Piercing the veil. *Yale Law Journal, 112*(6), 1399.

Tjaden, P., and Thoennes, N. (2000). *Full report of the prevalence, incidence, and consequences of violence against women: Findings from the National Violence Against Women Survey.* Washington, DC: U.S. Department of Justice. Retrieved from http://www.ncjrs.gov/pdffiles1/nij/183781.pdf on June 1, 2010.

United Nations General Assembly. (1993). Declaration on the elimination of violence against women. *Proceedings of the 85th plenary meeting, Geneva.* Retrieved from United Nations Web site, http://www.un.org/documents/ga/res/48/a48r104.htm, on May 15, 2010.

Violence Against Women Act of 1994, 42 U.S.C. § 13701. (House, Office of the Law Revision Counsel 2001).

Violence against women: A priority health issue. (1997). *World Health Organization.* Retrieved from World Health Organization Web site, http://www.who.int/gender/violence/prioreng/en/print.html, on June 12, 2010.

Walker, L. (1989). Psychology and violence against women. *American Psychologist, 44*(4), 695–702. doi: 10.1037/0003-066X.44.4.695.

Weber, B. (2009). Freedom from violence, freedom to make the world: Muslim women's memoirs, gendered violence, and voices for change in Germany. *Women in German Yearbook, 25,* 199–222.

13

Transformational Leadership: Is This the Way to the Top?

Michele T. Cole

In the forward to Carol Hooks Hawkins' 2009 book, *American Women Leaders*, her husband, Walter L. Hawkins, writes, "These women leaders have shown their competitive edge by using the full potential of their individual abilities ... The long-held belief of a glass ceiling does not appear to be unbreakable" (n.p.).

Really? Carter and Silva (2010) report that despite the promising increase in numbers of women graduating with advanced degrees and "swelling" the ranks of managers in corporations worldwide, women represent but 3 percent of *Fortune* 500 CEOs and 15 percent of *Fortune* 500 directors. In publicly traded companies, they state, less than 14 percent of top executives are female (p. 1).

Yet, as Eagly and Carli point out in their 2007 article, *Women and the Labyrinth of Leadership*, the fact that there are women CEOs, heads of state, Supreme Court justices, and university presidents demonstrates that the glass ceiling is not an absolute barrier to success—assuming that success is defined as reaching the top. However, note the authors' less-than-rosy assessment of women's struggles to get there: "... the glass ceiling fails to incorporate the complexity and variety of challenges that women can face in their leadership journeys. In truth, women are not turned away only as they reach the penultimate stage of a distinguished career. They disappear in various numbers at many points leading up to that stage" (p. 64).

Why are women lagging behind men in achieving top positions? Is it a question of leadership style? Are women less able to lead than men? And what is "leadership"? Is it defined differently for a woman than for a man? Rohmann and Rowall posed those questions in their 2009 survey of German workers in the public and private sectors. The authors asked participants to evaluate their leaders with respect to leadership style. They also asked students to comment on the perceived leadership styles of various historical world leaders. They found that participants viewed women more often than men to be transformational leaders. Participants viewed men more often than women to be transactional leaders. They note that despite a finding that transformational leadership is credited with greater worker satisfaction and greater management effectiveness, men are still rated more qualified for management roles than women (Rohmann and Rowold, 2009).

Contrary to Rohmann and Rowold's findings, Kalid and Amjad (2009) found no significant difference in leadership styles between men and women in their study of educators in Pakistan. But they did find that leaders, regardless of gender, relied on transformational leadership more than they did on transactional leadership.

In a discussion of transformational and transactional capability sets used in higher education recruitment and selection, Moss and Daunton (2006) cite numerous studies in support of transformational leadership producing greater long-term organizational results across sectors and in various countries than transactional leadership. Yet, if transformational leadership is the more successful style and is more often linked with women leaders, why then are there still relatively few women at the highest levels of public and private sector organizations? Is it that, regardless of gender, there is a preference for transactional leadership over transformational leadership? Or, as Moss and Daunton argue, is there in fact a glass ceiling that prevents women from advancing at the same pace as men in the same field?

In his review of leadership theories, Van Wart (2010) notes that it was not until James MacGregor Burns's 1978 seminal work, *Leadership*, and his emphasis on "transformational" characteristics of leadership, that the focus of leadership studies shifted from middle management to the executive suite. Models of transformational leadership stress vision and organizational change (Van Wart, p. 81). Traditional models of transactional leadership are based on a system of rewards and punishment. London (2008) describes Burns's conception of transformational leadership as the promotion of the common good by a mutual exchange between the leader and the follower.

Arguably, the characteristics more often associated with transformational leadership are "feminine" (collaboration and cooperation, intuitive problem solving, shared control), while those associated with transactional leadership are "masculine" (competitiveness, control, hierarchy, analytical problem solving) (Jogulu and Wood, 2006). However, defining leadership styles in gender-specific terms may not be very helpful in understanding why more women are not in leadership positions. The real issue remains equity in choosing the right person for the position (Trinidad and Normore, 2006).

Fairholm (2001) explains Burns's philosophy of leadership as one grounded in the development of interpersonal relationships consistent with the motives and values of the leader and the followers. These are characteristics associated with transformational leadership. While transformational and transactional leadership are often presented as opposing styles, Van Wart (2010) reminds us that effective leadership can as easily be thought of as a blend.

In one study focusing on improving the status of women in higher education administration, several women administrators and faculty from different institutions explored the factors surrounding the leadership challenges they faced in their careers (Ransdell et al., 2008). As a result of their discussions, they proposed a transformational leadership model to address the constraints placed on female administrators. They argue that developing personal and professional characteristics and understanding environmental characteristics will lead to transformational actions that result in organizational transformation. Their hope is that successful implementation of the model will help attract and retain women in leadership positions in academia.

Schyns, von Elverfeldt, and Felfe (2008) tell us that even when women lead "transformationally," that by itself does not contribute to the female leader's belief in her efficacy as a leader. ". . . Women do not gain from showing female behavior" (p. 609). The significance of this finding lies in its relationship to the reluctance of women to promote themselves in the workplace. Is it possible that some are not trying hard enough to reach the top, acknowledging the inevitability of the glass ceiling? Or, is it that the road to the top is littered with obstacles less easily overcome by women because of their professional and personal preferences, their family values, and the perception that those preferences and values are not compatible with climbing the career ladder? Eagly and Carli (2007) say that it is not the glass ceiling that holds us back; rather, it is "the sum of many obstacles along the way" (p. 63).

In an earlier piece on gender differences in management skills and leadership styles, Burke and Collins (2001) examined the relationship among management skills, the development of subordinates, clear communication of organizational goals, resolution of conflict, analysis of problems and decision making, and leadership styles. They found differences in style based on gender; however, unlike Schyns, von Elverfeldt, and Felfe, they identified a positive relationship between transformational leadership and effective management.

Management is the process of getting things done, effectively and efficiently, with and through people (Robbins, Decenzo, and Coulter, 2011, p. 6). It is planning, organizing, leading, and controlling resources to achieve organizational goals efficiently and effectively (Jones and George, 2009, p. 5). Leadership is also a process. It is one in which a person influences, motivates, inspires, and directs others to achieve stated goals (Jones and George, p. 321).

Managers direct a set of activities in support of accomplishing the chosen objective. That is relatively easy to do, assuming one understands what needs to be done and how it can be done, and one can access the resources to do it. Leadership, on the other hand, is more difficult. To lead is to make positive change happen. Change, whether on the individual, organizational or societal level, as we all know, is very difficult to effect. I seem to recall that those of us who were in college in the 1960s thought we could change the world.

Leadership opportunities can present themselves in a variety of settings—inside the workplace as well as in volunteer work, sports, recreational activities, etc. What seems to be critical to being effective though is whether one has the authority—informal or formal—to effect change or inspire others to achieve the objective.

Is transformational leadership a means to the top? Will transformational leadership prove to be a means of breaking through the glass ceiling? Writing about women leaders and the women's movement, Astin and Leland

(1991) remind us that ". . . leadership involves a diversity of effective styles, strategies, risks, and initiatives" (p. xvii). Effective leadership, whether transformational or transactional or some combination of the two, regardless of gender, requires self-confidence. Ideally, that confidence springs from a realistic assessment of capabilities and possibilities. We can control the part of the equation that rests on capabilities. The challenge is in changing what is possible.

References

Astin, H. S., and Leland, C. (1991). *Women of influence, women of vision: A cross-generational study of leaders and social change.* San Francisco: Jossey-Bass Publishers.

Burke, S., and Collins, K. M. (2001). Gender differences in leadership styles and management skills. *Women in Management Review, 16*(5), 244–256.

Carter, N. M., and Silva, C. (2010). Pipeline's broken promise. *The promise of future leadership: A research program on highly talented employees in the pipeline.* New York: Catalyst.

Eagly, A. H., and Carli, L. L. (2007). Women and the labyrinth of leadership. *Harvard Business Review, 85*(9), 63–71.

Fairholm, M. R. (2001). *The themes and theory of leadership: James McGregor Burns and the philosophy of leadership* (Working Paper CR01-01). George Washington University Center for Excellence in Municipal Management.

Hawkins, C. H. (2009). *American women leaders: 1,560 current biographies.* Jefferson, North Carolina: McFarland and Company, Inc.

Jogulu, U. D., and Wood, G. L. (2006). The role of leadership theory in raising the profile of women in management. *Equal Opportunities International, 25*(4), 236–250.

Jones, G. R., and George, J. M. (2009). *Essentials of contemporary management,* 3rd ed. Boston: McGraw-Hill.

Khalid, S., and Amjad, S. (2009). Gender influence on leadership styles: A case study of education sector at district Abbottabad, Pakistan. *FWU Journal of Social Sciences, 3*(1), 66–78.

London, S. (2008). Leadership by James Macgregor Burns [Review of the book *Leadership*]. Retrieved from http://www.scottlondon.com/reviews/burns.html on May 17, 2010.

Moss, G., and Daunton, L. (2006). The discriminatory impact of non-adherence to leadership selection criteria: The case of higher education.*Career Development International, 11* (6), 504–521.

Ransdell, L. B., Toevs, S., White, J., Lucas, S., Perry, J. L., Grosshams, O., et al. (2008). Increasing the number of women administrators in kinesiology and beyond: A proposed application of the transformational leadership model. *Women in Sport and Physical Activity Journal, 17*(1), 3–14.

Robbins, S. P., Decenzo, D. A., and Coulter, M. (2011). *Fundamentals of management: Essential concepts and applications.* New York: Prentice Hall.

Rohmann, A., and Rowold, J. (2009). Gender and leadership style: A field study in different organizational contexts in Germany. *Equal Opportunities International, 28*(7), 545–560.

Schyns, B., von Elverfeldt, A., and Felfe, J. (2008). Is there a male advantage in the effects of feedback and leadership on leaders' occupational self-efficacy? *Equal Opportunities International, 27*(7), 596–612.

Trinidad, C., and Normore, A. H. (2005). Leadership and gender: A dangerous liaison? *Leadership and Organization Development Journal, 26*(7), 574–590.

Van Wart, M. (2010). Public-sector leadership theory: An assessment. In Perry, J.L. (Ed.). *The Jossey-Bass Reader on Nonprofit and Public Leadership* (pp. 73–107). San Francisco: Jossey-Bass.

14

Leading a "Dis-Organization": Being a Queen Mother of a Red Hat Society

Sharon W. Hurley

The Red Hat Society was formed by Queen Sue Ellen Cooper in 1988. The society was inspired by Jenny Joseph's poem, "Warning," which begins with the phrase: "When I am an old woman I shall wear purple / With a red hat which doesn't go . . . ." The poem basically idealizes a time when a woman can break away from the shackles of a responsible life, act naturally without regard to convention, be silly, and have fun away from the "sobriety of my youth." The basic premise is that we women have paid our dues as we have juggled our careers, family, and homes for years and now, as we have grown older, we deserve to take time for ourselves and to do new, different, and fun things.

After joining another Red Hat chapter, I discovered that there are all kinds of groups. Some meet once a month for lunch or dinner. Some have a special interest, like line dancing or quilting. And others engage in a variety of activities, try new experiences, and find creative ways to laugh, be silly, and have a great time.

Six of us gathered in 2006 to create our own style of group. After some trial and error, we came up with the name "Rowdy Scarletts." We wanted to develop an active, fun-loving chapter. We needed someone to register and apply for a charter; by default, I became the founding queen mother.

The values of the Red Hat Society describe a "dis-organization," or an organization with no rules, few organizational responsibilities, and no penalties for participation on your own basis. Our sole organizational guideline is that members must wear a red hat (or red feather, ribbon, or flower) on her head and something purple on her body.

At first, being queen of the Rowdy Scarletts was nothing but a fun title that allowed me to wear a rhinestone pin that says "Queen" on my purple dress, or a tiara if I so chose. We made decisions and plans by consensus; each member shared ideas and plans for us to undertake. We each quickly learned that wearing purple and red caused people to notice us as we went out. The attention was almost universally positive. Donning our regalia became a sort of costume that freed us and enabled us to act without our usual deference to convention and the norms of our upbringing.

We found that we laughed more, acted sillier, tried new things, and, as we got to know each other better, we became close friends. As the group grew, however, the role of queen changed rather markedly. It is my belief that in order to have a welcoming group, members must know each other personally and be comfortable sharing a table or a ride. Even as a dis-organization, the women are only willing to be members of a group that they feel a part of. It has become the queen's role to manage the acceptance of new members at a rate such that they can be assimilated by the group and to develop fun, interactional experiences to integrate new members.

Another one of my roles is to develop and maintain an environment that promotes free exchange of ideas: all ideas are accepted and evaluated and brainstorming can flourish. We are looking for ideas, events, and experiences that are outside of our day-to-day life. We want to be open to try new and different activities, cross things off our "bucket lists," and have fun as often as possible. We also need to plan activities that are accessible to members and affordable for different budgets. And, just to complicate things a bit, it has become the queen's role to share the task of planning and organizing across the membership so that members can just join in the silliness without any responsibility most of the time. But perhaps the most important role of the queen is to model fun and frivolity! This is by far the easiest and best part of being queen. I get to wear the most outra-geous, over-the-top, crazy red hats with purple outfits befitting a queen, along with tons of rhinestone bling that would have been embarrassing at my junior prom.

I get to dress up as often as I like in a society where casual is the norm. I get to freely laugh at fun things, and enjoy the company and sisterhood of a group of fabulous women whom I otherwise would never have met. I can be as queenly as I like, with a queen's wave and elegance. I am able to enjoy spending time with others, sharing funny stories, learning about the members' very interesting lives and histories, and developing great friendships.

I get to lead kazoo parades at gatherings and use silly, loud noisemakers at functions. I get to have a wonderful time with a group of close friends while at the opera, rodeo, comedy clubs, Renaissance fairs, garage sales, boat cruises, ball games, Victorian teas, auto races, horseback riding, movies, picnics, Elvis shows, theater performances, pool parties, luaus, museums, TV tapings, tubing, festivals, birthday parties, racinos, and weekend conventions of hundreds of similarly clad Red Hat ladies. And I will get to do a lot of fun things I haven't even thought of yet—with a group of terrific women.

Appendix: Organizations Concerned with Women and Leadership

Renay Dworakowski and Michele A. Paludi

We have compiled a list of resources dealing with women and leadership. We believe this is a good starting point for those who seek additional information about women and leadership in the United States and globally. We recognize that this list is neither complete nor exhaustive.

Advocates for Youth
  http://www.advocatesforyouth.org/about/ywoclc.htm

Advancing Women in Leadership Journal
  www.advancingwomen.com/awl/awl.html

National Council of Negro Women
  http://www.ncnw.org/centers/height.htm

African Women's Development Fund
  http://www.awdf.org

Grand Rapids Opportunities for Women (an alliance of women entrepreneurs)
  http://www.awe-westmichigan.org/

Association for Women's Rights in Development
  http://www.awid.org/

Athena Foundation
  http://www.athenafoundation.org/

Black Career Women
  http://www.bcw.org/

Black Women's Leadership Council
http://www.bwlc.com/

Business and Professional Women's Foundation
http://www.bpwfoundation.org/i4a/pages/index.cfm?pageid=1

Caribbean Institute for Women and Leadership
http://www.ciwil.org/

Catalyst
http://www.catalyst.org/

Center for Creative Leadership
http://www.ccl.org

Center for Leadership and Change Management
http://leadership.wharton.upenn.edu/

The Center for Asian Pacific American Women
http://www.apawomen.org

Center for Women & Enterprise
http://www.cweboston.org/

Center for Women's Business Research
http://womensbusinessresearch.org/

Center for Women's Global Leadership
http://www.cwgl.rutgers.edu

Center for Women's Intercultural Leadership
http://www.centerforwomeninleadership.org/#/

The Center for Women's Leadership, Babson College
http://www.babson.edu/cwl

Centre de Leadership Féminin
adfm@casanet.net.ma

Chattanooga Women's Leadership Institute
http://www.cwli.org/index.php

Community of Women Entrepreneurs
http://www.reformsnetwork.org/women/

Council of Women World Leaders
http://www.womenworldleaders.org

Courageous Leadership Consortium
   http://www.courageousleadership.org/Leadership-Resources.cfm

Executive Women International
   http://www.executivewomen.org/

Feminist.com
   http://www.feminist.com

Foundation for Women's Resources
   http://womensresources.org/LT.asp

Global EXEC Women
   http://www.globalexecwomen.com

Harpswell Foundation Leadership Centers for Women
   http://harpswellfoundation.org/center/index.html

Home-Based Working Moms
   http://www.hbwm.com/

Institute for Women's Leadership
   http://www.womensleadership.com

Invent Your Future Enterprises
   http://inventyourfuture.com

International Committee of Women Leaders for Mental Health
   http://www.cartercenter.org/health/mental_health/intl_women.html

Leadership California
   http://www.leadershipca.org

Leadership Illinois
   http://leadershipillinois.org

Leadership Texas
   http://www.womensresources.org/LT.asp

Mobility International USA
   http://www.miusa.org

Mompreneurs Online
   http://www.mompreneursonline.com

National Association for Moms in Business
   http://www.mibn.org/

National African-American Women's Leadership Institute, Inc.
http://www.naawli.org

National Association for Female Executives
http://nafe.com/?service=vpage/1474

National Association of Women Business Owners
http://nawbo.org

National Council of Women's Organizations
http://www.womensorganizations.org/

National Hispana Leadership Institute
http://www.nhli.org

National Organization for Women
http://www.now.org/

National Women Business Owners Corporation
http://nwboc.org

NEW Leadership Development Network
http://www.cawp.rutgers.edu/education_training/NEWLeadership/
newleadership_devnet.php

Orange County Women's Leadership Fund
http://www.womensleadershipocny.org

Organization of Women Leaders
http://owls.wordpress.com/

Rutgers University Center for Women and Politics
http://www.cawp.rutgers.edu/education_training/trainingresources/
index.php

Seattle Women's Commission
http://www.seattle.gov/womenscommission/resources.htm

Soroptimist International of the Americas
http://www.soroptimist.org/Leadership/Resources.html

South Asian Women's Leadership Forum
http://www.southasianwomen.org/

Susan B. Anthony Center for Women's Leadership
http://www.rochester.edu/College/WST/

The Coaching & Mentoring Network
  http://www.coachingnetwork.org.uk

The White House Project: Vote, Run, Lead
  http://thewhitehouseproject.org/voterunlead/

U.S. Women's Chamber of Commerce
  http://www.uswcc.org/

Virginia Women's Institute for Leadership
  http://www.mbc.edu/vwil/

Women Executive Leadership
  http://www.womenexecutiveleadership.com/

Women's Executive Network
  http://www.wxnetwork.com

Women in Leadership Foundation
  http://www.womeninleadership.ca/

Women's Foundation of California
  www.womensfoundca.org

Women's Leadership Circles
  http://www.w-l-c.org/content/print.php

Women's Leadership Exchange
  http://www.womensleadershipexchange.com/

Women's Leadership Forum
  http://www.exed.hbs.edu/programs/wlf/

Women's Leadership Institute
  http://www.mills.edu/WLI/wli.home.html

Women's Leadership Network
  http://wlnhelena.org/

Women's Leadership Program
  http://www.ccl.org/leadership/programs/WLPOverview.aspx

Women of Color Leadership Institute
  http://www.nmac.org/index/wocli

Women's Executive Leadership Retreat
  http://executive.berkeley.edu/programs/women-leadership/

Women Presidents' Organization
   http://www.womenpresidentsorg.com/

World Association for Women Entrepreneurs
   http://www.fcem.org/home.php?lang=en

Worldwide Guide to Women in Leadership
   http://www.guide2womenleaders.com

WomenWatch
   http://www.un.org/womenwatch

Zonta International
   http://www.zonta.org/

About the Editors and Contributors

Editors

Michele A. Paludi, PhD, is the series editor of "Women's Psychology and for Women and Careers in Management" for Praeger. She is the author/editor of 38 college textbooks, and more than 170 scholarly articles and conference presentations on sexual harassment, campus violence, psychology of women, gender, and discrimination. Her book, *Ivory Power: Sexual Harassment on Campus* (1990, SUNY Press), received the 1992 Myers Center Award for Outstanding Book on Human Rights in the United States. Dr. Paludi served as chair of the U.S. Department of Education's Subpanel on the Prevention of Violence, Sexual Harassment, and Alcohol and Other Drug Problems in Higher Education. She was one of six scholars in the United States to be selected for this subpanel. She also was a consultant to and a member of former New York State Governor Mario Cuomo's Task Force on Sexual Harassment. Dr. Paludi serves as an expert witness for court proceedings and administrative hearings on sexual harassment. She has had extensive experience in conducting training programs and investigations of sexual harassment and other equal employment opportunity (EEO) issues for businesses and educational institutions. In addition, Dr. Paludi has held faculty positions at Franklin & Marshall College, Kent State University, Hunter College, Union College, and Union Graduate College, where she currently directs the human resource management certificate program. She is on the faculty of the

School of Management. She was recently named "Woman of the Year" by the Business and Professional Women in Schenectady, NY, and is currently the Elihu Root Peace Fund Professor in Women's Studies at Hamilton College.

Breena E. Coates, PhD, is chair of the Department of Management, College of Business and Public Administration, California State University, San Bernadino. She has been a professor of strategic management, planning, and organizational behavior in the Department of Command, Leadership, and Management at the U.S. Army War College. Dr. Coates has also served as interim associate dean and divisional chairperson at San Diego State University. Her research includes market controls on corporate social responsibility, women in the military, culture and cognition in a complex megaorganization, and an understanding of stress on social systems in dynamic organizational environments. Dr. Coates's current teaching interests include organizational behavior, strategic management, planning and leadership and the impact of public management, and the policy and law of organizations. In 2009, she received the Commandant's Award for Outstanding Teaching and Service from the U.S. Army War College. She also received the Outstanding Professor Award from San Diego State University's Imperial Valley Campus in 2005.

Contributors

Susan A. Basow is the Charles A. Dana Professor of Psychology at Lafayette College. A licensed clinical psychologist, Dr. Basow focuses her teaching and writing on gender issues. She is the author of the textbook, *Gender: Stereotypes and Roles*, as well as chapters on gender socialization, gender and education, body image, gender identity development, and gendered communication. She has conducted numerous research studies on gender issues in students' evaluations of female and male faculty as well as on such topics as women's body objectification and gendered perceptions of relational aggression. A fellow of the American Psychological Association in three divisions (Society for the Psychology of Women; Society for the Psychological Study of Lesbian, Gay, and Bisexual Issues; Society for the Psychological Study of Social Issues), Dr. Basow is currently on the executive committee of Div. 35, the Society for the Psychology of Women.

Terry A. Beehr, director of the PhD program in industrial/organizational psychology at Central Michigan University, earned a PhD in organizational psychology from the University of Michigan. He is a fellow of the Society for Industrial and Organizational Psychology, Association for Psychological Science, and Midwestern Psychological Association and an associate editor for *Human Relations* and *Journal of Organizational Behavior.*

Karen Dill Bowerman is dean of the College of Business & Public Administration at California State University, San Bernardino. She has taught leadership in U.S. and Asian businesses, as well as in university management education courses. Her scholarly work is in the fields of leadership, strategic management, human resources, and organization theory. Before earning her doctorate at Texas A&M, where she was named Outstanding Graduate for Academics, Leadership, and Service, she led organizations in business and served as the executive director of the Texas Commission on the Status of Women. Some observations in her chapter, "Living the Questions," are adapted from personal experiences and from a 2011 leadership textbook that Dr. Bowerman coauthored, titled *The Business of Leadership.*

Megan A. Brewer is a graduate student in the clinical psychology program at the University of Texas at Tyler. She earned a BS in criminal justice from the University of Houston-Downtown. While pursuing graduate studies, she has participated in various types of research projects. Her career plans involve forensic psychology and a role with the Federal Bureau of Investigation.

Michele T. Cole, JD, PhD, is the director of the master's program in nonprofit management and an associate professor of nonprofit management at Robert Morris University, Moon Township, PA. Her research interests include distance education, nonprofit sector curriculum development, legal issues and the application of business best practices and research to the nonprofit sector, and the application of technology to learning strategies.

Nicole L. Cundiff, PhD, earned a doctorate from Southern Illinois University Carbondale in 2010. She is the director of the Northern Leadership Center and an assistant professor of management at the University of

Alaska-Fairbanks. She specializes in gender in leadership and organizational diversity. Dr. Cundiff's articles have appeared in such publications as the *Journal of Leadership and Organizational Studies* and *Management Research Review.*

Renay Dworakowski, MBA, earned a graduate degree from Union Graduate College in 2010. She graduated from the State University of New York at Albany with a BA in English and women's studies. She currently is employed by Community Care Physicians as the training and systems administration lead.

Tina C. Elacqua, PhD, teaches graduate-level business courses and undergraduate business and psychology courses at LeTourneau University. She earned graduate and undergraduate degrees in industrial and organizational psychology from Central Michigan University. Her research interests include leadership, career development, and faith-based management of postviolent death.

J. Harold Ellens is a retired university professor of philosophy and psychology, a retired U.S. army colonel, a retired Presbyterian pastor and theologian, executive director emeritus of the Christian Association for Psychological Studies International, founder and editor in chief emeritus of the *Journal of Psychology and Christianity,* clinical psychotherapist in private practice, and the author, coauthor, or editor of 175 volumes and author of 166 professional journal articles. He continues in his role as adjunct professor of philosophy and biblical studies at the University of Detroit Mercy and adjunct professor of classics at Wayne State University and is a research scholar in the Department of Near Eastern Studies at the University of Michigan.

Jeanine M. Galusha is a graduate student in the MS clinical neuropsychology program at the University of Texas at Tyler. Her academic goals include earning a doctorate in psychology and to continue doing research in dementia. She earned a BS in psychology and graduated *magna cum laude* from the University of Texas at Tyler in 2010. As an undergraduate, she was accepted as a member of Psi Chi, the national honor society in psychology and worked with several professors on various research projects.

Ayelet Giladi, PhD., is a pioneer and recognized expert on the harassment of young children in Israel. Dr. Giladi, a professor at Kibbutzim College, teaches her students how to recognize the sexual harassment of children, conduct qualitative research, and report on the phenomenon. In addition, she conducts research on the issue, consults with a variety of organizations, and conducts training about sexual harassment at an early age. She has authored five prevention programs for use with children: Getting Along Together, for children aged 4–7; Getting Along Together 10, for children aged 8–10; Getting Along in Big Time, for children aged 11–13; Getting Along in Junior-High, for seventh to ninth graders; and Getting Along in High-School, for ninth to twelfth graders. These prevention programs are widely used in kindergartens as well as public and private schools throughout Israel.Dr. Giladi is the chief executive officer of the Voice of the Child Association for the Prevention of Sexual Harassment Among Young Children. The association serves young children with visual impairments; children from various religious backgrounds; and new immigrant children, especially from Ethiopia. She is the author of book chapters and several articles in professional journals about the sexual harassment of young children. She has been featured on Israeli television, radio programs, and newscasts and in Israeli newspaper articles.

Dr. Giladi has spoken about sexual harassment at an early age to the Knesset (Israeli parliament) and at international conferences in the United States and England. She trains family judges, physicians, nurses, psychologists, educators and schools administrators, social workers, parents and children about the phenomenon. Dr. Giladi has a doctorate in sociology education from England ARU University, a master's degree in sociology and education, and a bachelor's degree in education. She has been an activist in developing awareness about sexual harassment at an early age since 1996.

In 2008, Dr. Giladi received a certificate of recognition from the International Coalition Against Sexual Harassment (ICASH) for her contributions to sexual harassment research. In 2010, she won an award from the Israel Sociological Society (ISS) for being a practicable sociologist.

Veronica L. Gilrane is currently pursuing a doctoral degree in industrial-organizational psychology at George Mason University. Working closely with her advisor, Dr. Eden King, Ms. Gilrane conducts research in the area of workplace diversity and inclusion. A primary focus of her research explores the experiences and perceptions of women and minorities in leadership positions. Ms. Gilrane has presented her research at the annual conference for the Society for Industrial and Organizational Psychology. In addition to her scholastic endeavors, Ms. Gilrane has also gained applied research experience relating to the retention of officers in the U.S. Armed Forces.

Desiree L. Glaze is a graduate student in the MS clinical psychology program at the University of Texas at Tyler; she anticipates graduating in 2011. While at UT-Tyler, she has participated in research projects. Her academic goals include becoming a licensed professional counselor and obtaining a doctorate in psychology. She hopes to conduct research with and provide therapeutic intervention for children who have experienced sexual abuse. She earned a BS in psychology from Abilene Christian University in 2009. As an undergraduate, she was accepted as a member of Psi Chi, the national honor society in psychology, served as a research assistant, and was a member of Abilene Christian University honors program.

Katie E. Griffin received a master's degree in forensic psychology at CUNY John Jay College of Criminal Justice. Her research interests include microaggressions and mental health, as well as hate crimes and their associated legislation.

Sharon W. Hurley is a retired mental health administrator and rehabilitation counselor for the New York State Office of Mental Health, where she worked for 35 years. She earned a bachelor's and a master's degree from the University at Albany. She is currently is founding queen of the Rowdy Scarletts Chapter of the Red Hat Society, a volunteer wish granter for the Make-a-Wish Foundation, a volunteer with Proctor's Theatre in Schenectady, New York, and a member and former board member of the Schoharie Colonial Heritage Association. She lives in Schoharie County, New York, with Steve, her husband of 38 years and their two little dogs. She has two adult married daughters who are fabulous young professionals.

Eden B. King joined the faculty of the industrial-organizational psychology program at George Mason University after earning a PhD from Rice

University in 2006 Dr.. King is pursuing a program of research that seeks to guide the equitable and effective management of diverse organizations. Her research, which has appeared in such publications as the *Journal of Applied Psychology, Human Resource Management, Perspectives of IO Psychology,* and *Group and Organization Management,* integrates organizational and social psychological theories in conceptualizing social stigma and the work–life interface. This research addresses three primary themes: 1) current manifestations of discrimination and barriers to work–life balance in organizations, 2) consequences of such challenges for its targets and their workplaces, and 3) individual and organizational strategies for reducing discrimination and increasing support for families. In addition to her academic positions, Dr. King has consulted on applied projects related to climate initiatives, selection systems, diversity training programs and has worked as a trial consultant. She is currently on the editorial board of the *Journal of Management* and the *Journal of Business and Psychology.*

Paula K. Lundberg-Love, PhD, is a professor of psychology at the University of Texas at Tyler (UTT) and was the Ben R. Fisch Endowed Professor in Humanitarian Affairs for 2001–2004. She earned an undergraduate degree in chemistry and worked as a chemist at a pharmaceutical company for five years prior to earning a doctorate in physiological psychology with an emphasis in psychopharmacology. After a three-year postdoctoral fellowship in nutrition and behavior in the Department of Preventive Medicine at Washington University School of Medicine in St. Louis, she assumed her academic position at UTT, where she teaches classes in psychopharmacology, behavioral neuroscience, physiological psychology, sexual victimization, and family violence. Subsequent to her academic appointment, Dr. Lundberg-Love pursued postgraduate training and is a licensed professional counselor. She is a member of Tyler Counseling and Assessment Center, where she provides therapeutic services for victims of sexual assault, child sexual abuse, and domestic violence. She has conducted a long-term research study on women who were victims of childhood incestuous abuse, constructed a therapeutic program for their recovery, and documented its effectiveness upon their recovery. She is the author of nearly 100 publications and presentations and is coeditor of *Violence and Sexual Abuse at Home: Current Issues in Spousal*

Battering and Child Maltreatment as well as *Intimate Violence Against Women: When Spouses, Partners, or Lovers Attack.* As a result of her training and expertise in psychopharmacology and child maltreatment, she has been sought as a consultant on various death penalty appellate cases in the state of Texas.

Silvia L. Mazzula is an assistant professor at John Jay College of Criminal Justice in the Department of Psychology. She received a PhD in counseling psychology from Columbia University (BS and MA, The College of New Jersey; MPhil, Columbia University) and completed her formal clinical training at the University of Medicine & Dentistry of New Jersey-UBHC Newark Campus. Dr. Mazzula's research interests focus primarily on multicultural issues in psychology, including multicultural competencies in research and practice, acculturation, racial/ethnic identity development, and mental health disparities, particularly among Latino/a Americans. She has worked in a variety of clinical settings, predominantly servicing underserved and underrepresented populations.

Tracy C. McCausland is a second-year doctoral student in the industrial-organizational psychology program at George Mason University. She earned a BS from Davidson College in 2009. Her teaching responsibilities include undergraduate psychology research methods as well graduate advanced statistics and research methods. Her research interests include leadership, teamwork, training, and age diversity. In addition to her academic responsibilities and pursuits, Ms. McCausland also serves as the president of the Industrial-Organizational Psychology Student Association (IOPSA) at George Mason University.

Whitney Botsford Morgan, PhD, received a doctorate in industrial-organizational psychology from George Mason University in 2009. She is currently an assistant professor of management at the University of Houston-Downtown.Dr. Morgan teaches organizational behavior, principles of management, and leadership. The overarching goal of her program of research is to provide theoretical and empirical evidence guiding the advancement of women and mothers in the workplace. Her line of research touches a variety of content areas, including performance appraisal, developmental opportunities, extrarole behavior, and retention. She has published in *Human Resource Management Review, Journal of Occupational Health Psychology, Equal Opportunities International*, and *Sex Roles*; she is also a reviewer for *Equal Opportunities International, Human Relations* and for the annual conferences of the Academy of Management and the Society for Industrial and Organizational Psychology. Dr. Morgan has consulted on several applied projects related to selection, competency modeling, and leader development initiatives.

Kevin L. Nadal, PhD, is an assistant professor of psychology and mental health counseling at John Jay College of Criminal Justice-City University of New York. He earned his doctorate in counseling psychology from Columbia University. He has published several works focusing on Filipino American, ethnic minority, and LGBTQ issues in the fields of psychology and education. He is a fellow of the Robert Wood Johnson Foundation and is the author of the books *Filipino American Psychology: A Handbook of Theory, Research, and Clinical Practice* and *Filipino American Psychology: A Collection of Personal Narratives*.

Margaret S. Stockdale, PhD, is a professor of psychology and program director of applied psychology at Southern Illinois University Carbondale. She is the author and editor of over 40 publications, including five books primarily in the field of employment justice and gender issues in the workplace. Dr. Stockdale is a fellow of the American Psychological Association and an associate editor of *Psychology of Women Quarterly*.

Susan Strauss, EdD, is a national and international speaker, trainer, and consultant. Her specialty areas include management/leadership development, harassment and bullying, and communication. Dr. Strauss is an organization development consultant specializing in management coaching, teambuilding, and workplace bullying. Her clients are from business, education, health care, law, and government organizations in the public and private sectors. Dr.Strauss has held positions in training, organization development, and middle and senior management. She has authored book chapters, articles in professional journals, curriculum, and training manuals, as well as the book, *Sexual Harassment and Teens: A Program for Positive Change*. Dr. Strauss has been featured on *The Donahue Show, CBS Evening News, 20/20,* and other television and radio programs and has been interviewed for such newspaper and journal articles as the *Times of London, Lawyers Weekly,* and *Harvard Education Newsletter.*

Josephine C. H. Tan is an associate professor with the Department of Psychology, Lakehead University, in Thunder Bay, Ontario, Canada. She is involved with the graduate collaborative women's studies program and is a part of the multi-institutional research Centre for Biological Timing and Cognition. She is active in service to the profession, having been elected and served on the council and various committees of the Ontario provincial professional psychology regulatory board, and is the past president of the Canadian Council of Professional Psychology Programs (CCPPP). She received the CCPPP Award of Excellence in Professional Training (Academic) in 2008 for her work and mentoring as the director of clinical training in her program and was elected to fellow status by the American Psychological Association in 2009.

Jennica Webster is an assistant professor in the Department of Management at Marquette University. She received a PhD from Central Michigan University and a master's degree from the University of Wisconsin Oshkosh. Her research interests are in the areas of gender stereotypes in leadership, occupational stress and health, and career issues.

Yinglee Wong received a master's degree in forensic psychology from CUNY-John Jay College. Her research interests include microaggressions, as well as eyewitness identifications and eyewitness descriptions.

Karen Gross is the president of Southern Vermont College (SVC), a small, private, affordable four-year college located in Bennington, Vermont. SVC has more than 60 percent first-generation students, over 45 percent of whom are Pell eligible. The college offers a career-launching education with a liberal arts core; many of the college's graduates enter the fields of health care, criminal justice, entrepreneurship, and social service. Gross also holds the position of Distinguished Visiting Professor of Law at New York Law School, where she was a tenured law professor for more than two decades prior to becoming SVC's president. Gross's academic area of expertise is consumer finance, overindebtedness, and community economic development. She has earned a national and international reputation as a scholar, teacher, administrator, and community leader dedicated to improving the lives of those less privileged. She has a special research interest in women and money and student debt loads. Gross's legal scholarly work has been published in leading journals. Visit her blog, Higher Education Matters, at http://blogs.svc.edu/president/.

Index